CAMBRIDGE STUDIES IN RUSSIAN LITERATURE

Novy Mir

CAMBRIDGE STUDIES IN RUSSIAN LITERATURE

General editor HENRY GIFFORD

forthcoming titles

Word and music in Andrey Bely's novels
ADA STEINBERG

*The enigma of Gogol:
an examination of the writings of N. V. Gogol
and their place in the Russian literary tradition*

*Three Russian writers and the irrational:
Zamyatin, Pil'nyak, and Bulgakov*
T. R. N. EDWARDS

Novy Mir

A CASE STUDY IN
THE POLITICS OF LITERATURE
1952–1958

EDITH ROGOVIN FRANKEL

Director, Soviet and East European Research Centre
Hebrew University of Jerusalem

CAMBRIDGE UNIVERSITY PRESS

CAMBRIDGE

LONDON   NEW YORK   NEW ROCHELLE
MELBOURNE   SYDNEY

Published by the Press Syndicate of the University of Cambridge
The Pitt Building, Trumpington Street, Cambridge CB2 1RP
32 East 57th Street, New York, NY 10022, USA
296 Beaconsfield Parade, Middle Park, Melbourne 3206, Australia

First published 1981

Printed in Great Britain at the
University Press, Cambridge

British Library Cataloguing in Publication Data
Frankel, Edith Rogovin
Novy mir. – (Cambridge studies in Russian
literature)
1. Russian literature – 20th century – History
and criticism
I. Title
891.74′4   PG3016   80-42152
ISBN 0 521 23438 7

For my parents
SAMUEL AND DORA ANN ROGOVIN
with affection

Contents

Illustrations

Preface

My interest in the interaction of politics and literature in the Soviet
Union developed when I was a graduate student at Columbia
University and some of my basic conclusions on the subject were
initially worked out in my doctoral dissertation, completed in 1974.
When writing the present book, however, I was able to draw on the
ever-growing supply of materials – often circulated in *samizdat* form
or published in the Russian *émigré* press – which began to appear in
the mid seventies. Furthermore, the recent emigration of citizens
from the USSR, some of whom had been active in literary life there,
has added a significant new source for a work which would,
otherwise, have had to rely almost entirely on Soviet publications.
Perhaps I should add that, while the first part of the book concentrates
on *Novy Mir* in the period 1952–58, the last two chapters undertake
an over-all (non-chronological) analysis of the publishing process.
There, free use has been made of relevant materials drawn from more
recent years.

All along the way I have received encouragement and help of all
kinds and I would like to express my appreciation for at least some
of it. This list will not, unfortunately, be exhaustive.

First and foremost I would like to express my gratitude to a
number of people at Columbia University, where I did much of the
research for this book. The late Rufus Mathewson meticulously went
through early drafts of my work and filled yellow legal sheets with
careful comments and encouraging remarks, which were of enormous
help. John N. Hazard, with his never-failing warmth and enthusiasm,
gave me the impetus to persevere in my work when the end was far
out of sight. Joseph Rothschild and Peter Juviler also read and
commented on this study, while Robert Maguire performed the
major task of reading through the entire completed manuscript and
devoting a great deal of time to commenting on it.

In general, I received the best of service from the Columbia
University Library, but in particular I would like to thank two

extraordinary librarians who went well beyond the call of duty in providing me with bibliographic help: Eileen McIlvaine Koerner and Mary Ann Miller. Sonya Sluzar of the Research Institute on International Change at Columbia, apart from other help, saw to it at a crucial stage that I could work in a comfortable office.

It was at that time, when my children were smaller, that I relied on the good offices of several baby-sitters, without whom I could never have spent the required time on research. I still recall with gratitude the help of Laurie Weinstein, Elka Gould and, above all, the late Mrs Kathleen McLoughlin.

The New York University Russian Library, administered by Bernard Koten, provided an excellent source of Soviet newspapers and periodicals, readily available to the reader in their original form.

I am extremely grateful to the people who shared with me their first-hand experience in the Soviet literary world: Veronika and Yury Shtain, Grigorii Svirskii, Boris Zaks and Andrei Sinyavsky; and Igor Sats, David Dar and Arkady Belinkov, all three of whom have since died. Their testimony gave my study an added dimension. My colleague Ted Friedgut gave me invaluable help in obtaining some of my source information. And I would also like to thank Martin Dewhirst, who advised me on various matters of Soviet literary policy, as well as Peter Reddaway, Sheila Fitzpatrick and Tatiana Babchina-Herzenberg.

Rose Raskin, Martin Horwitz and Maurice Friedberg all generously gave me of their time and skill in advising me on the translation of Russian poetry in the text, and Stanton Eckstut gave inestimable help in preparing the charts.

While I would like to thank many of my colleagues at the Hebrew University, I will single out here Galia Golan and Gur Ofer, who headed the Soviet and East European Research Centre at the University during the academic year 1977–78 when I was given a fellowship there, thus receiving the opportunity to finish a considerable portion of the book. Also at the Hebrew University, Mikhail Agurskii's comments and suggestions and Ada Steinberg's help are very much appreciated.

My mother-in-law, Ella S. Frankel, went over the entire manuscript and this book is much the better for her good eye and wonderful ability to effect major improvements through seemingly minor changes.

While my daughters, Leora and Rachel, cannot be said to have actually helped the progress of this book, they do nevertheless deserve a word of thanks for the fortitude and good humor with which they withstood the rigors of life with a book in progress. And last, but by no means least, I thank my husband, Jonathan, who gave me every encouragement, help and advice from start to finish and whose fine judgment and historical sense added so much.

Jerusalem, September, 1980

A note on transliteration

Two systems of transliteration are used in this book. Bibliographic references to Russian works are generally transliterated according to the Library of Congress system. However, for the sake of non-specialist readers, the spelling of Russian names and words both in the body of the book and in the text of the notes is rendered in a simplified form of the 'British' system. Thus, Tvardovskii is also given as Tvardovsky and *Novyi Mir* becomes *Novy Mir*. Names which have a generally accepted English spelling are given in that form, e.g. Ilya Ehrenburg. The following table sets out the differences in transliteration.

Transliteration table

		Simplified British (used in text)	Library of Congress (used in bibliographic references)
А	а	a	a
Б	б	b	b
В	в	v	v
Г	г	g	g
Д	д	d	d
Е	е	e	e
Ж	ж	zh	zh
З	з	z	z
И	и	i	i
	ий	y*	ii
Й	й	i	i
К	к	k	k
Л	л	l	l
М	м	m	m
Н	н	n	n
О	о	o	o

* When appearing at end of word.

		Simplified British (used in text)	Library of Congress (used in bibliographic references)
П	п	p	p
Р	р	r	r
С	с	s	s
Т	т	t	t
У	у	u	u
Ф	ф	f	f
Х	х	kh	kh
Ц	ц	ts	ts
Ч	ч	ch	ch
Ш	ш	sh	sh
Щ	щ	shch	shch
	ъ	″	″
	ы	y	y
	ый	y,	yi
	ь	,	,
Э	э	e	e
Ю	ю	yu	iu
Я	я	ya	ia

Glossary

agrogorod	an urbanized center, advocated by Khrushchev, designed to unite several neighboring collective farms, thereby introducing the amenities of the city into rural life
aktiv	the active Communist Party members at any institution or organization
apparat	professional Communist Party administration
apparatchik	full-time paid Party official
derevenshchiki	prose writers who take the village and rural life as their primary subject
Glavlit	Chief Administration for the Preservation of State Secrets in the Press; the censorship. Regional and local subdivisions of Glavlit are: *krailit, oblit, railit, gorlit*
ideinost	ideological content; along with *narodnost'* and *partiinost'*, the three fundamental requirements of socialist realism
ispolkom	executive committee of a soviet; responsible for local government
kolkhoz (pl. -y)	collective farm
kolkhoznik	member of collective farm
MTS	Machine Tractor Station; provided neighboring collective farms with heavy agricultural equipment and the accompanying manpower; discontinued in 1958
muzhik	peasant
narodnost' (*narod*)	of the people, folk character
NEP	the New Economic Policy (1921–28)
nomenklatura	those posts in the various branches of administration which are filled through nomination by the Party; prerogatives and privileges attached to such appointments

obkom	Party committee of an *oblast* (region)
ocherk	essay, sketch
okhrana	Tsarist secret police
partiinost'	Party spirit
poryadochnost'	decency, honesty (*poryadochny*, adj.)
samizdat	literally, self-publishing; unofficial (hence, uncensored) reproduction of written materials, circulated from hand to hand
tolkach	pusher, fixer (in Soviet industrial enterprises), expediter
Zhdanovism	associated with pronouncements on Soviet literature and the arts made by Andrei Zhdanov between 1946 and 1948; hence, severe restrictions on cultural life as in Stalin's time

1 Aleksandr Tvardovsky during the first period in which he edited
Novy Mir (reproduced by courtesy of Novosti)

Introduction

The relationship between literature and politics has been more pronounced in modern Russia than in any other major European country. This is not to say that there have not been Russian critics who have been concerned with the intrinsic artistic merit of a work, or Russian writers who have been guided by purely aesthetic norms. However, at least from the time of Radishchev and Pushkin, the state has imposed controls on the writer, and even in tsarist times this fact persistently undermined the concept of literature as falling within the strictly private domain. Apart from critics and writers consciously committed to the cause of social change, for example, Chernyshevsky and Gorky, there were others of a religious or conservative bent (Gogol, Dostoevsky, Tolstoy) or of a more detached nature (Turgenev, Chekhov) who found themselves involved in politics and political issues.

Despite the profound changes which have taken place in Russian politics and society since the October Revolution, the tsarist era has left its mark on Soviet literary life in at least three basic respects. First and most obviously, the tradition of censorship was taken over without break by the new regime – although since the 1930s it has proved far more inclusive and efficient than in the pre-1917 period. Second, and ironically, the concept of literature as didactic and utilitarian, associated in the nineteenth century with the radical opposition – Belinsky, Dobrolyubov and Pisarev – has been adopted into the Soviet theory of literature. As a result, to the prohibitions imposed by the *ancien régime*, under which statements of a certain type were forbidden, have been added a series of positive demands on the writer: his work must be imbued with the spirit of the one authorized aesthetic doctrine, socialist realism.

Finally, however, the legacy of the nineteenth-century Russian intelligentsia has survived in the thinking of members of the intellectual community. The idea that the creative artist owes his ultimate loyalty to his own vision of the truth, that he belongs to his own sub-group which has its own rules different from and even superior to those of the state – has survived through the Soviet period and reasserts itself given the slightest opportunity.

These three factors combined to shape a journal such as *Novy Mir* in the period after the rise of Stalin. The journal at once reflected imposed limitations, ideological demands and restiveness within the literary community.

The 'thick' journal has had a long and distinguished history in Russian literature.[1] The tradition of this kind of publication has continued from the tsarist era, in modified form, to the present day and a number of such journals are published monthly in the Soviet Union. Of these, *Novy Mir* was the best known and had the most interesting contents in the postwar years. (Besides works of literature, *Novy Mir* has carried on the tradition of the 'thick' journal by regularly publishing articles on science, current affairs, economics and literary criticism.)

However, given the fact that its freedom of publication is so limited, what is the value of studying a Soviet periodical?

For a variety of reasons the journal provides an excellent yardstick for gauging the relationship of the regime to the creative intelligentsia at any given time. First, as a publication which appears every month, *Novy Mir* is in a good position to reflect any variations in official policy. Within a period of some two months, the journal can respond in its pages to the latest political changes, demands, relaxations. Rapid shifts in policy can be made far more quickly in a periodical than by the book-publishing houses. And while the daily press clearly is even more subject to instantaneous change, it does not publish *belles lettres* to any significant extent, is more overtly political and therefore even more closely watched.

Because of the frequency of a journal's appearance, the critics also have the opportunity to respond rapidly to its contents. Critics are, in a way, the last stage of the official control system over literature. At best, they do provide a relatively spontaneous reaction to what is published. But very often they make the final pronouncement over a work which, perhaps hastily or inadvertently, was allowed through the censor's sieve. Thus, even the official decision to publish a work can be reversed *ex post facto* by a series of negative articles by key critics.

On the other hand, the liberal intelligentsia has the opportunity to exploit any relaxation of official policy by responding quickly to changes in the air. And for two decades *Novy Mir* made use of this opportunity more consistently than any other Soviet journal.[2] Assuming that strict adherence to long-established Party policies is the easiest option in Soviet Russia (and that which is usually chosen), we can learn most from a journal which showed a predilection for change, which seized every opening to publish intellectually and artistically challenging material.

This is a study of *Novy Mir* during one of the most politically crucial periods of Soviet history. Starting with the year 1952 – the last year of Stalin's life – it opens with a study of literary politics under Stalin and then traces developments during the years of political flux – generally termed the 'thaw' – which culminated in the overthrow of Khrushchev's opponents. For purposes of this investigation, the span from 1952 to 1958 is broken into three periods, each of which saw *Novy Mir* publish exceptional or ground-breaking material only to be attacked and eventually forced to retreat. But, despite the important resemblances, each of these three crises was in many essential ways unique. The detailed study of these official campaigns against the journal casts light on Soviet literary policy in general as it has developed since the nineteen fifties.

Recognized as the best literary journal of the nineteen fifties and sixties, *Novy Mir* played a significant role in intellectual developments during the thaw and in the following years, partly as a barometer of policy change but also as a pioneer in the formulation of publishing policy. Indeed, at a time when publishing abroad was a rare practice for Soviet authors and the institution of *samizdat* was at best nascent, *Novy Mir* performed an indisputably significant function: it was the principal forum for the liberal Soviet intelligentsia. This was expressed succinctly by Andrei Sinyavsky, who described *Novy Mir* as:

such a decent, interesting journal with which the liberal intelligentsia lived for a long time, and a journal which somehow resounded abroad and, in general...the best Soviet journal.[3]

1

Literary policy under Stalin, 1952–1953

> I have been looking through the files of *Literaturnaya Gazeta* [1952]: everything appeared most satisfactory. The paper noted that Grossman's novel *Za pravoe delo*...had appeared in *Novy Mir*, but the reviewers ignored it.
>
> Ilya Ehrenburg, *Post-War Years: 1945–54*

In recent years Western scholars have been deeply interested in determining the nature and degree of change which has taken place in the Soviet Union since Stalin's death.[1] Numerous works have analyzed and assessed the transformation of post-Stalin Russia: changes in economic policy, in the effectiveness of group pressures on policy-making, in the use and role of terror, and in the area of public discourse, debate and cultural creativity. But relatively little effort has been made to establish a reliable gauge with which to measure change.[2] Studies of what was happening in specific areas of interest during the late Stalin years – studies in detail – have been few and far between, so that comparisons have often been based on well-documented research covering the recent period but on generalizations in discussing the Stalinist era. One exception has been Marshall Shulman's study of Stalin's foreign policy,[3] which emphasized its complexity and broad range of options.

The field of literature under the Stalinist regime likewise was not monochromatic. A study of literary developments during the last year of Stalin's life – as evidenced both in general literary publications and specifically in *Novy Mir* – illustrates an intertwining of political and literary policies, each motivated by its own set of interests.

The general view of internal Soviet politics in the early nineteen fifties is that the increasing repression and pre-purge tension were irreconcilable with a loosening of literary bonds. And yet an examination of the period shows that both trends – a policy of mounting intimidation by the state and an officially sanctioned 'liberalization' in the literary sphere – coexisted in the Soviet Union in 1952.

4

Soviet internal policy at this time was characterized by the renewed attack on bourgeois nationalism, the instigation of the Doctors' Plot and the proliferation of the vigilance campaign. On the other hand, foreign policy provided a contrast – the broad alliance policy and the development of the peace movement after 1949 represented a 'rightist' approach.[4] A similar absence of consistent correlation between all aspects of Soviet policy had been seen at other times: in the mid nineteen thirties, for example, the beginning of the Great Purge was coupled with an official veneration of law and order, with propaganda for the new constitution and, in foreign affairs, with the pursuit of the Popular Front.

In 1952 the contrast was not limited to an emphasis 'on "peaceful coexistence" in foreign policy and strict ideological conformity at home'.[5] A multi-level policy was also to be seen in the field of literature, where, for approximately ten months, an atmosphere of relaxation, albeit strictly limited, was to be felt.

This modification in the firm attitude of the Party towards literature was first felt as early as February, 1952.[6] Although prose was the object of some of the reforming criticism, the main brunt of the campaign was felt by drama. There ensued a series of articles condemning the so-called 'no-conflict theory' which had dominated postwar Soviet drama.[7] The single most famous – and most outspoken – statement on the subject was made by the playwright Nikolai Virta in March of that year. In it he tried to explain his own role in the development of the 'theory'.

It arose as a consequence of 'cold observations of the mind'[8] on the manner in which those of our plays which contain sharp life conflicts passed through the barbed-wire obstacles of the agencies in charge of the repertoire... everything living, true to life, sharp, fresh and unstereotyped was combed out and smoothed over to the point where it was no longer recognizable. Every bold, unstereotyped word in a play had to be defended at the cost of the playwright's nerve and the play's quality...each of us has accumulated a great deal of bitter experience in ten years about which, for some reason, it has been the custom to keep quiet.[9]

Virta placed much of the blame on those people who destroyed plays and who were guided 'not by the interests of Soviet art but by a wild rabbit fear of the hypothetical possibility of a mistake, mortal fear of taking any risk or responsibility for risk'. His own initial adherence to the no-conflict theory had been the result of his search for 'a creative way out'. Perhaps, he had thought, the period of sharp conflicts in drama really had passed. But, no, this stupid and spurious theory did not arise because 'everything was fine!' It is not because 'everything is fine' that Pogodin writes a play about the beginning of the century, while Virta, who spent two years in a Russian village, wrote a play about peasants of the People's Democracies!

Although, of course, the atmosphere of suppression which Virta here described does not surprise us, what is notable is that he expressed his views publicly – and in the way that he did. His candid remarks during what was assuredly an extraordinarily repressive period, his attack on problems of censorship and publication policy, and the fact that his statement was not a unique utterance but part of a concerted campaign in the press to revise established literary doctrine all make this a most noteworthy article. What is interesting is not that a writer in the Soviet Union in the early 1950s should have felt bitterness and helplessness at his plight, nor necessarily that he should have committed these thoughts to paper, but that a publication such as *Sovetskoe Iskusstvo*, of conservative leanings and quite orthodox editorial policy, should have taken it upon itself to publish them. One can only assume that the editors – and there had been no recent significant changes of the board – deemed the article appropriate to the current literary mood.

Although Virta's article, and others, were subsequently attacked in the Soviet press,[10] the crusade against the no-conflict theory continued throughout the summer and into the autumn of 1952, with concomitant demands for the portrayal of more well-delineated negative characters and for more and better comedies. It proceeded with varying degrees of fervor beyond the 19th Party Congress and extended to include not only drama but other prose forms as well. Malenkov's speech at the 19th Party Congress in October did little to clarify the literary situation.[11] Nothing really new was said in the few paragraphs devoted to the subject. One thing that his speech did not do, however, was put any further brake on the limited process of innovation which had been emergent since the previous spring. Literary events were apparently to proceed along their course without a strong directive from the top at this point.

In January, 1953 – on the same day that the Doctors' Plot was announced in the press – I. Pitlyar published an article demanding that more attention be paid to the material details of life: 'What enormous artistic and editorial possibilities open up before the writer who is not afraid to be truthful in portraying the material conditions of people's existence... Those writers who wave aside the so-called "details of life" are sinning against the truth of life."[12] This sentiment, uttered here at the beginning of a repressive swing in Soviet literature, would later be a central theme in the literary criticism of the early thaw.

A situation in which articles calling for conflict, for innovation, for a description of negative characteristics of Soviet life appeared simultaneously with attacks on nationalism in literature, with Great-Russian chauvinism, with virulent anti-semitism and a campaign to induce mass paranoia was clearly anomalous. There was a build-up of fear and distrust, but there was the opposite, too, which cannot be ignored. Explaining this concurrence of apparently contradictory trends is by no means simple.

There are a number of possible explanations and there is probably some truth in each. First, there was the state of drama itself. It is certainly plausible that the attack on the no-conflict technique was nothing more than an attempt to cure the ills which had beset the theater for some time. Evidence of the low level of dramatic endeavor (half-empty theaters and the popularity of the classics over contemporary plays) is overwhelming, and it is not unlikely that a main goal was to raise the theater to the point where it could at least be a meaningful instrument of education or propaganda. Demands for more constructive criticism, for a reorganization of responsible committees, and attacks on dull, insipid plays all point in this direction.

If, however, one considers the period preceding Stalin's death as a whole, and not just in terms of literary development, one perceives other possibilities. Seeing the build-up of insecurity and tension throughout the year 1952, which reached a frenzy early in 1953, one is struck by a certain similarity between the vigilance campaign and the attack on the 'no-conflict' theory. The vigilance campaign, in essence, warned that no one was to be trusted, that all sorts of subversive elements lurked in the background of Soviet society, that one should be on guard against every conceivable danger, whether from doctors, embezzlers, bourgeois nationalists or petty criminals. Implied in the campaign against the doctrine of no conflict was the assertion that it was wrong to assume that Soviet society had reached that point of development where there was no socio-political danger left. Drama could not yet be written in which the only opposition present in a play was that between good and better. Evil remained in society and ought to be presented in the theater, with the aim of rooting it out. In other words, in order to expose enemies the Soviet citizen had to know how to recognize them.

There is, finally, the possibility which we cannot entirely discount: that this 'liberal' swing was simply to be used as a bait to draw out those whom Anatoly Surov had referred to as the 'keepers of silence'[13] from their lairs, with the ultimate intention of repression. It is widely held that a major purge was in the offing on the eve of Stalin's death; perhaps this campaign was simply to be used as a mouse trap.

Whatever the ulterior motives may have been, the fact is that in 1952 writers and editors did find that they had somewhat more scope, more 'elbow room', limited though it still was. This became evident not only in the remarkable candor of some writers, but also in the demands made on the writers as a whole. The attack on the no-conflict theory permitted a less stereotyped publication policy. In order to demonstrate this point, let us look at the output of *Novy Mir*, the most experimental journal in the fifties and the one quickest to reflect a change of policy.

Two major works appeared in its pages in the summer and early autumn of 1952 – as well as some lesser items – which distinguished that literary season and differentiated it from the Stalinist model. Almost predictably, *Novy Mir* was to be the object of a severe concerted attack launched against it by the Party press and the Writers Union several months later.

In the July, 1952 issue of *Novy Mir* the first instalment of Vasily Grossman's *Za pravoe delo* (For the Just Cause) appeared.[14] This was a lengthy novel which centered on the Battle of Stalingrad and followed a number of individuals and families whose lives were caught up in the war and whose fates were interrelated. Long sections of the book were devoted to discussions of a philosophical nature among the participants – soldiers, professors, students – on the causes of the war.

It is indicative of the indecisive official attitude – and the amount of permissiveness – that the novel received some excellent, or at worst mixed, reviews at the end of 1952.[15] Indeed, *For the Just Cause* was virtually ignored in the beginning. Ilya Ehrenburg noted this fact in his memoirs, recalling that he considered this a positive development. 'I have been looking through the files of *Literaturnaya Gazeta* [for 1952]', he wrote. 'Everything appeared most satisfactory. The paper

2   Vasily Grossman, author of *For the Just Cause*

noted that Grossman's novel *Za pravoe delo*. . . had appeared in *Novy Mir*, but the reviewers ignored it.'[16]

In fact – as Ehrenburg clearly understood – the novel did contain sections which could well have been alarming to the Soviet reviewer. The following excerpts are from a passage in which an academic, Chepyzhin – one of the central characters – propounded his views in a conversation with Professor Shtrum.

Look, imagine that in some little town there are people known for their learning, honor, humanity, goodness. And they were well known to every old person and child there. They enriched the town life, enlarged it – they taught in the schools, in the universities, wrote books and wrote in the workers' newspapers and in scientific journals; they worked and struggled for the freedom of labor. . . But when night fell, out onto the streets came other people whom few in the town knew, whose life and affairs were dirty and secret. They feared the light, walked stealthily in the darkness, in the shadow of buildings. But there came a time when the coarse dark power of Hitler burst into life, with the intention of changing its most fundamental law. They started to throw cultured people who had illuminated life into camps, into prisons. Others fell in the struggle, others went into hiding. They were no longer to be seen during the day on the streets, at factories, at schools, at workers' meetings. The books they had written blazed. But those who had been hidden by the night came out noisily into the light and filled the world with themselves and their terrible deeds. And it seemed that the people had been transformed, had become a people of evil and dishonor. But look here, it isn't so! Understand that it isn't so! The energy contained in a people's wisdom, in a people's moral sense, in a people's goodness is eternal, whatever fascism might do to destroy it. [It continues to live, temporarily dispersed. It accumulates in nodes. It gathers around itself indestructible microscopic diamond crystals which can cut both steel and glass. And those popular champions who were killed transmitted their spiritual strength, their energy to others, teaching them how to live and how to die. And their strength was not destroyed together with the corpses of the dead, but continues to live in the living. I am convinced that the Nazi evil is powerless to kill the energy of the people. It has only disappeared from view, but quantitatively it is undiminished in the people. Do you understand me? Do you follow my line of thought?][17]

Chepyzhin then went on to discuss the psychology of social change:

You see, all sorts of things are mixed in man, many of which are unconscious, hidden, secret, false. Often, a man, living under normal social conditions, doesn't himself know of the vaults and cellars of his soul. But a social catastrophe occurred, and out of the cellar came every evil spirit, they rustled and ran out through the clean, light rooms. [The flour fell and the chaff rose outside. It wasn't the relationship of things that changed, but the position of the parts of the moral, spiritual structure of man which was altered.][18]

It is not at all surprising that, when the attack finally came, the critics singled out these passages. Chepyzhin, wrote one, taught an 'idealist philosophy', which the author himself obviously espoused.[19]

It does not require much imagination to see Grossman–Chepyzhin's description of the coming of Hitlerism as a commentary on Stalinist Russia. Especially in the light of his later work *Forever Flowing*,[20] it is clear that Grossman was highly sensitive to, and understandably obsessed with, the evils which had been committed in Soviet Russia during his lifetime. His concentration in this section on the intelligentsia and its difficult fate was at least as applicable to the Soviet as to the German situation. This is a striking example of the not-infrequent practice of political criticism by analogy, in which the dissenting writer attacks a feature of his own contemporary society through reference to tsarist times or to foreign and hostile countries. Of course, the official critics could not directly expose this type of invidious comparison, for to do so would be to admit that they themselves had recognized the forbidden parallel.

The critics in general – and the February article in *Literaturnaya Gazeta* was in this typical – had therefore to confine their criticism within safe ideological bounds. Specifically, in the case of Grossman, they concentrated most of their fire on his universalistic moralism, his apparent indifference to Marxist dialectics and his preference for a class-free, science-based philosophy. 'It adds up', said *Literaturnaya Gazeta*,

to the idea that there is an eternal struggle of good and evil, and good is the personification of perpetual energy – whether the cosmic energy of the stars or the spiritual energy of the people. It is completely clear that these ideological, unhistoric fumblings of reasoning can in no way explain the existence of social phenomena.[21]

Chepyzhin, the article went on, talks abstractly, and unhistorically, about fascism and the idea of war. He measures everything according to his 'unhistoric categories' of the struggle of light and darkness, of good and evil. Shtrum, it continued, nods his agreement, and not one of the main characters replies to this argument with a Marxist–Leninist explanation of the war and the nature of things. So one may assume that Grossman did not want Chepyzhin's reactionary philosophy refuted. Grossman, through Chepyzhin, seemed to follow the idea of the Pythagoreans that there is an eternal rotation of events, that 'there is an eternal circulation of the very same beginnings, conditions, events'.[22]

It should be noted that when the novel was published in book form, as it was after Stalin's death and again in the 1960s, the two passages quoted above had been considerably altered. Moreover, the entire dialogue between Chepyzhin and Shtrum had been transformed, toned down and attenuated – Shtrum here emerged as an advocate of Soviet Marxist orthodoxy. For example, in the new version he objected vigorously to the idea that Nazism was to be explained as the work of 'a handful of evil men with Hitler at their head', arguing instead that it was the result 'of specific peculiarities of German imperialism'.[23] Again, Shtrum now pointed out that Chepyzhin's theory of science and history, if applied 'not to fascism... but to progressive phenomena, to liberating revolutions... [implies that] the revolutionary struggle of the working class also cannot change society, also cannot raise man to a higher level'.[24]

Besides the criticism of the excerpts quoted here, many general features of Grossman's novel were attacked. Grossman had not 'succeeded in creating a single, major, vivid, typical portrait of a hero of the battle of Stalingrad, a hero in a grey greatcoat, weapons in hand'.[25] He 'had not shown the Communist Party as the true organizer of victory'.[26] A feeling of doom pervaded the work.[27]

The campaign continued unabated until a month after Stalin's death.[28] In fact, pressure became so great that several members of *Novy Mir*'s editorial board – Tvardovsky, Tarasenkov, Kataev, Fedin and Smirnov – publicly apologized for their 'error' in publishing Grossman's novel.[29] It was a vain attempt to stem the tide of criticism directed at the journal. The climax of the letter was the admission by the editors that the fault lay with the editorial board – that is, with themselves – for not having gone into the work more thoroughly, for having failed to ferret out its ideological–artistic faults. They asked the secretariat of the Writers Union as soon as possible to 'take measures towards strengthening the composition of the editorial board of *Novy Mir*'. As for Grossman, he never made any kind of apology.[30]

The last major attack on Grossman's novel – and on the journal which had published it – was made by Fadeev at the end of March. Thus the end of the campaign against *Novy Mir* – and against *For the Just Cause* – was not simultaneous with the death of Stalin. Indeed, it is interesting to note that the literary campaign extended longer than the other onslaughts characteristic of the last months of Stalin's life. Even after the official halt of the Doctors' Plot, articles criticizing *Novy Mir* continued to appear. Ehrenburg later discussed Fadeev's role in the publication of and subsequent attack on Grossman's novel:

In March, 1953, soon after Stalin's death, I came across an article in *Literaturnaya Gazeta* in which Fadeev sharply attacked Grossman's *Za pravoe delo*. This puzzled me because I had several times heard him speak well of this novel *which he had managed to get published*. It had aroused Stalin's displeasure and there had been some scathing reviews of it. But Fadeev had continued to defend it...And now suddenly Fadeev had come out with this article.[31]

Only by mid April had the attacks on *Novy Mir* finally stopped. Ehrenburg mentioned the continuation of the literary campaign in his memoirs:

The announcement about the rehabilitation of the doctors appeared: changes were obviously in the air. Fadeev came to me without ringing the bell, sat down on my bed and said: 'Don't be too hard on me...I was frightened.' 'But why after his death?' I asked. 'I thought the worst was still to come', he replied.

The focus of Fadeev's criticism at the end of March had not differed sharply from preceding censure, except for a rather pointedly anti-semitic undertone. But significant for the historian is his account of the publication process through which the novel had passed.

According to Fadeev,[32] the novel had been discussed for a number of years before its appearance in print, and there had been numerous objections to it. But the discussion did not reach the broad public. 'It was conducted in the narrow circle of the editorial board and the secretariat [of the Writers Union], and only after the novel was printed did it creep into the presidium of the Writers Union – the body which should have decided these matters of principle.'

Evidently, when the novel first came to the editorial offices of *Novy Mir* it had been strongly criticized by B. Agapov, then a member of the board.[33] As we know that Agapov left the editorial board of *Novy Mir* in February, 1950, it is clear that the novel must have been under discussion for a minimum of two-and-a-half years, and probably for much longer. It was when the new editorial board was appointed that discussion of the novel flared up again. The new editorial board, which brought out its first issue in March, 1950, had been significantly changed. Tvardovsky took the place of Simonov as editor-in-chief. Agapov and Aleksandr Krivitsky were replaced by three new members: M. S. Bubennov (an abject conformist under Stalin – and after him), S. S. Smirnov and A. K. Tarasenkov.[34]

When the manuscript of *For the Just Cause* was submitted for examination to the new board, Bubennov brought the issue to the secretariat of the Writers Union. Fadeev reported: 'The novel was changed many times. Discussion once more developed in the secretariat and the above-mentioned comrades[35] held to their point of view.' Fadeev then asked why the novel had been published despite all the adverse criticism.

Because a situation has arisen in the Union of Soviet Writers and in editorial boards in which the solution of many ideological questions – the evaluation of works, the formulation of one or another serious problem – very often depends on the opinion of a few leaders. We rarely apply the normal collegium principle in our work.

It must be assumed that, in the face of a good deal of opposition, someone on the *Novy Mir* board had been keen on seeing *For the Just Cause* published. The likelihood is – in view of his reputation and courage – that that man was Tvardovsky. Had he, as editor-in-chief, been unfavorably inclined towards the novel there would never have been a struggle to have it printed.

One cannot ignore the basic facts of the Grossman affair. First, the author was not an unknown. On the contrary, he had a reputation and, by the official standards, a dubious one. Born in Berdichev in 1904, Grossman had been a war correspondent during the Second World War for both *Krasnaya Zvezda* and for *Eynikeyt*, the Yiddish-language journal of the Jewish Anti-Fascist Committee. His story 'The People are Immortal', which appeared in *Krasnaya Zvezda* in 1942, was one of the earlier, more powerful works on the war. However, his play *If We Believe the Pythagoreans* – written before the war, but not published until 1946 – had been severely criticized by the press. After the war he had collected materials on heroic and tragic facts concerning Jewish victims of the Nazis. They were to have been published in what was to be called the Black Book, as a tribute to the Jews who had suffered during the war. The book, although set in type, was never published in the Soviet Union, and the plates were destroyed in 1949, when the Soviet Jewish cultural community was closed down.[36] Grossman was hamstrung by Soviet criticism during the postwar Stalin years. Disliked by Stalin[37] and dogged by hack critics, Grossman never won the acclaim he deserved.

Second is the undeniable fact that, as the novel had been under consideration for so long, the *Novy Mir* editorial board, members of the Writers Union and of the literary – and censoring – community must have been well aware of the objections to it. It was thus a deliberate, and not a random, decision to publish that particular novel by that particular author during the summer of 1952. It is quite clear that Tvardovsky took the step of publishing the novel then because he felt – correctly – that this was an opportune time, that the literary atmosphere warranted it.

Indeed, another remarkable aspect of this case is that *For the Just Cause*, published during a period of mounting fear, under the unyielding influence of the Zhdanov tradition, was never republished in its original form in Russia. As has been noted above, passages published under Stalin were considered unfit to print in later years.[38] Nor did Part II of the book ever appear at all, even in the 'best' of literary periods to follow. Grossman died in 1964, some six months after the manuscript of the second part had been confiscated by the secret police.*

* See, for example, Svetlana Alliluyeva, *Only One Year* (London: Hutchinson, 1969), p. 44: 'In the USSR one could expect anything: the search of one's home by warrant, the confiscation of books from one's shelves, of manuscripts from one's desk. In

3   Valentin Ovechkin in 1955, three years after the
publication of his remarkable sketch

All this indicates that the literary situation during 1952 was in a
state of flux. The Virta statement provided one example of the subtle
change which was evident and *Novy Mir*'s publication of *For the Just
Cause* another. Whatever the motivation behind the anti-'no-conflict'
campaign, the end result had been a different publishing policy.

One of the outstanding literary events of the whole decade was the
publication in 1952 of Valentin Ovechkin's '*Raionny budni*' (District

this way the government had confiscated the second part of Vasily Grossman's
novel.' See also Efim Etkind, 'Sovetskii pisatel' i smert'', *Vremia i My* 26. 1978,
pp. 132–44: 'Thus Vasily Grossman died from cancer in 1964, a deep and tragic
writer, not surviving arrest – but this time it was not the author who was arrested
but his novel' (p. 136). Other sources report that the KGB confiscated the
manuscripts after the author's death. One copy at least was preserved by friends.
Although Part II has never been published in Russia, excerpts of the novel have
begun to appear in the West. See, for example, *Posev*, no. 7, 1975, pp. 53–5; *Grani*,
no. 97, 1975, pp. 3–31; and *Kontinent*, nos. 4, 5.

Routine), the first of a series of sketches on contemporary kolkhoz life.[39] It was concerned primarily with Party work in a rural area and specifically attacked the complacent attitude of the district secretary, Borzov, whose sole aim was to see that the plan was fulfilled. Ovechkin contrasted him with the second-in-command, who was interested in the long-term goal of achieving communism and in treating fairly those kolkhozniki who did manage to fulfil their quota. He supported the principle of incentive, if this would encourage the kolkhozniki to work harder and more effectively.[40] Ovechkin emphasized the fact that these characters were not products of his imagination, but real people. The implication was that the Borzov approach was not uncommon and that the political direction of rural work was a real problem which the Party must solve.

It is significant that the sketch, far from being passively accepted, was warmly received in spite of the fact that it incisively censured the work of Party officials in the rural areas.[41]

Tvardovsky would later note the innovative nature of Ovechkin's sketch. In his article on the occasion of the fortieth anniversary of *Novy Mir* he called the appearance of 'District Routine' a literary turning point.[42] Noting that it had been published before the September plenum of the Central Committee in 1953 (which dealt with problems of agriculture), Tvardovsky said that its 'truthfulness [and] ideological orientation' were only fully appreciated afterwards. He pointed out that until then criticism had tenaciously attacked the slightest deviations of prose writers from 'conventional and legitimized norms, as it were, of interpreting rural life in literature. It seemed that maintaining these norms of well-being in the reflected picture was more important than reality.'[43] The fact is that 'District Routine' was to serve as a model for works on the rural scene throughout the mid fifties, and that it became symbolic of the 'new approach' of thaw writing. Tvardovsky's other mention of 'District Routine' was in a letter to Fedin about *Cancer Ward*.[44] The letter, written in January, 1968, came after the refusal to publish Solzhenitsyn's novel. Tvardovsky wrote: 'Solzhenitsyn, incidentally, outstanding as he is, is not unique or unprecedented in our literature. We should not forget the courage of Ovechkin's ['District Routine'], which appeared in *Novy Mir* as early as 1952 and marked a turning point.'[45]

All indications – Tvardovsky's remarks, Malenkov's discussion of agriculture at the 19th Party Congress, and the very fact of the publication of Ovechkin's sketch[46] – point to the fact that the ruling group had recognized the serious weaknesses of the agricultural situation and was seeking remedies. The coincidence of Ovechkin's first sketch and Malenkov's speech in the autumn of 1952 indicates a coordinated introduction of forthcoming changes in agricultural policy. (In fact, however, agricultural problems and a corrective program were to be dealt with only six months after Stalin's death, beginning in September, 1953.)

There were other items published in *Novy Mir* during the last year of Stalin's life which contributed to the general feeling of moderation in publishing policy.* Thus, the combination of the Virta statement, the concerted attack on the no-conflict theory, the publication of Vasily Grossman's novel and of Ovechkin's first sketch in the series, as well as the appearance of some lesser articles in *Novy Mir*, establishes a view of the Soviet literary scene clearly redolent of variety, limited experimentation and chance-taking on the part of the editors. Whatever was in the offing – and by January, 1953, attacks on *Novy Mir* had already begun – the fact remains that an atmosphere of some give-and-take had existed in 1952.[47] In literature (as well as in the field of foreign affairs) official policy did not on the surface proceed in consonance with the obviously repressive environment.

We are thus confronted by some curious, but surely not random, facts. The events described do present a cumulative image of literary life in 1952 which is far more variegated than is usually recognized. The year selected for examination was one that is generally assessed as oppressive to a degree at least typical of Stalin's postwar years. And there is no reason to doubt this over-all judgment. On the contrary, indications do point to a vicious situation in the internal life of the Soviet Union, one headed towards a new phase of mass terror. But our recognition of this fact should not lead us to the conclusion that there was complete uniformity in all aspects of Soviet

* See, for example, V. Komissarzhevskii, 'Chelovek na stsene', *Novyi Mir* 10, 1952, pp. 210–24, in which the author was relatively outspoken in extending the general lines of the attack on the no-conflict theory; N. K. Gudzii and V. A. Zhdanov, 'Voprosy tekstologii', *ibid.* 3, 1953, pp. 232–42, which discussed the censor's arbitrary destruction of texts in nineteenth-century Russia – a veiled comparison between that censor and his Soviet counterpart; V. Ognev, 'Iasnosti!' *ibid.* 1, 1953, pp. 263–7; E. Kazakevich, 'Serdtse druga', *ibid.* pp. 3–125. Much of the criticism levelled against Grossman was applied to Kazakevich as well, although the works were distinctly different and the Kazakevich story departed less from the ideological norm.

life. Comparative studies which cover both the Stalinist and post-Stalinist years – Ploss's work on agriculture, for instance, or Conquest's on politics[48] – have shown in specific cases the intricacies and contrasts present within the monolithic Stalinist system, thus providing a realistic basis on which to assess the actual changes which subsequently took place. Certainly, the literary life in the one year examined here suggests that there, too, complexity was the norm.

There is often an assumption in Western writing, encouraged by the image of the totalitarian model, that the Stalin period must have been monochromatic. Thus, whenever one meets a clash of opinion, or an indication of variety or innovation in the post-Stalin period, the natural tendency is to assume that it is 'new'. But the presence of terror did not necessarily mean an absence of variety. People willing to take a chance – and the risks were far greater then – could still manage, as Tvardovsky did with Grossman's novel, to find the means of publishing a particular work. And men like Grossman could still refuse to bow to official criticism, though his bravery could well have been suicidal had Stalin not died when he did. The examples provided were from the last year of Stalin's life, but detailed studies of other years would probably yield similar 'anachronisms'.

Let there be no misunderstanding. The absence of arbitrary terror in the post-Stalin years made an enormous difference in the lives of people in all spheres – the difference between night and day, between madness and a measure of normality. But the absence of terror no more signals the existence of a 'pluralistic' society than the fact of a 'totalitarian' regime implies complete uniformity. Certain people in certain fields were able on occasion to publish or say what was important to them even at the worst of times. The abandonment of the mass purge as a method of attaining compliance has not put an end to the coercive pressure enforcing conformity on the writer (or scientist, or lawyer). He is not at an opposite pole from his colleague of Stalinist times, but must still toe the line if he wishes to be published and paid. The writer who sticks his neck out is still taking a grave chance, even if this is not usually a chance of life or death. In the literary sphere, as in many other areas of Soviet life, the dichotomy between the Stalinist and post-Stalinist periods should not be taken for granted, but analyzed and measured.

Here in 1952–53 the seeds were being sown which were to germinate after Stalin's death and become central themes of the thaw during the following year. The attack on the principles of the no-conflict theory, the emphasis on human values in literature and the concentration on the 'trifles of life' in criticism would all be taken up again in the new era. That these central elements of thaw literature should have had their beginnings in the criticism of 1952–53 is a fact of startling import.

2

The 'economic thaw'

> I decided to publish these remarks on the work of the writer after prolonged
> doubts. They contain, of course, much that is controversial... I asked myself:
> Is this the time to raise questions connected with the work of the writer?
> It seems to me that this is the time.
>
> Ilya Ehrenburg, 'Concerning the Writer's Work',
> *Znamya*, October, 1953

After Ilya Ehrenburg gave the title *The Thaw* to his famous novel
of 1954, the word became generally accepted not only as applying
to the portent of spring, at the story's close, to the relaxation in the
personal lives of the book's characters, but also as a symbol of the
general moderation in the political climate which Russia had been
witnessing during the first year after Stalin's death. Later the term
was used to embrace the post-Stalin years until the end of 1956, with
a variety of dates given as the starting point. In fact, an examination
of material published in *Novy Mir* between 1953 and 1956, as well
as of official policy and discussions during those years, indicates the
wisdom of dividing the literary thaw into two main periods for the
purpose of more profitable analysis.

These periods correspond to two separate, but related, stages in the
post-Stalin struggle for power and attempts at political adjustment,
and the concomitant literary responses to these stimuli. The first stage
began in the summer and autumn of 1953 and continued until the
end of the spring of 1954. It was thematically dominated in the public
sphere by economic considerations, and it was this subject which had
a profound influence on literary productivity. The second stage,
which is primarily associated with the year 1956, was mainly
concerned with particular political revelations and demands, both in
the public and literary worlds. This is not to say, of course, that
themes from one period did not appear in the other, or that there
is no continuity between the two stages of the thaw – for there
indubitably is – but simply that in their general aspects the two
periods were characterized distinctly as, first, an economic and,
second, a political thaw.

The first stage of the thaw, which is the subject of this chapter, was distinguished not only by its emphasis on economic considerations but also by the fact that most of the notable *Novy Mir* works characteristic of 1953–54 were in the field of literary criticism. In 1956, on the other hand, far more works of fiction appeared devoted to the dominant political theme.

Dating the specific beginning of a particular trend or movement is often impossible. The most obvious milestone in the case of the thaw was, of course, the death of Stalin in March, 1953. It was only in the autumn of 1953, however, with the September plenum of the Central Committee and the October plenary session of the board of the Soviet Writers Union that events took place which were to have an immediate and significant impact on literary affairs. Thus a survey of the contents of *Novy Mir* during the summer months shows a few interesting developments, but no dramatic over-all changes.

The single most outspoken work to appear in *Novy Mir* in the summer of 1953 was a poem, '*Za dal'yu dal*'' (Distance beyond Distance), by Tvardovsky himself. The first instalment of the poem appeared in June and described the author's trip by train across the Soviet Union. Particularly striking were his stanzas on literature and literary criticism, which he incorporated as the subject of a night-time conversation among the passengers – two members of the reading public and the writer himself – of the railway compartment. One of them accuses the writer of not having an intimate tie with life:

> And how many of you are there in Russia alone?
> Probably five thousand or so.
> After all, it's not numbers that really matter,
> But life is passing you by
> While you probably lock yourselves up in your studies
> And guzzle vodka.[1]

Another passenger complains of the standard socialist–realist novel:

> But their novels are all written
> Before they drop in, sniff the dust,
> Poke the concrete with a walking stick,
> Thus verifying volume one against life itself.
> Before you know it the novel and all that goes with it are in top shape:
> A new method of bricklaying is properly depicted
> As is a backward deputy, a go-getter chairman,
> And a granddad marching on toward communism.
> She and he are both model workers,
> Then, the motor switched on for the first time,

> A party organizer, a snowstorm, a breakdown, an emergency,
> A minister visiting the shops, and all
> Going off to a ball.[2]

> And everything looks real enough, everything resembles
> That which is or which could be[3]
> But as a whole it is so indigestible
> That you want to howl out in pain.[4]

One reader becomes more outspoken as the conversation continues:

> No, say what you will, but voluntarily
> I will not agree, I will not give in.
> Life to me is pain and joy,
> I believe, I suffer, I love.
> I am happy to live, to serve my native land;
> I went and fought for it.
> I was born into this world for life –
> Not for editorials.
> I finish a book with irritation.
> My soul is sick: where is the ending?
> But there is no ending. There is a continuation.
> No, brother, that's too much. Have some decency.

And one nods:

> True, true.
> It's understandable, the criticism is well taken.[5]

The writer finds that his own thoughts are ignited by this talk with his readers and feels that he himself would like to deserve their love, to reach 'where the heat of living, truthful speech, and not the cold smoke of lies' is found. And so, for the sake of

> that priceless love,
> Having forgotten the bitterness of many years,
> Ready to work day
> And night – you are ready to burn up your soul.
> Ready to face
> All gossip and slander and to say
> Who gives a damn...[6]

But there is another passenger in the railway compartment besides the writer and his readers:

> Suddenly – a new voice from the upper berth:
> – It won't be published...
> – Meaning what?
> – I won't let it...

This is not a stentorian outcry,
No, but the particularly tough tone
With which superiors usually
Utter a refusal into the telephone.
– It won't be published, he drawled a second time.
– But who are you up there?

– You know very well yourself...
– But who?
– I am your editor.[7]

The irony in the situation is becoming apparent now. Tvardovsky the poet is portraying himself as a writer being hounded by readers because of the poor state of literature. But he suddenly finds himself being bullied by a demanding editor in the upper berth. As Tvardovsky was himself an editor as well as a poet we thus have Tvardovsky the writer fighting with his alter-ego, Tvardovsky the editor, and finding it difficult to work out a solution. The editor calls down mockingly from the upper berth:

Well, it's incredible how ardent,
How brave! And how you go back
On your own words,
How having amused yourself for a while,
You sound your own retreat.
What for? Because I am with you –
Always, everywhere – I, your editor.[8]

Tvardovsky attributes to his editor thoughts which he himself could only have regarded with dismay – is this criticism of some unnamed editors or an expression of self-criticism?

You see, when bent over a blank sheet of paper,
You're filled with creative thought,
But you can't go a step without me, wise guy,
Not a line and not a comma.[9]

Although the writer tries to place the blame on the editor, accusing him of taking too much upon himself, the editor rejects the allegation, referring to the time-honored system of self-censorship:

And lowering his voice ingratiatingly
He answers:
– I don't remove anything.
Not at all. I delegate everything
To you and your pen.

It makes no sense for me
To sweat over, to cross out, cursing fate.
Understand? All my work
You will do for me.
...
I prefer you above all,
I set you up as an example: here's a poet
Whom I simply do not read:
There's no need to worry there.

And he winked at me slyly
As if to say, you and me, buddy, we're together all the way...[10]

Tvardovsky has here identified himself as the 'I' by having the editor refer to him not as a writer, but, suddenly, as a poet. He is becoming more entangled in his own literary figure and the dual nature of his own, Tvardovsky's, dilemma becomes increasingly poignant.

The conversation on the train remains unfinished and the problems unresolved. But the bitter quarrel between reader and poet, between poet and editor, has thus been introduced in the post-Stalin period, and well before the landmarks of the autumn Tvardovsky was thus outspokenly expressing the major conflicts of literary life. These were later to be picked up and enlarged upon by Pomerantsev and published in Tvardovsky's own journal.

Critical response to '*Za dal'yu dal''* reflected approval of the poem as a whole and of his stanzas on literature in particular. In fact, the reviewers tended to adopt an even more vigorous stand than he had taken on the subject. Chivalikhin enthusiastically wrote in July that, 'Apart from polemical sharpness, the value of these stanzas is that the poet talks about his understanding of the writer's duty and, in our view, speaks in a way in which not one of the contemporary Soviet poets has spoken since Mayakovsky.'[11] The following month Vladimir Ognev – the same Ognev whose *Novy Mir* article, 'Clarity!', had been severely criticized only months earlier – wrote a long article in *Literaturnaya Gazeta* praising Tvardovsky's latest poem.[12] He singled out the same stanzas on literature as being the best, although he suggested that they could have been even more significant had the poet emphasized the fact that art and time-servers were incompatible. No review seems to have appeared which quarreled with the tone or tenor of the poem.

In a book review which appeared in the September issue of *Novy Mir* the subject of the limitation of self-expression was again discussed in very bold terms, this time by Mikhail Lifshits. Lifshits, who was a staff member of the journal and a literary critic of long standing, reviewed a book on eighteenth-century serf artists by A. Kuznetsov.[13] He clearly used the article as a vehicle for discussing the experience of the artist under the Stalinist regime. Arguing that a true artist could never be intimidated into actively falsifying his vision and would always preserve his inner freedom, Lifshits expressed his thoughts in a most outspoken way. 'For a true artist,' he wrote, 'it is better to be a shepherd than to falsify... Better to be a shepherd than such an artist.' 'One should not persuade the reader', he continued, 'that art is some kind of tool which can be adapted as it suits one.' Arguing against the author of the book, Lifshits asserted that 'A. Kuznetsov forgets that artistic creation demands a certain level of freedom and human dignity even in slavery.' Finally, discussing the peasant artist, Ivan Argunov, Lifshits wrote, 'Rendering unto Caesar that which is Caesar's, he remained internally a free man, a true artist and an honorable son of the people.' These sentiments were very much in keeping with the general drift of Tvardovsky's poem and also very much consonant with the 'Novy Mir style' and its affirmation of a liberal, humanistic attitude towards the creative spirit. In the early autumn days of 1953 no critical comment on Lifshits' review appeared.

Indeed, the general tenor of literary criticism in the summer and early autumn of 1953 reflected the line which criticism had taken the previous year, before the start of the vigilance campaign. Thus, threads of the attacks on the 'no-conflict' theory were picked up and articles once again called for the depiction of 'living human characters' and a 'multi-faceted description of the inner world of Soviet people'.[14] In August, Literaturnaya Gazeta published an article on its front page attacking 'play-it-safe' literary critics.[15] Critics, wrote the author, should help the writer to speak up in the name of truth, not hinder him. The term 'play-it-safe' is one generally used for editors of magazines who are unwilling to risk publishing controversial material. While the article basically dealt with problems generated by the no-conflict theory, its terminology and advice to the individual writer transcended earlier, more dogmatic, statements of the previous year.

Soviet drama, forever the bête noire of the critics, was still the focus of attack in this period.[16] The interest in drama reached a high point in October, a month during which liberalizing influences in the general sphere of literature had culminated in a semi-official indication that there was not to be a return to Stalinism in literature, at least not for the present.[17]

Thus, during the first six months after Stalin's death, while literary criticism spoke for a more personal, a more humanistic involvement of the writer in his work, the pattern upon which this proceeded was not a fresh one, but, rather, one from the last year of Stalin's life. Whether or not this resulted in something qualitatively new is another question. Other influences dominated the atmosphere, and literature and literary criticism did not, and could not, develop within a vacuum.

During the summer and autumn of 1953 the political struggle was characterized by an emphasis on economic problems. The two facets stressed at this time were a demand for more and better consumer goods and a quest for dramatic progress in agriculture. The first of these was expressed quite early in articles demanding an improvement in the quality of goods.[18] In July, for example, a series of articles called 'Criticisms of Things' was launched in *Literaturnaya Gazeta* and appeared thereafter every two weeks.[19] The first article criticized a variety of consumer products – poor-quality hats and umbrellas, pyjamas that shrank, baby carriages that were worthless but cost a fortune – and demanded improvement. Other articles elsewhere also dealt with what were called the 'trifles of life' and attacked bureaucrats who regarded the public's demands as a nuisance and only cared about 'the plan'.[20] These newspaper complaints were given substance in October in a joint statement of the USSR Council of Ministers and the Central Committee of the Communist Party, which affirmed that they 'consider it necessary in the next two or three years to speed up in every way possible the development of light industry in order to have a sufficient quantity of manufactured consumer goods in the country and to increase markedly the supply of these goods to the population'.[21]

The emphasis on a need for more and better consumer goods had a direct effect on the literature and literary criticism which appeared before the Second Writers Congress. First, writers sought to put greater emphasis on the ordinary details of human life.[22] This necessarily involved an exposure of the shortcomings in material life in postwar Russia – crowded communal apartments, difficulties in obtaining products, impoverished families, poor educational facilities. As the fifties progressed, the 'trifles of life', which had earlier been glossed over, ignored or misrepresented, took on an increasingly significant role in fiction, but the beginning of this trend was undoubtedly in the autumn of 1953.

The second effect of the demand for consumer goods was that the literary image of Soviet man was altered. Having generally appeared in fiction as a worker, a farmer, a citizen, he now appeared with more frequency at home instead of at the factory, talking to his family and friends instead of to his fellow-workers. And his conversation was more often devoted to problems of a private, or a human, nature, unrelated to the fulfilment of the plan or snags in work at the factory or on the farm.

The writer, however, did not treat the 'trifles of life' only at their face value. Better pots and pans and baby carriages were inextricably linked to man's personal life and from here there was but a short jump to his inner life. In stressing the importance of consumer goods and material conditions, literature was thus putting them on an equal footing with the industrial goals and impersonal political priorities which had previously occupied an elevated position all of their own. It was the personal and emotional side of man's life (expressed in material terms by the politicians) which gradually came to dominate fiction during the ensuing decade.

The second economic campaign which influenced literary development centered on Khrushchev's pronouncements on agriculture in the autumn of 1953 and the winter of 1954. Agriculture, which had long been in a critical state, became Khrushchev's vehicle in his fight for power, just as the production of consumer goods was Malenkov's. This was a natural focal point for Khrushchev to choose, as he had already established his expertise in propounding theories for agricultural improvement under Stalin. Some of these ideas, such as the development of the *agrogorod*, became popularized in the year following Stalin's death.

Briefly, Khrushchev, in a report to the Central Committee on September 3, 1953, discussed the failings of previous agricultural policy, specifically in the field of animal husbandry and in the production of certain farm staples, and suggested solutions to these problems. These included the encouragement of the farmers' private plots and the use of incentives. Later, in his speech at the February–March plenum in 1954, he expanded his suggestions and introduced the great Virgin Lands project for increasing the grain yield.

The discussion of and emphasis on agricultural problems were reflected in literature in two important directions. First, we see an intensified interest in kolkhoz fiction, although the kolkhoz had, of course, already provided much background and subject matter in fiction. Ovechkin, for example, had paved the way with his sketch in *Novy Mir* the previous year, and his fresh approach had introduced a whole school of kolkhoz fiction-writing. Developments in kolkhoz fiction continued over the next few years. These were accompanied by more demanding articles by literary critics: indeed, the new trends in criticism developed at a faster pace than the works of fiction embodying them.

Second, in articles of the period, and most specifically in Abramov's article in the April issue of *Novy Mir* in 1954,[23] one finds not only a literary critique of various stories and novels with rural themes, but a definite appraisal of the opinions stated or implied in them on questions of agriculture. Thus Abramov can be considered to have a partisan view not only of literary style – which is understandable in a literary critic – but of actual agricultural policies.

Moreover, the statements on agriculture, as well as those on consumer goods, exerted a further influence. In his exposé of the true state of affairs, Khrushchev emphasized past disappointments and failures in the organization of agriculture. It is difficult to control a trend once begun, and this admission of inadequacy in the field of agriculture did not stop there. It gradually developed into a questioning, probing attitude towards other features of Soviet life which had also previously been gilded over, and this came to be reflected in literary works. Thus, the two competing economic platforms of Malenkov and Khrushchev not only gave literature subject matter, but also provided the spirit of criticism and forthrightness which infected works of fiction and which in fact became more significant than the actual material goals themselves.

At the end of October the 14th plenary session of the board of the Writers Union was held. It opened on October 21st in the Moscow Cinema House, with writers from all over the Soviet Union participating. The plenary session had been preceded for almost two weeks by a campaign towards improving Soviet drama.[24] As a repetition of what has been observed in 1952, the appearance of this spate of articles reinforces the impression that the discussion and criticism of the state of drama, clearly a weak rung in the literary ladder, served in both cases as a signal for an increase in literary innovation. The earlier campaign had called forth the attack on the no-conflict theory and the related loosening of other bonds. This one came only weeks before the publication of literature which was a harbinger of the thaw.

The plenary session, which lasted for four days, was attended by P. K. Ponomarenko, Minister of Culture. Conquest sees his presence at the plenum as a positive sign towards liberalization.[25] The previous March, Ponomarenko, who had been a secretary of the Party's Central Committee, was transferred to the post of Minister of Culture. Conquest, who associates Ponomarenko with Malenkov, sees this transfer as an intentional strengthening of the state apparatus in the cultural–ideological field as against the Party bureaucrats of the Agitprop and Science and Culture departments of the Central Committee.[26] The hypothesis that Ponomarenko's presence represented a liberalizing influence and that this tendency could be associated with Malenkov himself does seem to be borne out by the facts. While the Zhdanov decrees passed almost unmentioned, Malenkov's address to the 19th Party Congress was quoted by almost every speaker.[27] Furthermore, October does appear to have been a watershed – the subsequent months witnessed the publication of a spate of innovative material, items which were not to be criticized harshly in the press until the end of January, 1954. Significant here is that it was in February, 1954 that Ponomarenko was relieved as Minister of Culture, though he remained a candidate member of the Party Presidium until 1956.[28] From February to May we see an increase in the number and scale of critical articles directed against *Novy Mir* and its contents, reaching a high point in May and June, and then tapering off. This early connection of the thaw with Ponomarenko as Malenkov's man and the later conjunction of dates in literary policy and fluctuations in the political sphere can provide a link between the rhythms of literary policy and Malenkov's changing political fortunes.

The October plenum decided to hold the Second Writers Congress in the autumn of 1954. Furthermore, Fadeev was chosen to be chairman of the board of the Union, and Surkov the first secretary of the board secretariat.

Fadeev's speech at the 14th plenum, bearing almost the same title as his speech the previous spring, was markedly different in tone and provided a striking contrast.[29] Most of the invective was gone, criticism centered upon the work of the Writers Union, and there was an almost conciliatory note in his mention of the two writers whom he had sought to destroy seven months before. Towards Kazakevich, whom Fadeev had accused of gross ideological errors and inexcusable political statements, he now adopted a patronizing tone. 'However profound the mistakes of Kazakevich,' he wrote, 'they are only individual errors and cannot obliterate the virtues of the story as a whole. However, not one publishing house, including our own Sovetsky pisatel', took it upon itself to work over the story with the author and publish it.' Similarly, Fadeev's attitude towards Vasily Grossman, whom he had attacked viciously in March, had changed radically. He now appeared helpful and anxious not to confuse artistic and ideological criticism.

The 14th plenum reflected, then, a broad change of climate. Most important, perhaps, was Ilya Ehrenburg's article 'Concerning the Writer's Work', published in the October issue of *Znamya*.[30] In it Ehrenburg made an impassioned plea for the right of the writer to describe man's inner world as he sees it, for critics to provide more than a shallow catalog of vices and virtues, and for the writer to write only when he is motivated by artistic considerations.

A writer is not an apparatus mechanically recording events. A writer writes a book not because he can write or because he is a member of the Soviet Writers Union and might be asked why he has not published anything for a long time, not because he must earn a living, but because he is compelled to tell people something he personally feels, because he has 'begun to ache' from his book.[31]

This same plea was echoed and reinforced in Pomerantsev's article on sincerity in literature, published in *Novy Mir* the following month, but handed in for publication before he could have seen this issue of *Znamya*.[32]

In the wake of the October plenum there also appeared a remarkable series of articles in *Sovetskaya Muzyka* which clearly paralleled what was being increasingly demanded by liberal literary critics, and which coincided with similar items in the literary field. Perhaps the most outspoken article was the first, written by Aram Khachaturian, and published in the November issue of *Sovetskaya Muzyka*.[33] In his demand that music be judged by its compositional and harmonic qualities and not by the theme given in its title and subtitles, his assertion that 'creative problems cannot be solved by bureaucratic methods', his reviling of the composer's use of only well-known and commonplace artificial musical phraseology as 'an attempt to sell the public used goods from the second-hand store or pawnshop', Khachaturian proved himself at least as bold in the field of music as writers had been thus far in the field of literature.

However, such articles were only exceptions to the standard criticism which persisted, perhaps in not so virulent, but at least in a very dogmatic, form. They by no means took over the critical field. It was with its November, 1953 issue that *Novy Mir* began to register the significant changes of the previous months. This issue had been handed in for typesetting at the end of September and was put into print – that is, approved by the censor – on October 13th. First, there was the modest listing on the last page, with no prior announcement, of a new editorial board. Nine months before, there had been a palpable threat that the too-'liberal' board of *Novy Mir* was to be removed. Stalin had died before the expected replacement had taken place, leaving the editorial board intact. Until the November issue, the board was composed of the following members:

A. T. Tvardovsky (editor-in-chief)
M. S. Bubennov
V. P. Kataev
S. S. Smirnov
A. K. Tarasenkov
K. A. Fedin
M. A. Sholokhov

This had been the composition of the *Novy Mir* editorial board since March, 1950, when Simonov had been replaced by Tvardovsky as editor-in-chief. In November, 1953 the board gained three new members and lost two. This was the new board:

A. T. Tvardovsky (editor-in-chief)
S. P. Antonov
A. G. Dement'ev (assistant editor)
V. P. Kataev
S. S. Smirnov (assistant editor)
S. B. Sutotsky
K. A. Fedin
M. A. Sholokhov

Antonov, Dement'ev and Sutotsky were all new additions. Missing were Bubennov and Tarasenkov. In Bubennov's removal the journal was obviously losing one of its most conservative, Stalinist members.[34] None of the new members fulfilled the watchdog function which he had performed.

Sutotsky and Dement'ev, as new members of the 'liberalized'

board, later both proved their mettle in defending *Novy Mir* against the critics. Dement'ev, particularly, distinguished himself in this early period as a liberal editor and spokesman.[35] When called upon the following spring to admit his 'guilt' in helping to formulate *Novy Mir*'s faulty publishing policy, he staunchly refused. His career roughly followed that of Tvardovsky: he left the editorial board somewhat after Tvardovsky (in 1955) and returned only at the end of 1959, after Tvardovsky himself had been reinstated as editor-in-chief. An article which he published in 1956 with A. Metchenko and G. Lomidze[36] has been cited as one of the extremely liberal ones of that eventful year.[37] However, Dement'ev was also a 'reliable' literary figure, having been a member of the Communist Party since 1941. He had held various literary posts, including that of directing the criticism section of *Zvezda* from 1951 to 1953.

The third new member, Antonov, later defended further discussion of the question of sincerity in literature, a stand which was to be unacceptable to the conservative critics in the summer of 1954.

Assuming that Fedin, Kataev, and Sholokhov were on the board primarily for their reputations as recognized and popular writers and that they contributed more name than energy to their positions,[38] we may attribute a neutral role to their membership. Finally, S. S. Smirnov certainly played a moderate-to-liberal part in later literary politics and may well, even at this point, have tipped the balance toward new liberalized policies.

Thus, as it was composed in November, 1953, the *Novy Mir* board was predominantly liberal. There was a majority of five editors who went along with the spirit of reform, and these five, plus various staff members, were presumably the most active in editorial work, the leading guide of editorial policy being Tvardovsky. The change in the board coincided with a quickening in the tempo of the journal's liberalization which was eventually followed by the attack culminating in Tvardovsky's removal as editor.

It was in the November issue of *Novy Mir* that the first half of Vera Panova's novel *Vremena goda* (Seasons of the Year) was published, the second half appearing the following month.[39] Panova was already an established and very popular writer at the time and had given readings or published various excerpts of the novel previously.[40] She apparently wrote *Seasons of the Year* between 1951 and 1953,[41] so the major themes of the novel must be seen largely as a product of the Stalinist period, although particular details and certainly the publication itself can be attributed to the thaw atmosphere.

4 Vera Panova, whose *Seasons of the Year* was
published in *Novy Mir* at the end of 1953

Seasons of the Year is a novel about two families, the Kupriyanovs
and the Bortasheviches, implicated in the crime of embezzlement –
one for perpetrating it and the other for peripheral involvement. The
action takes place in 1950. Dorofea Kupriyanova is a Party member
who holds an important post. It is her son, Gennady, a man of no
moral sense, who eventually consorts with gangsters and embezzlers.
By the climax of the novel Gennady has sunk so deep in a morass
of criminal involvement that the possibility of his eventual moral
rehabilitation is highly questionable. He never shows any remorse.

In the Bortashevich family it is the wife, Nadezhda, a woman of
bourgeois origin, whose greed has motivated her husband's embezzlement from the All-Union Trust. Their two children, Katya and
Serezha, are affectionate and exemplary young Soviet citizens.

Stepan Bortashevich leads a double life – a good communist and solid family man, but at the same time involved with a gang of embezzlers who, to cover their traces, commit further crimes, including arson and attempted murder. When the police finally arrive to arrest him, Bortashevich shoots himself.

Several striking departures from the norm of acceptable Soviet literature are immediately evident. First, one of the villains is a young man, born in the Soviet period, whose parents are not only of proletarian origin but are even loyal members of the Party. His lack of moral fiber clearly goes back to childhood and his tendencies are seen to have flourished in the very home where his parents had set so different a tone. The children of the other villains, on the other hand, are, in spite of parental influence, model Soviet citizens. This situation contradicts the standard theory that under the Soviet system the moral dilemmas and criminal acts existing in capitalist society will disappear, that whatever crime there is in the Soviet Union must be attributed to 'survivals' of bourgeois society.[42] There is no way to assess Gennady's way of life without seeing it as a development within Soviet society itself. Somehow, for some reason, Gennady had grown up in a 'good' home in Soviet Russia and had developed into a Soviet criminal.* Furthermore, at the novel's end we are left in doubt as to whether Gennady will ever be reformed; there is a clear probability that Dorofea will again use her influence to save her son from his deserved punishment. This is a distinct contrast to the socialist–realist 'happy ending'.

In describing Gennady's involvement with criminals Panova was taking up a problem which was a genuine phenomenon in postwar Soviet Russia. An actual case which was remarkably similar to that in the novel was discussed in *Komsomol'skaya Pravda* in November, 1953.[43] In a feuilleton entitled 'Blight', the authors described a group of young men – 'gilded youth', children of important people – who passed the time carousing, spending huge sums of money, and who eventually turned to robbery and murder. One member of this group bears a strong resemblance to Dorofea's son. This young man, unlike the others, was not fully identified in the newspaper report. Although the others were given stiff sentences he was not even tried. The

* Leonid Kupriyanov notes this anomaly when he says,
  I see Gennady hasn't changed a bit...He's just the same. It's amazing! If we'd been former landowners or capitalists, you could understand it. But I've worked on the railways since I was fourteen and his mother used to go out scrubbing floors. And yet he's a typical exploiter.

similarity between him and Gennady and the protection given each
is striking.

In a study written ten years later, Zoya Boguslavskaya suggested
that *Seasons of the Year* was a very contemporary novel when
published in 1953 – contemporary in its ideas, in the 'moral character
of the generation, its mode of thought and the pattern of experience'.
It was, she wrote, contemporary in its central problem – 'on the
interconnection of generations, on their responsibility to each other
and to the common cause'.[44]

Describing the difficult path of Gennady Kupriyanov, the history of his fall
and regeneration, Panova, perhaps for the first time in our literature, so
clearly said something about the appearance of scepticism among a small
part of postwar youth, and about the sources of its indifference to common
causes and about those whose idea of a good life was identified with an
understanding of an easy, thoughtless life.[45]

In another study of Panova's work, Lev Plotkin noted that in
providing the history of the two couples, Panova had devoted a good
part of the novel to a description of life in the nineteen twenties. He
sees the character growth of Dorofea Kupriyanova and Stepan
Bortashevich in the twenties as 'the ideological center of the novel'.[46]
These were the years when native talent, like that of Dorofea,
developed.

The personal aspect of man's social behavior is an underlying
theme of the novel. Social origins and political ideology are not in
themselves the determining factors in the development of character.
Panova suggests the variety of influences at work in character
formation, and in doing so she takes educational theory away from
the Party and the political theorists and treats each case individually
as it varies from family to family.

Seasons of the Year marked a clean break with the 'no-conflict'
novels of the early fifties. A Soviet critic, Sarra Fradkina, has noted
that 'in *Seasons of the Year* Panova not only does not avoid difficult
judgments, complicated psychological situations, but actually over-
indulges in them. Thus, in a heavily populated novel there is actually
not a single happy family in the full sense of the word.'[47] A welcome
departure from standard Soviet literature of the day was Panova's
reluctance to present wholly 'positive' and 'negative' characters.
Thus, even 'villains' are more than cardboard stereotypes. For
example, Stepan Bortashevich, though clearly a scoundrel in terms
of his deception of the Party and the Trust, is portrayed as a warm,

humorous, affectionate man, well loved by his children, who are themselves very positive characters. Similar balance is given to the depiction of Churkin, one of the top officials in the town of Ensk. In his official status Churkin is in control of the distribution of new apartments in the town. However, we discover that he is simply unable to resist the demands of 'important' people for better apartments and, although he knows that many people are desperately in need of housing, Churkin always finds himself in the position of having already assigned the new apartments not to the neediest but to those who pressured him the most and used the most influence. Panova herself is very indulgent toward Churkin and shows more sympathy than ire. This more balanced portrayal of characters as well as certain themes – problems of individual morality and the education of the young – were to typify the thaw literature which followed Panova's novel.

Another characteristic of the novel and of thaw literature was the change in attitude towards man's material existence. The assertions in the press that material things did matter and that Soviet citizens deserved better than they received were echoed in *Seasons of the Year*. Panova went a step further and insisted that without decent living conditions man cannot attain the ideological heights which the Party intends him to reach. In fact, housing, in one way or another, provides a secondary theme throughout the novel.

The pleasant Kupriyanov home and the luxurious Bortashevich apartment present a striking contrast with some of the other dwellings described in the book. In the sixth chapter Dorofea receives a complaint in her office that couples are living in an all-women's hostel. On going to visit it, 'She was hit by an antiseptic smell and dazzled by the glare of a lonely naked bulb shining on the white-scrubbed floorboards of the bare, deserted hall.' There is no trace of 'embellishing' in the description of Dorofea's looking into the rooms as she walks down the hall. 'The room contained four beds, four bedside tables, four chairs, and one table. Clothes hung on the walls and bedrails.' She and the Warden pass an obviously pregnant young woman. 'That's Tanya', says the Warden.

Just take her case. Suppose I separate her from her husband and he gets used to being parted from her and runs off with another woman? You know they say families break up if there's no love. Well, I'll tell you something else. Families break up if there's no living space. Love doesn't last without floor space, you can take that from me. I've seen enough of that sort of thing.

This is a jolting recognition of the importance of material conditions and an admission of the squalor in which a large number of people were living. And no miraculous solution to the couples' problems is forthcoming. While Dorofea promises to look into the possibility of finding them living quarters, she makes a temporary arrangement which is only marginally better than the previous one. Later Dorofea speaks again of the housing problem: 'I believe that it's only when every single person has a proper place in which to live that culture will really flourish...Just think of it nowadays – all the people who haven't room for a bookcase.'

Besides problems of housing, other difficulties of Soviet life are mentioned starkly: abortion, abandonment, financial hardships. Another innovative feature comes at the end of the novel when one of Panova's characters is chided for not looking after the interests of the Bortashevich children. 'Are you telling me', Dorofea bursts out, 'that they have to be punished for their father?'

Seasons of the Year thus quietly set the stage in atmosphere and emphasis for thaw works to come. Initially accepted and praised when noted – but largely ignored – the novel was reprinted in book form in February, 1954 in a Leningrad edition of 30,000.

In December, 1953 a startlingly outspoken article of literary criticism appeared in *Novy Mir* under the title '*Ob iskrennosti v literature*' (On Sincerity in Literature).[48] The author was a forty-five year old writer–critic by the name of Vladimir Mikhailovich Pomerantsev.[49] His article and those of Mikhail Lifshits, Fedor Abramov and Mark Shcheglov which appeared in the ensuing months came to be lumped together under the rubric of the *Novy Mir* 'series' and were considered by adverse critics to express the *Novy Mir* 'line'.

That the article was considered to be potentially troublesome is clear from the fact that the issue in which it appeared was handed in to the typesetter on October 1, 1953 and was actually put in the press on November 12, 1953.[50] Tvardovsky, evidently sensing that the journal might have problems getting past the censor, handed in the manuscript unusually early. This, plus the fact that it took six weeks to get through, indicates the difficult nature of the material. The early date of handing it in also points to the possibility that the new editorial board, officially acknowledged only in the November issue, had already been at work at least as early as September.

I. Sats, who was the staff member in charge of literary criticism at the time, provided the following information on *Novy Mir*'s acquisition of the Pomerantsev article.

Vl. Pomerantsev did not work at the journal. His article 'On Sincerity' was not commissioned by the editorial board: he brought it in...As a man he was distinguished by impulsiveness, was even hysterical. Constancy was not one of his characteristics. He was somehow carried away in this article which was called a *cri de cœur* in the English Pen Club's *Criterion* – in this was its merit. His thoughts were confused: when for example he demands that literature be a confession and not a sermon the thought lacks specificity – that is, a confession (J. J. Rousseau, L. Tolstoy) was always a sermon. The editing of the article was entrusted to me. It was then read by all the board members. As always, I was limited in my editing by what the author would agree to. With all its failings the article played a certain beneficial role, awakening critical thought from slumber, although it provoked displeasure. In fact, Fedor Abramov's article...on 'kolkhoz literature' was more significant, not to speak of M. Lifshits' article 'Marietta Shaginian's Diary', N. Leont'ev's 'Sorcery instead of Science' (on pseudo-folklore), and the very talented works of Mark Shcheglov...It was these articles [*sic*] that impelled Pomerantsev to turn to *NM*; in other journals it would not have been printed.[51]

The first feature of the article to strike the reader is its style. Pomerantsev plunged directly to the core of his subject, with not so much as a ceremonial bow to accepted Soviet literary theory, presenting 'disjointed thoughts, some of them doubtless debatable, concerning shortcomings in our literature'. Written impressionistically, this very informal and readable article was the antithesis of the usual piece of literary criticism found in Soviet journals.[52]

What Pomerantsev had to say was exciting to the reader, not only for its content, but for the boldness with which he stated his ideas. Fundamentally, the article was about sincerity, the touchstone of good literature. Arguing against the contrived novel, the stereotype in literature, which becomes synonymous with insincerity, Pomerantsev wrote that 'The degree of sincerity, that is, the directness of things, must be the first test. Sincerity is the basic item in the sum total of qualities which we call talent.' Everything he said beyond this was an enrichment of the theme. What Pomerantsev sought was an emotional foundation to literature, a spontaneity, a 'confession and not merely a sermon'. Thus the essentials of socialist realism, *narodnost'*, *ideinost'* and *partiinost'*, were ignored and presumably occupied an inferior position in Pomerantsev's scale of values.

In listing qualities which are the opposite of sincerity, Pomerantsev included the author's omission of all problems from his subject matter. Referring to an unnamed novel, he wrote,

The author said nothing about the dormitories and dining rooms of the factory which he had in mind when writing the novel; and they were atrocious. The author did not put earrings and brooches on his characters, but he left out everything unsavory and nasty.

(Panova had already made a giant step in the direction towards which Pomerantsev was heading – she did not omit the grimmer side of life, but matter-of-factly described the minute but significant details he deemed necessary in a sincere novel.)

Pomerantsev feared that writers would continue to be disoriented by critics with their 'notorious charge of "untypical"'. He exhorted the writer,

Don't write until you have explored thoroughly. Know what you are fighting for. Don't think about the prosecutors. Don't spell out conclusions, but don't let yourself write a single line that you do not feel. Be independent. And then my truth will correspond with our common truth.

This corresponds to Ehrenburg's sentiment that the writer writes a book 'because he is compelled to tell people something he personally feels, because he has "begun to ache" from his book'.[53]

Though Pomerantsev's call for sincerity in literature had a fresh ring in 1953, the demand had been heard by the Soviet public before. It bore remarkable similarity to the demands for sincerity expressed by the Perevaltsy in the 1920s. The Pereval, a group of young writers, had issued a summons for sincerity and humanism in literature. 'They emphasized the primary importance for the writer not of "the Party spirit", but of "the human spirit"', as Edward J. Brown has written.[54] Just as Panova harked back to the nineteen twenties as the fertile ground in which the individual could flourish, so Pomerantsev sought a literary principle from that period to bring to life the moribund literature of the fifties.

Pomerantsev's attitude towards literature with a rural theme was symptomatic of the new trends in thinking. Instead of enumerating the classic works of Soviet literature in a standard practice which was *de rigueur*, he named only one work as a major contribution to recent Soviet literature. This was Valentin Ovechkin's 'District Routine', which he used as a yardstick against which he measured other, inferior, books such as Babaevsky's novels and Nikolaeva's *Harvest*. He criticized works in which 'things shoved man aside', and described an essay in which the human side of a kolkhoz had been ignored although the essayist had personally noticed certain details which might have helped to present a balanced picture. In his notes, for example, the author had written that his landlady, though the kolkhoz was a wealthy one, had neither cow nor garden – 'nothing but potatoes and cucumbers'.

Unheard of! It turns out she destroyed the cherry trees herself! She explained it to me this way: 'When there is a good harvest, the cherries are worth nothing; when the trees produce little, the tax must still be paid on each tree. So I cut them down. Many people have done the same here.[55]

This, and other human details, had been omitted in the essay. Pomerantsev, in citing this case, was asking of literature what was being demanded in the economic sphere: a recognition of the shortcomings in Soviet man's material life – in this case in agriculture – and an attempt to overcome them. He reminded the reader that material existence and the human aspect of life are intertwined and cannot be viewed separately. His demand for sincerity emphasized humanism and an honest interpretation of Soviet reality. In the field of economics Soviet political figures were viewing the situation in a more realistic and openly critical fashion; Pomerantsev was only asking for the same approach in literature.

His article was to have far-reaching effects in the literary debate which raged on and off over the next few years.[56] Although sincerity was not officially recognized as the ultimate criterion of good literature, his literary taste did come to be widely recognized as the Babaevskys of literature lost their popularity with literary critics.*

The second article of the *Novy Mir* 'series' appeared in the February, 1954, issue of the journal. This was a review by Mikhail

---

* In a caustic passage in *Cancer Ward*, Solzhenitsyn portrays a conversation which takes place in the late winter of 1955 in which Aviette discusses Soviet literary criticism.

Take the case of Babayevsky. At first everyone loved him, then everyone hated him, they all renounced him, even his most faithful friends. But that's only a temporary phase: they'll change their minds, they'll come back to him. It's just one of those delicate transitions life's so full of. For instance, they used to say, 'There must be no conflict.' But now they talk about 'the false theory of absence of conflict'. If there was division of opinion, if some people were still talking the old way while others were using the new style, then it would be obvious that there had been a change. But when *everyone* starts talking the new way all at once, you don't notice there's been a transition at all.

(Alexander Solzhenitsyn, *Cancer Ward*
(New York: Bantam Books, 1969), p. 282)

Lifshits of Marietta Shaginyan's *Dnevnik pisatelya 1950–1952* (A Writer's Diary).[57] In the *Diary* Shaginyan described her travels around the Soviet Union and discussed literary techniques, offering practical advice to young writers.

An earlier review had appeared in *Literaturnaya Gazeta* in December.[58] The critic, Sergei L'vov, had been largely favorable toward the *Diary*, but expressed three main criticisms. First, the book had been so poorly edited that geographic names and technical terms were frequently of dubious preciseness. Second, Shaginyan had failed to excise insignificant material from the book. Finally, in some parts of the *Diary* he felt that the aim to know as much as possible was accompanied by a desire to know as quickly as possible, thus leading to premature generalizations on Shaginyan's part. The *Novy Mir* review, while duplicating L'vov's criticisms, was longer, more detailed and harsher in tone.

The author of the review, Mikhail Lifshits, was a frequent contributor to *Novy Mir*. Two years younger than Pomerantsev, he had been a member of the Communist Party since 1938 and had been active in literary and philosophical spheres for almost two decades. He had earlier been a board member of *Literaturny Kritik*.

The motif running throughout Lifshits' review was that Shaginyan's enormous range of interests and great versatility had led to a dilettante approach in her writing. Thus a high degree of superficiality characterized her work. In presenting numerous examples of this, Lifshits used a style which was brisk, accusatory and often sarcastic.*

His most profound criticism of Shaginyan's *Diary* emerged in a discussion of human problems and values. Here his attitude reflected points made earlier by Pomerantsev and, before him, Tvardovsky. Lifshits, in describing one scene in the *Diary* in which Shaginyan displayed a cavalier attitude towards a village woman's complaints, attacked writers who make lightning visits to the countryside: 'Surely tomorrow they will drive off in their car and carry off with them a

---

* For example: 'With all her education she has the right not to know what a compressor is. But how can she not be afraid to write on something she knows nothing about?' And, he added, if she feels she must write about these things, why not check with someone for accuracy?

We also do not have any special familiarity with technology and judge the shortcomings of her story only on the basis of accessible sources. However, accessible sources are accessible to everyone and it is not understandable why such a simple thought did not enter the head of the writer herself.

(*Novyi Mir* 2, 1954, p. 209)

pleasant recollection and nothing more.' Shaginyan, he writes, 'in her constant enthusiasm... has an element of indifference to people'.

Lifshits demanded that a writer, in this case Shaginyan, write because she is deeply motivated to write and that she desist from writing simply to write. A shallow, superficial understanding of subject matter is tantamount to insincerity. Although Lifshits never used the word, he was clearly setting the same requirement of sincerity, of strong motivation and of personal involvement that Pomerantsev had established two months before. Although these points had already been made in the earlier review of the *Diary*, in a moderate way, the tone and emphasis of Lifshits' article later helped to make it controversial.

An entirely different aspect of Lifshits' attack on Shaginyan should be noted here. The previous year Shaginyan had come out with a provocative assault on Vasily Grossman's *For the Just Cause*.[59] (Indeed, Grigory Svirsky, in his interview, recalled the particular vehemence of Shaginyan's review and singled it out in his recollections as the most shocking of all the attacks on Grossman.) There could certainly have been an element of revenge in Lifshits' strongly worded, sarcastic review of the *Diary*, out of annoyance with Shaginyan's participation in the campaign and out of loyalty to a *Novy Mir* author. Other examples of such solidarity in defense of *Novy Mir* writers would occur later.

In his article on 'People of the Kolkhoz Countryside in Postwar Prose' Fedor Abramov departed from purely literary considerations and discussed economic policy decisions as well.[60] Thus his review article contained criticism, not only of literary style, but of the agricultural policies which form the background of the rural theme. Indeed, Abramov introduced his subject with a discussion of the September plenum and agricultural problems and then tied in the shortcomings of agriculture with those of literature containing a rural theme. Critics, he wrote, had eagerly welcomed new works on the countryside and were sometimes ready to forgive the author his mistakes.

However this should not hide from us the serious shortcomings of postwar literature on the kolkhoz countryside. They have become particularly evident in the light of the latest party and government decisions on questions of agriculture.

Abramov proceeded with a wholesale condemnation of kolkhoz fiction of the postwar period, including the works of Stalin Prize winners.* In criticizing them for embellishment, for pastoral romanticism and for ignoring the true situation on the collective farms, Abramov described the shocking state of postwar farming in the Soviet Union: lack of manpower, the drought of 1946, severe shortages. The basic failing of the novels was an inability or unwillingness to portray the great suffering endured.[61]

Abramov illustrated the lack of reality in kolkhoz fiction by citing Babaevsky's *Cavalier of the Golden Star*. In this novel the collective farm set aside important farm work in order to build a hydroelectric station.

The first stage of construction of the electric station – the floating of timber – begins *at the very height of the grain reaping*!

Although the cutting of grain cannot be delayed and every hand is necessary for the task, in Babaevsky's novel brigades were formed among the best workers of the village for the floating of timber, which was at least a month's work.†

However, Abramov's criticism went beyond accusing Soviet authors of an unrealistic portrayal of rural life. His comments included an implied attack on past policy and on Khrushchev's present agricultural policy.[62] He was in effect questioning the practicability of the grandiose ideas which had been expressed since September.

Throughout the article, Abramov criticized the fact that writers

* Among the writers attacked were Babaevsky, Mal'tsev, Voronin, Laptev and Nikolaeva. The main criticism of all of these authors was their unrealistic portrayal of kolkhoz life just after the Second World War. In his article Abramov did have praise for a few individual recent writers on kolkhoz themes – Ovechkin, Kalinin, Troepol'sky, and Tendryakov. Their works had all appeared in 1952–53.

† In spite of a difference in tone, there is marked similarity between Abramov's view of Babaevsky and that of Konstantin Simonov as expressed at the 14th plenum of the board of the Soviet Writers Union in October, 1953:

In 1947–48 Babaevsky came out with the novel *Cavalier of the Golden Star*, where he described the lively and strong central character, Sergei Tutarinov, and in a talented way showed the difficulties of the postwar rehabilitation of agriculture and the persistence and victories of the Soviet people in the struggle with these difficulties. However, later, in the first and especially in the second book of *Light over the Earth*, it seems to me that the writer gives in with some softened description of life. His heroes constantly – easily and off-handedly – cope with any difficulties, the description of the struggle changes into an enumeration of victories, and the general picture of life at the end of the novel begins to acquire a hue of rosy tenderness and, in places, of improbability. Having started his novel well, at the end the writer noticeably spoils it, embellishing life and people, smoothing over conflicts, closing his eyes to the shady sides of life.

(Konstantin Simonov, 'Problemy razvitiia sovetskoi dramaturgii', *Literaturnaia Gazeta*, October 22, 1953, pp. 1–3)

created situations in which their characters ignored the obvious facts
of the agricultural season – planting or harvest time – or of
agricultural problems – shortage of working hands, low crop yield –
and permitted them to participate in non-agricultural activities at the
very time that they should have been devoting all of their labor to
the collective farm. He constantly reminded the reader that the main
object of agricultural workers is the production of crops. In referring
to the non-agricultural job of building hydroelectric stations he
persistently asked the same questions: Where did they find the labor
for it? Where did the capital come from? Who was doing the work
of paramount importance – agricultural work – while the station
was being built? Whom was it being built for?

Postwar reports indicate that there had been, indeed, a vigorous
drive to build hydroelectric stations in the rural areas.[63] If one can
believe the daily accounts in the press, the novelists had been only
too accurate in sending their collective farmers out of the fields and
into the forests for timber. Abramov was thus attacking, not the
novelists' solutions to problems – though there was, of course, severe
criticism of the literary material – but the actual solutions of the
immediate postwar years.

In a searing attack on *Cavalier of the Golden Star* Abramov singled
out the question of how a kolkhoz could have managed to build a
station in such hard times. This problem should have been considered
in the novel.

How strange in a novel not to broach the far from unimportant question –
from where will the kolkhoz take the means for the construction of a
powerful electric station sufficient for servicing several villages. Surely the
main source of revenue of this kolkhoz is the harvest, but we know from the
novel that it is very low; even after reaping the new harvest Sergei Tutarinov
confesses: 'Things are bad with our harvest, grandpa.'[64]

Not only literature, then, but also agricultural policy was at issue
here. By implication, Abramov was also criticizing Khrushchev's
recent pronouncements on agriculture.

In calling for a material improvement in the lives of collective
farmers Khrushchev had revived his concept of the *agrogorod*, the
building of giant conglomerates of collective farms which would include all the best features of town life – good schools, fine dwellings,
parks, movie theaters, libraries. With this idea, originally suggested
in 1950, Khrushchev had sought to appeal to Stalin's obsession with
regimentation. In Edward Crankshaw's words, 'The factory workers

had always been easier to control than the peasants, if only because they were concentrated under the eyes of strong forces of police and Party functionaries and depended wholly on the state for their wages and means of subsistence.[65] Crankshaw sees the vision of the *agrogorod* as nothing more than blueprints of a Utopian dream, with no conceivable possibility of realization. The plan had been dropped in 1951 and only taken up again in Khrushchev's policy statements of recent months. But there was no reason to believe that the *agrogorod* as a Utopia was any more feasible in 1954 than it had been in 1950. Fundamental problems of agriculture could not be solved by sidestepping into another project, be it a new hydroelectric station or a new movie theater in a *agrogorod*. Funds and labor should be applied to farming, not diverted. Abramov, in demanding a realistic approach in postwar fiction, was also demanding a realistic approach in policy-making, and in this his view was significantly closer to that being advocated by Malenkov than that favored by Khrushchev.

The last author in the 'series' of critical articles in *Novy Mir* was Mark Shcheglov. Shcheglov, who died an early death in 1956, was a *Novy Mir* critic, closely associated with the journal. He was to publish some outspoken literary criticism in the celebrated literary almanac, *Literaturnaya Moskva* II, in 1956.

Two recent articles of Shcheglov's came in for criticism in the late spring and summer of 1954. One was a review of Osip Cherny's novel *Snegin's Opera*.[66] The other, which was more severely censured and labeled part of the 'series', was his review of Leonov's novel *The Russian Forest*.[67] In both reviews Shcheglov selected a key theme and attacked the author's approach, which in each case reflected the official attitude. *Snegin's Opera* dealt with problems of creative latitude encountered by a composer. Shcheglov accused the author of ignoring the implications of the Zhdanov period, 'when the Party interfered in great measure with the development of Soviet music',[68] and of attempting no constructive analysis. Cherny gave Party officials full rein in his novel and had his hero leave a Party meeting 'a different man'.

Shcheglov's review in May of Leonov's *The Russian Forest* found much that was unacceptable in a novel which previously had received quite a warm reception.[69] The most objectionable idea expressed in Shcheglov's review – from the Party viewpoint – and the one which was criticized so virulently afterward, was his discussion of the origins of Professor Gratsiansky's evil character. Shcheglov rejected the standard facile explanation that the source of evil lay in 'survivals of capitalism', that Gratsiansky's pre-revolutionary origins were sufficient cause.

It was not gendarmes who made Gratsiansky what he was, but a series of social conditions which created the post-revolutionary off-shoots of the old petty bourgeoisie. This petty bourgeoisie attempted to preserve tendencies alien to socialist society, but in adapting to the new conditions, as Leonov himself wrote, was especially aggressive and used the most poisonous of weapons. These social conditions were those of 'the years of decline' which preceded October, of the NEP, and of certain features and occurrences which have still not been rooted out in our life – features which our literature treats lightheartedly, declaring them survivals of the past which easily disappear and 'birthmarks' of capitalism and therefore not worthy of a serious attack. However, what we need, after all, is not only to note the existence of capitalist survivals, but also to examine them, to struggle against them and to know how to expose them in their occasional 'Soviet' form. Leonov's Gratsiansky balances for his whole life on the head of a pin, afraid that his criminal connection with the tsarist *okhrana* will be exposed: but this is only one of the possibilities, and that most suited to the detective novel. More often the Gratsianskys in life fear exposure in a more simple sense; they fear that those [good] qualities which they believe they have will be exposed as nonexistent, and then their ungifted, egotistical, lowly guilty core will be revealed.

After all, when all is said and done, thirty-seven years have passed since tsarism and the tsarist *okhrana* left this world.

We repeat once again, as this is an important question – has L. Leonov succeeded in depicting the doom not of Gratsiansky the tsarist secret policeman, but of that Gratsiansky who is a post-revolutionary petty bourgeois, a man by no means old in years, who has acquired Marxist terminology and studied all the obligatory aspects of our social behavior which have permitted him to make a career without having to take anything else into account?[70]

Insofar as the articles in the *Novy Mir* 'series' had certain fundamental ideas in common – though in the most general of terms – it might indeed be considered a series. Shcheglov's main offense, that of seeing Gratsiansky as more than a mere 'survival' of capitalism, ties him to Gennady in Panova's novel which, though not categorized as part of the 'series', did share the general censure levelled against *Novy Mir*. It should be briefly noted here that, in his Leonov article, Shcheglov referred very favorably to Panova's *Seasons of the Year*.[71] This was after she had been severely criticized in other reviews. (He continued to praise her in later articles.)

Lifshits, in discussing Shaginyan, was echoing Pomerantsev's plea for sincerity on the part of the writer. Abramov, too, demanded a truthfulness in kolkhoz literature which could be seen as a link with the ultimate demand of sincerity, and shared many of Pomerantsev's views on recent kolkhoz fiction.

Still, this is the most that can be said, for the articles, while having some vague overlapping themes, were really connected mainly by a fresh general approach and not by the specific details of an ideological thread clearly repeated and embroidered in each. If *Novy Mir* did have a 'line', it was that of producing new and more innovative critical articles by young men who did not toe the conservative line of the Surkovs and Kochetovs. The mere selection of these articles for the journal did constitute an editorial policy, but not a constricting editorial line. It was to set a precedent for later liberalizing attempts.

A survey of *Novy Mir* from the autumn of 1953 until the summer of 1954 reveals that the actual proportion of new, innovative, 'liberal' items to appear in the journal during the early months of the thaw was small. Each issue contained from 280 to over 300 pages. Thus, there was a total of over 2,000 pages published during this period. As the sum of the celebrated 'series' plus the Panova novel comes to only approximately 300 pages of material which was actually singled out later for attack, by far the major part of published material was either ignored or favorably reviewed. Neither *Novy Mir* nor any other journal of the time was completely devoted to items of exceptional political or literary interest.

What is true, however, is that – besides the *causes célèbres* discussed above – the journal did contain more controversial items between November, 1953 and March, 1954 than was usual. These did not attract critical attention but, cumulatively, contributed to the thaw atmosphere of liberalization. What was of interest might be a theme or particular details, the handling of subject matter or simply a paragraph or two setting the piece apart from ordinary literary fare. A few examples of this should suffice.

The November, 1953 issue of *Novy Mir* carried Tendryakov's '*Padenie Ivana Chuprova*' (The Fall of Ivan Chuprov).[72] Tendryakov used the genre so successfully employed by Ovechkin to portray kolkhoz life – the sketch (*ocherk*) – to describe a kolkhoz chairman who becomes involved in illicit arrangements in order to promote his own kolkhoz. Characteristic of the new, more candid, style is Tendryakov's realistic portrayal of the 'pusher' (*tolkach*), who manipulates the acquisition of required goods, doctors the books and so on. Also typical of the less restrained style is the author's attitude toward Chuprov. In his personal disintegration and his resorting to drink he becomes a pathetic, not a hated, figure. At the conclusion of the sketch emphasis is placed on the pathos of his situation, not on the 'just punishment' he should receive.

Three articles in the December issue of *Novy Mir* contained significant liberalizing elements. The first, by Vasily Rusakov, dealt with the importance of publishing propaganda, using the positive example of successful agricultural precedents.[73] Warning against the demand for the kind of planned novels which had been usual hitherto, Rusakov referred to a recent meeting between officials of the Ministry of Agriculture and writers. The demand of the former for the quick completion of a drama or novel about the MTS was met with 'noise in the hall'. This could be interpreted in only one way, wrote Rusakov: 'So, they are calling us again to "production" literature.' His distaste at this is evident.

The second item in the December issue was B. S. Emel'yanov's article on Soviet comedy.[74] Writing at length about Mayakovsky's plays *Banya* and *Klop*, he quoted Prisypkin's speech at the end of the last scene in *Klop* to illustrate the fine technique of laughing at the audience. At that time *Klop* had not been produced on a Soviet stage in over twenty years and was to be seen again only in 1954.

Furthermore, a book review at the back of the journal, in discussing the first eight issues of the journal *Sovetsky Kazakhstan*, published in Alma Ata in 1953, commented on the policy of republishing items:

In our opinion, the journal abuses the use of reprinting. For instance, what was the point of publishing in the journal's fourth issue of this year, which was printed only on May 8th, the speech of A. Fadeev, 'Several Questions about the Work of the Writers Union', which was already featured in *Literaturnaya Gazeta* on March 28th? In the same issue as well they republished the article of A. M. Egolin, 'I. V. Stalin and Questions of Literature', included in a collection which came out over three years ago.[75]

The Fadeev article referred to is the one which attacked *Novy Mir* in general and Grossman and Kazakevich in particular.[76] The reviewer, Turkov, was here not only pointing out the unsuitability of such Stalinist-type criticism by the spring of 1953, but adding his personal comment on the entire affair of the previous winter.

In another article, Mark Shcheglov called for a more enlightened view of historical figures: 'It is wrong to look at figures of the past with too contemporary an eye, to demand from them obedience to our moral principles'.[77] Yu. Karasev, in the February issue, made a brief contrast between the literature of Stalinist and post-Stalinist times.[78]

Finally, a story in the March issue of *Novy Mir*, about an agricultural official attracted to a young woman who worked in his office,[79] contained many of those features rapidly becoming typical of thaw literature: an accent on individual human distractions rather than on official or technical problems and a frank discussion of material failings in Soviet life. (The girl says at one point, for example, 'In our city we have such shortages that one rarely finds decent meat in the Gastronom...and at the bazaar you know yourself that you have to overpay.')

The more noteworthy contents of *Novy Mir* from the autumn of 1953 to the spring of 1954 thus represent two main, related, themes in subject matter. First, we find a continuation of a trend begun during the last year of Stalin's life: literature which reflects the attack on the no-conflict theory and thereby incorporates a more complex view of life, as well as a new emphasis on the individual, human, aspects of life. Second, and as an outgrowth of this earlier development, we see literature and literary criticism in the first post-Stalin year reflecting the economic debate being voiced by the major politicians, both in subject matter and in a broader spirit of criticism and analysis.

3

A temporary setback

The editors of the magazine *Novy Mir*, in printing these articles, forgot that this journal, as the organ of the Soviet Writers Union, has the duty of systematically and promptly combating any deviation from the principle of socialist realism and any attempts to direct Soviet literature away from the life and struggle of the Soviet people.

Resolution of the presidium of the board,
Writers Union, August 11, 1954

True to an established pattern of Soviet literary history, a campaign was launched against *Novy Mir* for having published unacceptable material. In spite of the fact that this was the first offensive since Stalin's death – it took place in the spring and summer of 1954 – there were similarities to previous campaigns. There can be little doubt, for example, that the attack, at least as it developed, was officially inspired and culminated in changes engineered by the Party. Again as in the past, criticism was not the initial spontaneous response of the reviewers but appeared only after a time-lag during which, presumably, hints or directives reached the appropriate editorial offices. Thus, the Panova novel, though appearing in the autumn of 1953, did not become the object of attack until several months later.

However, there were significant differences in the 1954 attack on *Novy Mir*. This time a variety of opinions on the works in question continued to appear, and criticism was interspersed with praise throughout more or less the whole period of the campaign. In earlier years, while there had sometimes been praise for an item later to be censured, the general pattern had been that once the official hacks had expressed their opinion, literary reviews followed a fairly standard pattern with very little variation. The new situation was clearly a product of the thaw atmosphere with its greater tolerance of at least moderate disagreement.

Another significant feature of the 1954 campaign was the respective parts played in it by the newspapers *Pravda* and *Izvestiya*. Here we see a clear contrast not only in the extent of their participation but

[The gentleman in the hat carries a piece of paper which reads: 'I won't be a lazy person, a hooligan anymore.']

'I'll powder you, iron . . .'
'And now, be so kind as to step into the novel!'

'Come on, first I'll do your hair . . .'

Writer (to a negative type): 'Well, what do you think you're up to, creeping into my novel looking like that?'

5 Cartoon reprinted from the Ukrainian magazine *Perets'* in *Literaturnaya Gazeta*, February 27, 1954

also in the viewpoints expressed. The contrast was sufficiently marked to suggest a differentiation between Party and government positions in this case. This dichotomy can presumably be traced to the power struggle then being waged.

A brief review of the critical response to *Novy Mir* and its contents between January and August, 1954 will illustrate the character of the new campaign. Criticism of *Novy Mir* items fell into distinct periods. The brunt of the attack on Panova's novel came in May and June. Pomerantsev, who had been published at the same time, was criticized mainly before May. Lifshits, Abramov and Shcheglov, who were published later, were criticized later, but in only a few individual reviews. Articles which attacked the journal as a whole came in the period from May to July.

The attitude towards Vera Panova's novel was typical of the new, thaw-style, campaign. Here we see a counterpoint of favorable and critical comment almost throughout the period. Furthermore, points of attack varied with reviewers, some concentrating on ideological 'errors', others selecting objectionable details. Perhaps the main ideological deviation singled out by critics was Panova's decision to portray a stalwart Party member as the mother of a criminal son. However, other faults, both literary and political, were highlighted by various critics.

Published in *Zvezda* in February, Pavel Gromov's review was the first significant article on the novel. It was generally favorable.[1] Forestalling what would be a major point of dissent later, Gromov defended Panova's assertion that a parent like Dorofea could have a son like Gennady, saying that 'it would be undisguised and hypocritical sanctimoniousness to deny this. One could deny the life-like authenticity and persuasiveness of Dorofea's drama only with an interpretation of the typical as a statistical mean.'[2] Gromov's criticisms dwelt on details rather than on the main fabric of the work.* The following month *Zvezda* published another item on *Seasons of the Year*, this time a letter from some students expressing a predominantly – though not entirely – negative view.[3]

At the end of March *Izvestiya* published a favorable review by Marietta Shaginyan.[4] With unstinting praise she expressed admiration for almost every aspect of the novel, even noting with approval

---

* Gromov felt, for example, that the contradictions in Bortashevich's character were not plausible and that Nadya was presented in a style 'more characteristic of melodrama than of a psychological novel'.

that Panova had ruthlessly described Soviet products in all their tawdriness. 'The clean, new Soviet furniture purchased with money saved from the pay envelope appeals to you', wrote Shaginyan: 'you forget that it lacks taste, that our life demands that attractive furniture should grace the living quarters of our young people'. In general, however, she preferred to skirt the controversial issues.

Six weeks later *Literaturnaya Gazeta* published a letter which complained of the contradictions evident in the novel: Dorofea has a ne'er-do-well son as well as a decent daughter; Sasha Lyubimov, one of the most attractive characters, is the son of a woman of dubious moral sense; an exemplary couple is treated callously by their grown-up daughters.[5] This letter was followed by a series of hostile articles which gained in virulence over the following month.

In an article with a title indicative of its viewpoint, 'Which Seasons?', Kochetov launched one of the most outspoken attacks on *Seasons of the Year*. It was published in *Pravda* at the end of May.[6] Declaring the author guilty of naturalism and objectivism, Kochetov concluded that the novel not only did not advance Soviet literature, but 'may even set some writers on the road of bourgeois literature'. *Inter alia*, Kochetov also attacked the reviews of Gromov and Shaginyan.

The book, he said, was essentially a NEP novel. The characters were most alive and vital in the sections dealing with their lives in the twenties.

When the novel's heroes are shown at the beginning of their life's journey, coinciding with the first years of the Soviet regime, they evince vigorous traits of character. But as soon as matters turn to the present, to the contemporary behavior of the heroes, they immediately pale and fade...The best pages of the novel give us a vivid picture of Dorofea's youth. We see a Soviet woman, energetic, vigorous, purposeful, growing. As soon as the author has to maneuver her from one epoch into another, however, the heroine immediately grows pale and lifeless, turns into a mediocre and essentially characterless worker who adds up to nothing, not only in the great Soviet cause but even in her own family.

Kochetov's other main objection was that Panova, in portraying her characters' past, skipped from the nineteen twenties to the year 1950, missing the intervening period entirely.

She left out the years of the first five-year plans, the years of the struggle to industrialize the country and collectivize agriculture, the years when socialist competition was developed extensively. These were the years which could not but influence the minds of the characters from the older generation in the novel, the formation of their outlooks and their fate...If none of this happened, if the heroes did not go through either the five-year plans or the war, it is quite natural that their characters are spiritually impoverished and do not bear the traits of our remarkable times.

The omission was also noted, years later – in 1963 – in Zoya Boguslavskaya's book on Panova, but with a different interpretation.

Panova did not reveal and analyze everything in *Seasons of the Year*. There were not yet the objective conditions required to disclose the phenomenon and all its roots. After the 20th Congress this would be done...but Panova was still in the period of the cult of personality and did not go beyond the attempt to solve the problem of education...It was difficult then for Panova to tell the truth about the late thirties in the life of Dorofea and Churkin, the time of the bitter violation of socialist legality which cost the lives of many, many leaders of the same type.[7]

Although Ehrenburg did make a brief reference to the camps of the thirties in *The Thaw*, the time was not yet ripe for the historical introspection which came a few years later. Panova had the choice at this point of treating the decade of the thirties only one-sidedly or ignoring it altogether.

Other negative reviews were published later in May, and in June. By this time most of the criticism had become repetitious.[8] *Literaturnaya Gazeta*, which was edited by the conservative Ryurikov (who had taken over from Simonov the previous summer), carried many of the articles attacking *Novy Mir*'s publications. On June 5th the paper published a report on the Party meeting of Leningrad writers.[9] The main speaker, V. Druzin, an editor of *Zvezda*, criticized both the *Novy Mir* 'series' and Panova's novel. As a caveat, Druzin mentioned another Leningrad writer who had been castigated and who had apparently failed to learn his lesson – M. Zoshchenko. Mention of this chapter in Zhdanovism could not have failed to make its point.

Remarkably, other points of view continued to be expressed in print during this period, in spite of the fact that the months of May and June were saturated with attacks on Panova's novel (as well as on other works from *Novy Mir*). Two examples are noteworthy.

On June 26th, the same *Literaturnaya Gazeta* published an article by V. Voevodin and I. Metter on a manuscript which had been sent to the publishing house Sovetsky pisatel'.[10] What is interesting here is not the history of the manuscript, but the fact that Vera Panova was one of the board members who had gone over it. According to

Voevodin, who had read it after her, Panova had done an excellent job of editing. The timing here is important, for this testimonial came at the end of a two-month period of attack. The authors of the article, while omitting any mention of Panova's own writing, had chosen this opportunity to support her publicly.

Another article which mentioned Panova, this time in one paragraph out of a half-page, is distinguished by its liberal outlook. It too appeared in *Literaturnaya Gazeta*, but in July.[11]

It seems to me that V. Panova should be reproached not for portraying the shady side of our life in the novel *Seasons of the Year*, but for the fact that she does so without sharp censure, not deeply, but superficially, not revealing the origins. Some critics want to deprive our literature – the literature of socialist realism – of its fighting qualities, but it is impossible to reconcile oneself to this approach. Of course literature is spiritual food. But it does not follow from this that one must assess it just by qualities of taste. This food fulfills medicinal functions; but medicine is not always sweet, and only children can think that the best medicine in the world is sweet syrup. The shallowly thought-out arguments of some of our critics create great hardships for prose writers and poets because there is always the chance that tomorrow once again reviewers and editors with such 'theories' in their heads will sit firm on our editorial boards and, indulging in their rights to excess, will worry writers needlessly and mutilate their works.

The timing of this outspoken piece is delicate, for although it followed two months of a hard drive by conservative critics and preceded by weeks the change in the editorial board of *Novy Mir*, it came during a month of lull when practically nothing of a critical nature against the journal was published.

Of all the articles in the series, Pomerantsev's essay was subject to the most vociferous and frequent criticism. The main objects of attack were his elevation of sincerity above other criteria and the opinions he expressed on modern Soviet literary works.

Unlike Panova's novel, Pomerantsev's article was not given a wholly favorable review by a major critic in any publication. The first review which appeared set the tone for the ones to follow and presented the main points of criticism. Neither sincerity nor craftsmanship was the decisive factor in judging literature, wrote Vasilevsky at the end of January.[12]

Sincerity and craftsmanship, taken separately or together, do not guarantee success if, underlying the creative work, there is no profound and true concept, serious knowledge and understanding of life and its laws, the desire to serve the great cause of the people, and a clear, militant world outlook on the part of the writer. But Pomerantsev completely overlooks the question of the writer's world outlook, his Party stand.

He claims that 'the degree of sincerity, that is, the directness of things, must be the first test'. No, the first test for the Marxist has been and will continue to be an evaluation of the ideological–artistic quality of the work. Thus, under close scrutiny the basis of the article can be seen to be false.

The main qualities of *narodnost'*, *ideinost'* and, above all, *partiinost'*, had been ignored by Pomerantsev, and this constituted his cardinal sin.

Another major article criticizing Pomerantsev was written before Vasilevsky's, but appeared only in the February issue of *Znamya*. By a well-known woman critic called Skorino, the article constituted an uncompromising attack.[13] Peppering her review with typically depreciatory terms such as 'subjectivism' and 'aesthetic cliché', Skorino held up to ridicule various points made by Pomerantsev which she had misunderstood, probably intentionally.

In reaction to these articles of Vasilevsky and Skorino, *Komsomol'skaya Pravda* published a letter from some students and a teacher at Moscow State University. Attacking Vasilevsky's obvious desire to suppress Pomerantsev's ideas, they went on to criticize *Literaturnaya Gazeta* itself which, while frequently calling for sharp discussion of urgent literary problems, had published an article 'which is largely erroneous and which avoids all discussion of acute problems in the development of our literature,...an article couched in a tone of crude vituperation'. They accused Vasilevsky of quoting out of context, of 'playing it safe', of lack of principle, and of demagoguery. They then went on to attack Skorino vigorously. In defense of their position, the students quoted the passage in Tvardovsky's '*Za dal'yu dal'*' in which the reader described the typical pattern of the Soviet novel.[14] It is a sign of the atmosphere of the time that this diatribe against two prominent critics, as well as *Literaturnaya Gazeta* itself, appeared in the official paper of the Communist Youth Organization.

Ryurikov himself then entered the fray. Although perhaps in language less violent than theirs, his line of criticism was similar to that of Skorino and Vasilevsky. But, presenting his own list of worthy writers – in contrast to Pomerantsev's concentration on Ovechkin alone – Ryurikov included both Vera Panova and Aleksandr Tvar-

dovsky. Thus, his criticism was not yet an all-out attack on *Novy Mir*
as a whole. Concluding his article, Ryurikov even went so far as to
say that for the thousands of young people then going out to the
MTS, a pure diet of films of the type of 'Cavalier of the Golden Star'
and 'The Kuban Cossacks' would only create rosy illusions which
real life would destroy.

In the April issue of *Zvezda*, B. Platonov wrote a general review
of items which had recently appeared and, *inter alia*, discussed
Pomerantsev's essay.[15] In linking Pomerantsev's views with other
dangerous tendencies which had been expressed in *Novy Mir*,
Platonov for the first time during the spring coupled what was, in
his opinion, the guilt of the writer with that of the journal which had
published his work.

Platonov argued that, rather than compare Ovechkin with such
writers as Nikolaeva and Babaevsky, Pomerantsev could have seen
other deeper and more dangerous contrasts than these.

It would have been enough for V. Pomerantsev to glance at the very same
Novy Mir in which he read 'District Routine', but to glance not only at the
most recent pages but at the earlier ones. There he would have found the
most appropriate object for a discussion of contrasts: V. Grossman's novel,
For the Just Cause. It is wrong that V. Pomerantsev does not compare two
works printed in one and the same journal: the *ocherk* of V. Ovechkin and
the novel of V. Grossman. Such a comparison could have illuminated far
more clearly the questions touched on in the article 'On Sincerity in
Literature'. The author would have seen that, with all his distinctions,
V. Ovechkin and S. Babaevsky and G. Nikolaeva share the same position
but that V. Grossman stands off to one side. But for some reason V. Pomerantsev did not notice this contrast.[16]

Platonov then went on to draw a connection between Pomerantsev's
and Grossman's 'philosophy – that there is nothing new in life, that
everything returns cyclically... This is where sincerity leads when it
is in conflict with truth.'[17]

Surkov's long article in *Pravda* at the end of May discussed
Pomerantsev's essay briefly and then mentioned the other articles –
those of Abramov, Lifshits and Shcheglov, which *Novy Mir* had
published recently – in order to show that Pomerantsev's article was
symptomatic of the journal's literary criticism, and not unique.[18]
However, his comments were by no means limited to *Novy Mir*. He
mentioned various other writers not connected with it, as well as
singling out the journal *Oktyabr'*, whose editor-in-chief was to be

replaced in June, two and a half months before the *Novy Mir* editorial board was changed.

Surkov's critical line can be seen as a conservative response to the proliferation of 'questionable' material which had been appearing in the major journals. Aside from those in *Novy Mir*, a number of interesting or provocative works had been published – Zorin's play *The Guests*,[19] Ehrenburg's novel *The Thaw*,[20] and a new cycle of poems by Pasternak.[21] By the end of May it was clear that the earlier, moderately *laissez-faire* policy of the late autumn and winter, which had been followed either intentionally or inadvertently, was being supplanted by a conservative line. Despite the dissonant voices, the dominant tone in the field of literature in May and June was that of reaction.[22]

During this period the other articles in the *Novy Mir* 'series' were also condemned, although rarely in full-scale review articles. A case in point is Lifshits' review of Shaginyan's *Diary*, which had only one article wholly dedicated to it. This was Boris Agapov's lengthy discussion in *Literaturnaya Gazeta*, published early in April.[23] Admitting that Shaginyan's *Diary* had been poorly edited, Agapov went on to say that the greater sin was the 'viciousness of methods and of the general ideological direction of [Lifshits'] critical article'. Agapov's central criticism of Lifshits lay in his general attitude toward Shaginyan, his tone of ridicule and contempt, the fact that he refused to recognize any positive aspect of the work, that he distorted what Shaginyan wrote, cited passages with the aim to mislead. Agapov, on the contrary, defended Shaginyan on every point on which Lifshits had criticized her.

He concentrated on attacking the attitude of the review, not on slandering either the reviewer or the journal in which he published.[24] His attitude toward *Novy Mir* was made plain when, in the last paragraph, he expressed surprise that Lifshits' article should have been found in the pages of a journal 'which is the best journal in terms of *ocherk* literature'.

While Abramov's article on kolkhoz literature was frequently mentioned in the press, no full-scale article was entirely devoted to it. Suffice it to mention two criticisms which are typical of the tone of the attacks on him. An editorial in the May issue of *Partiinaya Zhizn'* attacked his attitude toward postwar prose. Instead of recognizing the creative initiative of the Soviet people, it said,

Abramov wished to emphasize that which was backward and needed improvement in society.[25]

Later in May, Trifonova published an article in *Literaturnaya Gazeta*, part of which touched on Abramov's ideas.[26] She sought a *modus vivendi* between the 'no-conflict' writers and those who wished to expose every conceivable fault, without presenting anything positive. The latter, she said, failed to realize that the decisions of the September and the February–March plenums on agriculture rested on the previous triumphs of socialist industry and agriculture. Ovechkin knew how to combine both sides, showing both contradiction and success.

> But this is not understood by critics like F. Abramov from *Novy Mir*, to whom it seems that nothing valuable has been produced in rural literature, as if such characters as Mal'tsev's Grunya, Medynsky's Mariya, Babaevsky's Sergei Tutarinov, Nikolaeva's Vasily Bortnikov were utterly contrived, impossible, the result of a varnished reality. But who, if not such people, participated in the meetings of leading agricultural workers which took place not long ago, and isn't it about them that dozens of books on the advanced experience of machine operators, field crop cultivators, cattle breeders are written?

Though recognizing the shortcomings of even the best of these novels, Trifonova insisted that their significance, their social role and the sincerity of their authors be recognized.[27]

Noticeable by its absence was a serious discussion of Abramov's views on agricultural policy. This can be explained by the fact that by this time Khrushchev had clearly become the official Party spokesman on agriculture. If we assume that Abramov's views on the subject were in tune with those of Malenkov – and they were most certainly more akin to Malenkov's than to Khrushchev's – we can see that it was advantageous to the more conservative (Khrushchevian) forces to avoid a public discussion of Abramov's views on agricultural policy. Such a discussion would only serve to publicize the divergence of opinion a knowledge of which had, until now, been largely confined to the Party's inner sanctum. Thus, the critics concentrated on the literary and not the policy aspects of Abramov's article, adopting the frequent practice of ignoring a key area of dispute and selecting some standard error to attack.

Criticism of Mark Shcheglov came mainly in the context of more general attacks on *Novy Mir*, but very late in the season he was singled out in an article by Kedrina which did not appear until the end of July, when the campaign had almost completely petered out.[28] Kedrina tended to give an unfairly narrow rendition of Shcheglov's interpretation and to oversimplify what he had written, as when she took exception to Shcheglov's reading of Leonov. He saw in Leonov's forest, she wrote, 'a symbol for the eternal cyclical theory of life'. Her second main criticism echoed what other critics had earlier stressed: his attitude towards Gratsiansky.[29] Shcheglov's discussion of the origins of Gratsiansky's character was criticized along similar lines again the following month.* This later article also briefly found fault with Shcheglov's review of *Snegin's Opera*.[30] Shcheglov, it said, 'scoffs at the fact that the author of a novel showed the influence of the Party decisions in the sphere of music on the minds and creative work of musicians'. These were the main points of the criticism levelled against Mark Shcheglov, author of the last article in the *Novy Mir* 'series'.[31]

A significant *Novy Mir* article in economics, not designated as part of the 'series', was criticized separately at least twice during the spring. This was P. Mstislavsky's '*Narodnoe blagosostoyanie*' (The Well-Being of the People), which appeared in the November, 1953 issue.[32] What characterized the article was its consumerist line which, considering that this was the immediate post-Stalin period, took an extreme form. The article made two main points. First, as the result of the highly disproportionate investment in heavy industry since 1929 it was now possible and necessary to shift the emphasis to investment in light industry and agriculture. He noted the astounding figures illustrating this point – between 1929 and 1952, 638 billion rubles had been invested in heavy industry, 72 billion in light industry and 94 billion in agriculture.[33] Second, he emphasized the importance for a socialist economy of the proportional growth of all branches and sub-branches of the economy. This meant studying the patterns of consumer demand and foreseeing changes in that pattern. He argued that the value of a product could not be measured in quantitative terms alone but was also related to demand. If, he wrote, the production cost of one centner of wheat is one and a half times less than the production cost of a centner of cotton then the value ratio between them

---

* 'Shcheglov adduces the false idea that the Soviet way of life forms a flourishing milieu for corrupt types such as Gratsiansky...and criticizes Leonov for portraying the actions and cast of mind of Gratsiansky as manifestations of survivals of the past.' See 'Ob oshibkakh zhurnala "Novyi mir"', *Literaturnaia Gazeta*, August 17, 1954, p. 3.

is by no means 1:1.5. One also has to consider the relative use value of wheat and cotton, the relative social demand for them.

Granted that the cost of production of a pair of canvas shoes is less than that of leather shoes; nevertheless if the canvas shoes can be used for a shorter time than leather, then the former are both less elegant and less useful than the latter. Per unit of use value the production costs of canvas shoes will be higher than those of leather... All this confirms the necessity of knowing what the needs of society are. Unfortunately, in our economic literature this question is either disregarded entirely or is consciously relegated to the background.[34]

In his emphasis on consumerism and on the law of the balanced (proportional) development of the economy, Mstislavsky was clearly reaching back over the Stalin period to the ideas of Bukharin in the late nineteen twenties.[35]

As in the case of Panova and Pomerantsev, criticism came after a considerable lapse of time. Thus the article was written at a time when Malenkov was in a fairly powerful position, but was criticized when he was in eclipse. The general tenor – and even the title – of his article placed Mstislavsky in the Malenkov camp.

An editorial in *Kommunist* pin-pointed the main offense.[36]

One cannot ignore such facts as the revision of fundamental propositions of Marxist theory in some magazine articles. This occurred, for instance, in P. Mstislavsky's article 'The Well-Being of the People', in *Novy Mir* 11, 1953. The author of the article considers it a mistake that the concept of value hitherto has been confined to expenditure of social labor in material production; in his opinion, value is also determined by the usefulness of an article. Thus the author confuses a question which is clear and indisputable among Marxists, who hold that the value of a commodity is determined by expenditure of social labor in its production, while the usefulness of a commodity constitutes its use value.[37]

A month later Ya. Fomenko wrote an article in *Literaturnaya Gazeta* which dealt with the 'current affairs' sections of the thick journals.[38] He concentrated on *Novy Mir, Oktyabr'* and *Zvezda*, which, he said, had achieved greater variety of themes and genres. Among the articles he mentioned – and he concentrated equally on all three journals – was that of Mstislavsky. Referring to the *Kommunist* appraisal, Fomenko made the same point, but his review was more balanced.

There were also a number of articles attacking the journal as a whole, and Tvardovsky as its editor-in-chief. These all appeared between

May 4 and July 1, 1954, with most of them published in June. A number of meetings of local writers' organizations were held in June and the report of the Party meeting of Leningrad writers in *Literaturnaya Gazeta* described Druzin's attack on *Novy Mir* and its 'series' – 'a whole series of annihilating, abusive articles'.[39]

Following the Leningrad discussion there was a two-day meeting of the Party organization of Moscow writers, which both Party and non-Party writers attended. The report of this meeting, which appeared in *Literaturnaya Gazeta* in mid June, constituted the most serious and far-reaching attack on *Novy Mir* to date in the current campaign.[40] The official condemnation of the journal would later repeat the substance of what was said at this time. Surkov made the first major statement, concentrating on the 'series' with no mention of Panova's novel.

In the beginning one might have thought that these articles had appeared as a result of an accidental coincidence, or an oversight of the editorial board, but when their general context somehow coincided, it became clear that this was not an accidental coincidence, not an oversight, but an expression of a well-thought-out line – of a line which has its precursors in the history of our literature.

The criterion of 'sincerity', proclaimed by Pomerantsev, has the ring of the criteria of the 'theoreticians' of the 'Pereval' and is an attempt to take criticism away from the Marxist analysis of literature with its viewpoint of the class struggle and the laws of the development of society.

Following Surkov's lead, various other writers stepped forward and delivered their attacks. In the Soviet literary world a typical response to such criticism would be a confession, an apology or a statement from the editor. This did not happen. A statement was simply read out by the assistant editor, A. Dement'ev, and it failed to satisfy others who spoke after. (The report noted that at meetings of the Party group of the governing body of the Writers Union, the *Novy Mir* editors had defended the journal.)* The Moscow meeting was

* Another speaker at the meeting, N. Lesyuchevsky, chief editor of Sovetsky pisatel', also discussed the *Novy Mir* 'line' and expressed surprise that Dement'ev should have defended it. What all these articles had in common, he said, was
  that they are directed against principles of socialist realism in artistic literature and in literary criticism. This is especially clearly seen in V. Pomerantsev's article. It is surprising that the comrades from *Novy Mir* defended this article so stubbornly, that even the learned A. Dement'ev did not have the strength to recognize that the spirit of Pomerantsev's article is the spirit of idealism and subjectivism.

the first to repeat the kind of all-out attack on both journal and editor that had been seen in the campaign of the previous year.

The last major article on *Novy Mir* appeared on the front page of *Literaturnaya Gazeta* on July 1.[41] One-half page long, it was devoted entirely to the critical section of the journal and discussed *seriatim* the items in the 'series'. A few points distinguish it. First, in refuting Shcheglov's review of *Snegin's Opera*, the anonymous article referred to Zhdanov's statement on music in 1948.[42] Another retrogressive feature was a reference to Gurvich's 'The Power of the Positive Example', which had been published in *Novy Mir* years before and had also been referred to in the campaign of 1953. Here *Literaturnaya Gazeta* was following a standard pattern of culling out of the past various 'mistakes' associated with a journal in order to compound its present guilt.

Third, here alone did the criticism of Abramov's article touch on his central thesis of agricultural policy.

First, the most important duty of the critic is to support the new and progressive which the artist observantly portrayed in his work. Abramov must be reminded of this truth. In his article he attacked the innovative undertakings of Sergei Tutarinov, who had clearly recognized that the further advance of his own kolkhoz was impossible without electrification and mechanization. The critic essentially came out against the new and the progressive which are connected in the novel with the image of Tutarinov, against the task of the organizational–economic reinforcement of the kolkhozy under the Five Year Plan.

Following this article virtually nothing appeared attacking *Novy Mir* as a whole until the actual change of the editorial board in the middle of August.[43] In fact, except for Kedrina's attack on Shcheglov on July 29th, there was a six-week hiatus during which no material whatever against *Novy Mir* appeared in the press. This seems to coincide with the timing suggested by Conquest – that Khrushchev was in decline in the summer of 1954 and that Malenkov was then achieving some limited success. Malenkov's relative rise could well have been indicated by the absence of criticism.

Reflecting this situation, perhaps one other article which dealt with a *Novy Mir* item in July struck a sharp contrast with those of May and June. This was a review of a Tendryakov story which had appeared in *Novy Mir* in June.[44] The fact that it was a warm, positive review is not in itself unusual, as throughout this period various *Novy*

Mir works, outside the 'series', had been well reviewed. Noteworthy here is the attack made by the reviewer, Surovtsev, on another review of the same story which had appeared ten days before in *Moskovsky Komsomolets*.[45] The contrast in tone between the Surovtsev article and items which had appeared in May and June is striking.

Only as a result of a superficial acquaintance with the contents of the work could he [Nedosekin] come to this conclusion [that Tendryakov is impassive, objectivist], could he 'not notice' that the author is obviously on Fedor's side, is saddened by his sorrows, is gladdened by his joy...R. Nedosekin's article is unsubstantiated and incorrect. He deduces the real and fabricated shortcomings in V. Tendryakov's story from the fact that *Novy Mir* has published faulty articles.

The writers' community rejected the aesthetic articles in the journal *Novy Mir*. Why put honorable writers writing from their experience of life, even if they do have certain shortcomings, on the same shelf as aesthetic [critics]?

Two days later a *Literaturnaya Gazeta* editorial referred to the Nedosekin article. 'One must say straight out: articles written in such a tone in no way promote the establishment of a creative atmosphere.'[46] This was a clear attempt to put a damper on extremists in literary criticism.[47]

It is worth noting that even during the period of vigorous attacks, *Novy Mir* had not retreated completely. A few items are significant in this respect. First is a review by Mark Shcheglov which appeared in the July issue, indicating that the editors were not abandoning their critics while they were under fire. Second, in the same issue there appeared a review by K. Pozdnyaev,[48] in which he assailed a review which had been published in *Literaturnaya Gazeta*. By energetically finding fault with the critic – and even making her look a fool – Pozdnyaev succeeded both in attacking *Literaturnaya Gazeta*, which had been leading the campaign against *Novy Mir*, and in defending one of the *Novy Mir* authors (Panova) who had been subjected to the attack. This review – published at that particular time – was clearly a response to the treatment which was being meted out to the journal.

Finally, in the August issue of *Novy Mir*, the last edited by Tvardovsky, the editorial board demonstrated that even then it was not prepared to run for cover. The journal published a symposium on Soviet folklore which opened and closed with the board's own collective comment.[49] At issue was an article by N. Leont'ev which had appeared in *Novy Mir* the previous August.[50] Leont'ev had there attacked at length and in most outspoken language the use of such terms as 'folklore' and 'epic poetry' to describe crude, propagandist and usually untalented Soviet imitations of traditional folk genres. People, he wrote, should not be allowed to hide their lack of talent under the fig leaf of folk art. 'The fact is', he concluded, 'that Soviet folklore with the possible exception of some sayings and couplets does not exist as an independent form of Soviet art'.

Leont'ev's charges aroused a number of angry rejoinders which were published in *Novy Mir* 8, 1954. He was accused of having overlooked the importance of people's choirs, of popular songs collectively composed, and of contemporary folk poetry. Among other things, the attacks were marked by frequent references to Zhdanov, the Zhdanov decrees, Stalin and Surkov. To all this the *Novy Mir* editorial board responded with a calm but biting summing-up in which all mention of these political authorities was conspicuously omitted. Most notably, they sharply rejected the use by Leont'ev's critics of such epithets as 'nihilist', their unsubstantiated and downright misleading references to nineteenth-century authorities such as Belinsky and Chernyshevsky, and their self-satisfied complacency in general. It is perhaps not far-fetched to see in this editorial statement a refusal to yield voluntarily all the ground they had gained since March, 1953.

The campaign against *Novy Mir* was spearheaded by *Literaturnaya Gazeta*. However, a few of the main attacks were published in *Pravda* and, in examining the politics of the literary situation, it is instructive to compare the way in which *Novy Mir* was handled by the two major Soviet newspapers, *Pravda* and *Izvestiya*.

The most striking fact is that so little attention was paid to the whole affair. *Pravda* devoted minimal space to the literary field as a whole, and, of this, little to *Novy Mir*. An article appearing shortly after the February–March plenum dealt with the general subject of kolkhoz fiction.[51] In the same vein as Pomerantsev and Abramov, it criticized earlier works for embellishing life. Furthermore, it urged the necessity of principled criticism and self-criticism, an idea consonant with Khrushchev's recent assertions that agriculture was in a poor state and that vast improvements were required. Thus *Pravda* was simply discussing literature in the spirit of Khrushchev's position.

It was not until the end of May that *Novy Mir* was mentioned in *Pravda*, following a whole month when practically nothing about literature had appeared in the paper. Surkov's 'Under the Banner of Socialist Realism' of May 25 was followed by Kochetov's attack on *Seasons of the Year* two days later. On June 3, Ermilov's article on socialist realism which attacked, *inter alia*, Pomerantsev, was published in *Pravda*. In the middle of June came Abalkin's reference to Pomerantsev's 'harmful article' which had been republished in *Karogs*.[52] It is clear from this that while *Pravda* did not publish much on the issue, what it did print was clearly anti-*Novy Mir* and that two of the main attacks of the campaign did appear there.

Izvestiya provides a contrast. First, it contained more general material on literature. Considering this it is even more noticeable that there was a complete absence of any attack on *Novy Mir*. At the end of March *Izvestiya* published the highly flattering Shaginyan review of *Seasons of the Year*. Aside from this, *Novy Mir*'s problem items received no mention. The names of Pomerantsev and Abramov, of Lifshits and Shcheglov simply did not appear, even in May and June which were the key months of the campaign. In mid July there was a very brief mention of the 'political mistakes of *Novy Mir*' in a letter to the editor reporting on a writers' conference in Voronezh.[53] It was only on August 8, 1954, on the very eve of the removal of the editorial board, that there was finally a reference to the pot which had been boiling over months before. Having ignored the situation for so long, *Izvestiya* was finally forced into a minimal recognition of what was happening.[54] This reference was made in the front-page editorial, in a discussion of socialist realism. The editorial followed what was by now a fairly standard pattern: the past mistake of no-conflict, the important role of the writer, the fact that some favorite authors had produced no new works lately. The editorial took a stand against 'production' novels, 'where the description of the technology of production hides the living man'. It stressed the importance of literary style.

Only in the third-last paragraph was a brief acknowledgement of the *Novy Mir* 'affair', expressed in two sentences. Here *Izvestiya* declared that the writers' community had rightly condemned the highly erroneous position taken by *Novy Mir*, which had published 'a series of slanderous, nihilistic literary–critical articles. It is not right when the presidium and secretariat of the Soviet Writers Union actually withdraw from the leadership of the literary–artistic journals.' This was the sum total of *Izvestiya*'s participation in the attack on *Novy Mir*.

It would not be unreasonable to associate Khrushchev and Malenkov with *Pravda* and *Izvestiya*, respectively the organs of the Party and of the government. This corroborates Conquest's theory, mentioned earlier, that the early liberalization of literary policy can be associated with Malenkov's man Ponomarenko, and that subsequent attacks and policy shifts followed Ponomarenko's replacement as Minister of Culture by the lower-ranking figure of Aleksandrov.[55]

The timing of the campaign also substantiates what many political observers have already noted. Conquest, for example, sees the summer of 1954 as a time when Malenkov's position was strengthened.[56] Although he terms the period of Khrushchev's decline as the 'summer', Conquest does not give any examples from August. Indeed, it must have been in August that Khrushchev was recouping lost power, for Conquest cites September as the month in which one could see signs of an adequate anti-Malenkov majority in the delegation to China. Crankshaw does cite an indication in August that Khrushchev had regained the upper hand.

The turning-point was in mid-August when a great extension of the Virgin Lands campaign was announced and announced in a manner that showed that the Party had won formal as well as actual command of the government apparatus. For the first time since Stalin's death the Central Committee came before the Council of Ministers in the promulgation of a joint decree.[57]

The decree was published in *Pravda* on August 17, 1954. From the details of political maneuvering we can get a fairly good picture of the timing of literary politics during the spring and summer of 1954. As Khrushchev gained and consolidated power during the spring months, the attack on 'questionable' material published in *Novy Mir* intensified, reaching a peak in May and June. In July the highly active campaign of the previous months suddenly became moribund. This dovetails with the theory that at this time Khrushchev was suffering some setbacks.

Finally, the month of August was the time of Khrushchev's reassertion of power. We find this reflected in the specific situation of *Novy Mir*. After a month of respite – during which it appeared that the journal had escaped relatively unscathed – suddenly, in the middle of August, came the announcement that Tvardovsky had been removed from his position as editor-in-chief. The relaxation which might be associated with a Malenkov upsurge was apparently reversed by his decline and the original Khrushchev-related line simply continued after the interruption. There are some indices which do not fit into this general schematic view, but they are too few or too insignificant to undermine the basic premise.[58]

On August 17, 1954, the same day as *Pravda*'s announcement of the extention of the Virgin Lands Campaign, *Literaturnaya Gazeta* carried two large items about *Novy Mir* on its third page. The first was a report of a meeting of the presidium of the board of the Writers Union which had taken place on August 11.[59] The meeting had been called to discuss the mistakes of the *Novy Mir* editorial board. Surkov, as secretary of the board, had spoken first and singled out the articles of Pomerantsev, Abramov and Lifshits and both reviews of Shcheglov as errors of *Novy Mir*'s publishing policy. These authors, he said, particularly Pomerantsev, had tried to revive the practice of 'intuitivism', of divorcing art and literature from a part in the creative and constructive life of the people. He traced this principle back to the end of the twenties and the early thirties 'to literary groups which received inspiration from sources hostile to the Party program of the construction of socialism'.

Surkov also asserted that Pomerantsev's emphasis on sincerity 'directly echoes the platform of the "Pereval" group'. In concluding, Surkov recognized the responsibility of the leaders of the Writers Union for *Novy Mir*'s mistakes.

Following Surkov's speech Tvardovsky addressed the meeting. He took full responsibility 'for the grave political errors and the incorrect line taken by the magazine in literary criticism'. He added that when individual members of the editorial board had objected to some of the articles or particular statements in them he had refuted their objections with the one-man authority of the editor. The report then proceeded to criticize Tvardovsky's statement.

It must be noted that in taking the blame A. Tvardovsky uttered not a word concerning the weight and influence wielded in the magazine by I. Sats, former head of the book review and criticism department, and even by M. Lifshits,* who was a regular consultant of the department, though not a staff member. However, those who spoke in the subsequent discussion named these two and correctly evaluated their activity.[60]

---

* Of Lifshits, Zaks says, 'Tvardovsky treated him with great respect, because when Tvardovsky studied at the Institute of Philosophy, Literature and History, Lifshits was an instructor there and throughout his life he retained this attitude towards Lifshits, that of a student towards a teacher' (Zaks interview).

Two other members of the *Novy Mir* editorial board who spoke up at the meeting were S. Antonov and S. Sutotsky. Antonov began by suggesting how the journal could correct its errors. His suggestion, however, that something be published on the question of sincerity, but 'from the correct' standpoint, was assailed later by Ermilov, who denied that sincerity was at all a vital problem. In his statement, Sutotsky reported that the editorial board had fully recognized its mistakes.

These mistakes stem from the fact that the editorial board has not collectively worked out a point of view on various literary phenomena and on how to treat these phenomena in the magazine. While noting individual inexactitudes in articles carried, we did not give them a correct, over-all evaluation, did not delve as deeply as possible into the error of the stand taken in them.

He added that the secretariat of the Writers Union could have pointed out sooner that the policy was wrong. This attempt to involve the Writers Union in the blame, besides relieving *Novy Mir* of sole responsibility, can also be seen as a reminder that neither the editorial board nor the secretariat had been aware earlier of which way the wind would blow.

One critic, I. Lezhnev, sent a letter to the meeting, as he was ill. He devoted his letter

to the deep 'roots' of the recent mistakes of *Novy Mir*. Comrade Lezhnev showed convincingly how in a brief review carried in *Novy Mir* 9, 1953, M. Lifshits reverted to certain of the nihilist, antipatriotic 'conceptions' which at one time had brought lamentable notoriety to the magazine *Literaturny Kritik*. When three months after this review, V. Pomerantsev appeared in *Novy Mir* with an article on sincerity, wrote Lezhnev, 'one might say that he was setting forth on the track laid by M. Lifshits'.

It is clear from the report of the meeting that Sats and Lifshits emerged as the villains of the piece. There is no indication that either of them spoke, nor is there any impression that those *Novy Mir* board members who did speak were abject in their apologies. Tvardovsky's statement appears to have been controlled, accepting criticism but not seeking to ingratiate himself with the authorities.

According to the report, all the speakers censured *Novy Mir*'s 'line'. The meeting then unanimously adopted the resolution of the presidium of the board of the Writers Union.

This resolution was published below the report on the same page of *Literaturnaya Gazeta*.[61] Noting that the ideological errors of *Novy Mir* had been attacked in various forums, the resolution went on to condemn the literary criticism in *Novy Mir seriatim*, beginning with 'On Sincerity in Literature'. Pomerantsev, it stated, 'taking advantage of the justified dissatisfaction of readers and writers with certain artistic shortcomings in our literature, dishonestly levelled a wholesale accusation of insincerity against Soviet writers'.

Pomerantsev elevated the quality of sincerity...to the rank of a prime, fundamental criterion in evaluating a literary work, thereby substituting a moral criterion unrelated to any specific time or society for the ideological, class-social judgments universally recognized in our literature...he demoted literature from its elevated role – to educate the feelings and character of those building communism – to the level of the individual's 'confession', of his direct impressions recorded in detachment from the struggles and constructive labor of society.

In printing Pomerantsev's article, it continued, the editors of *Novy Mir* had 'adopted a policy of reversion to idealist tendencies long ago exposed in our literature'.

In criticizing Abramov's denigration of postwar fiction, the resolution also accused both the author and the editorial board for having misunderstood

the decisions of the September and February–March plenary sessions of the Party Central Committee. Their stern and ruthless criticism of shortcomings in the developing of our agriculture is based solidly on a recognition of the tremendous successes and unshakeable stability of the collective farm system and is directed toward the most rapid advance of the material well-being of the working people.

The paragraph dealing with Lifshits did not introduce any new points although it made use of more aggressive language than had hitherto been used.

Lifshits...analyzes the shortcomings of M. Shaginyan's book from a feudal–seignorial esthete's standpoint, rages against writers who try to plunge actively into life, and casts doubt upon the importance of turning to themes of labor, production and other topical themes of our life. Deserving of condemnation as unworthy of Soviet criticism is the ranting, jibing tone of the writer, who gleefully parades both actual and imagined shortcomings of the work under review and chooses to ignore favorable aspects of the book.

This passage was followed by the criticisms of Shcheglov which have already been discussed.[62] The resolution attacked the *Novy Mir* critics in terms familiar from earlier articles. Vera Panova and her

novel were nowhere mentioned, either at the meeting or in the resolution. Indeed, throughout the campaign she had been treated
separately from the *Novy Mir* 'series'.

Turning to the editors of the journal, the resolution accused them
of ignoring the duty 'to combat systematically and promptly every
deviation from the principle of socialist realism...every attempt to
cultivate decadent sentiments, and every tendency toward groundless
and nihilistic defamation of the accomplishments of Soviet literature'.
The editors had thus acted in opposition to the Party instructions
on literature and drama issued between 1946 and 1948. They had
drawn no conclusions from the Central Committee's criticism of the
journals *Zvezda* and *Leningrad*.

Further, the resolution noted that the governing bodies of the
Writers Union had until recently ignored the question of *Novy Mir*'s
ideological orientation. It also reiterated a criticism of the previous
year that, given the way editorial boards function, certain editors do
not take an active part in the decision-making process of journals.
Collective influence on the ideological stance of a publication is then
forfeited.

Thus, the resolution summarized the warnings issued during the
previous campaign and the criticism of the summer months. Sats had
already been removed. Now Tvardovsky himself lost his post. The
resolution concluded with a listing of decisions.

The Presidium of the Board of the Union of Soviet Writers resolves:

1. To censure the erroneous line of the magazine *Novy Mir* on
   questions of literature.
2. To relieve Comrade *A. T. Tvardovsky* of his duties as editor-
   in-chief of this journal.
3. To appoint Comrade *K. M. Simonov* editor-in-chief of *Novy Mir*.
4. To charge the Secretariat of the Board with the task of drawing
   up within two weeks and circulating among the members of the
   Presidium for discussion a set of proposals for fundamentally
   improving the guidance given to [Writers Union] organs of the
   press by the Presidium and Secretariat of the USSR Union of
   Soviet Writers.
5. To charge the Secretariat of the Board to take all measures
   towards a more active participation of the press in preparing for
   the Second All-Union Congress of Soviet Writers and the opening
   of broad pre-Congress creative discussion on the basis of comradely
   criticism of writers' work and comradely explanation.
6. To oblige editorial boards of all-Union organs to reorganize their
   work in such a way as to base it on the creative assistance and

support of the Soviet writers *aktiv* of these journals. By regularly calling together the writers *aktiv* of the journals they can transform these meetings into a lively tribune of discussion of new literary works and more vital general creative questions of the development of Soviet literature.

The resolution was reprinted in full on the first four pages of the September issue of *Novy Mir*. It was followed by a brief – one-paragraph – comment from the editorial board in which the editors recognized both the correctness of the resolution and the ideological-political mistakes of those critical articles which had been attacked. The editorial board listed at the back of the September issue showed a loss of two members: Tvardovsky and Sholokhov. Sholokhov's departure at this time appears to have been coincidental. He had certainly never been a target of the public attacks on the *Novy Mir* line. He was clearly one of those editors to whom the accusations of inactivity (first levelled in 1953 and now again) applied, but no statement was made giving this as a reason for his leaving the journal, and it seems likely that Sholokhov had simply removed himself from the board.*

Tvardovsky himself, having enjoyed a reprieve of a year and a half since the last threat of dismissal, finally lost his position at *Novy Mir*. Although he was not singled out for intensive criticism at the meeting of August 11, he must nevertheless have undergone great pressures behind the scenes. He himself referred to this over a decade later in a letter to Fedin in January, 1968. Writing to Fedin about Solzhenitsyn, Tvardovsky said he knew that Fedin was a man of honor who would stand up for a comrade.

I had proof of this myself when things were very bad for me in 1954 and you spoke up for me 'at the very top' – your words were quoted to me by people who were present at that memorable meeting.[63]

In place of Tvardovsky's name at the head of the list was that of Dement'ev, still with the title of assistant editor. (Smirnov was also listed as assistant editor.) The removal of Tvardovsky must have come too suddenly to permit the appointment of a new editor in time. Presumably Tvardovsky was at the helm until the August 11 meeting. Simonov was not listed as editor-in-chief until October.

* According to Zaks, Sholokhov had earlier announced his intention to leave *Novy Mir* because of disagreements with Tvardovsky's editorial policy. Following his departure from *Novy Mir* he joined the editorial board of *Oktyabr'*.

6 Konstantin Simonov, who returned to edit *Novy Mir* from 1954 to 1958

Konstantin Simonov, who replaced Tvardovsky, was an experienced editor. Until August 25 of the previous year he had been editor-in-chief of *Literaturnaya Gazeta* and before that, prior to March, 1950, he had been the editor-in-chief of *Novy Mir*. He had also been active in literary politics and an official of the Writers Union. Simonov had the reputation of being notably adept at supporting the predominant Party view at any given moment,[64] which might indicate the reason for his appointment to *Novy Mir* in August, 1954. He should not, however, be seen as a conservative or Stalin-type replacement. *Novy Mir* continued to maintain its image as a liberal journal and, though there was a lull, the journal did eventually take a leading role in the later stages of the thaw.[65]

Tvardovsky, though removed from his editorial position, was not destined for oblivion. At the Second Writers Congress only four months later he was named to the presidium of the Soviet Writers Union. He remained a member of the Communist Party. His relegation was in no way comparable to the total condemnation of such literary figures as Zoshchenko or Akhmatova in the forties, Pasternak in the fifties, or Solzhenitsyn in the sixties.

Within a year and a half *Novy Mir* had twice been the object of an organized campaign. One had been initiated during Stalin's lifetime and had been interrupted by his death. The other, after his death, was carried through to a definite conclusion. The contrasts between these two episodes are numerous.

The initial fact that Tvardovsky, having weathered the storm in 1953, was then removed from his post in 1954, is less than surprising in view of the fact that Stalin died before the whole earlier affair had been concluded. Tvardovsky's behavior during the two campaigns is notably different, however. At no point in 1954 did Tvardovsky or members of his editorial board try to make a public apology comparable to the letter which the former board had published in *Literaturnaya Gazeta* in March, 1953.[66] The only public admission of guilt was made at the actual meeting where the Writers Union board resolved to change the editorial board, and this was followed by the brief printed statement in the September issue. It still remains true, however, that these two statements of self-criticism were similar in both form and content. The chief difference is that the 1954 apology followed the *fait accompli*, while the 1953 letter tried to stave it off.

Another contrast is that the 1954 campaign did not involve personal attacks or innuendoes. In 1953 there was much emphasis on bourgeois nationalism, rootless cosmopolitanism and on the relation of some of the Jewish writers to these phenomena. These points did not arise in the second campaign, in spite of the fact that almost all of the criticized writers were Jewish.

Indeed the earlier campaign appears to have been linked with a far larger program which included, among other things, the Doctors' Plot, the increasingly violent attacks on bourgeois nationalism and the struggle against rootless cosmopolitans. In other words, it was part of the preparation for a new and far-reaching purge. The later campaign represented a clash between more moderate and more conservative literary views which in turn can be associated at least partially with the political struggle between the Malenkov and Khrushchev camps. In view of later developments the contrasting positions of Khrushchev and Tvardovsky during this period can be seen as transient. Several years later their interests were to coincide.

Unlike the 1953 attack when the Party press – *Pravda, Kommunist, Molodoi Kommunist* – took a far more active role, in 1954 *Pravda* evinced little interest. The 1953 campaign in general was waged by far more journals than that of 1954. Furthermore, the items criticized in 1953 covered a wider range. At that time numerous articles, many of which were completely harmless, were publicly attacked in an apparent effort to destroy the journal's reputation by any means possible. In 1954 the campaign concentrated on the 'series' limiting itself quite narrowly to a particular line of criticism. Even Panova's novel was omitted from the official condemnation of the editorial board.

The resilience of *Novy Mir* in 1954, both in refraining from an early public apology and in persisting in publishing outspoken and innovative material long after the critics had expressed their disapproval, contrasts with the understandably greater caution of the previous year.

Certain fundamental similarities recurred. In both cases there was a time gap between the publication of provocative material and the critics' response. In each case the criticism developed into a concerted attack with clear signs that it was perpetrated by higher authorities – the Party and, through it, the Writers Union. It was also true in both campaigns that there was a variety of critical opinion, but with a significant difference: in 1953 the favorable comments soon came to a halt, whereas there was a greater range of opinion throughout the period in 1954. In the later period certain writers defended themselves, or were defended by others.[67] And, even toward the end of the campaign, *Literaturnaya Gazeta* itself attempted to tone down the attack.

It was the nature of the campaigns rather than the material published in the journal which differentiates the two periods. Although it is true that in 1952 there was no article of literary criticism comparable to Pomerantsev's, it is likewise true that in fiction nothing published in *Novy Mir* from the time of Stalin's death until the summer of 1954 could match the originality of Ovechkin's sketch or the daring of some portions of Grossman's novel.

Significant here is that the campaign against *Novy Mir* in 1954, and even Tvardovsky's dismissal, did not constitute a complete reversal of the liberalizing atmosphere. Although the journal kept a fairly low profile during the following year, it did not revert to being a totally lifeless publication and it was the same *Novy Mir*, with the same Simonov editorial board, which in 1956 was to take a leading role in the next stage of the thaw.

4

The 'political thaw'

For me the lessons of Stendhal lie primarily in his exceptional truthfulness. Indeed, that is the most important thing for us – not only for writers, but for all people in the middle of the twentieth century.

Ilya Ehrenburg, *Inostrannaya, Literatura*, June, 1957

If a single moment in history can ever be designated a primary historical cause, then it was surely Khrushchev's Secret Speech at the 20th Party Congress which profoundly influenced literary developments in 1956 and gave the second stage of the thaw its unique character. The revelations made public by Khrushchev in the late winter of 1956 produced a two-pronged effect similar to that induced at the end of 1953: their very candor encouraged writers to seek and express the truth in their literature, and the facts disclosed became in themselves subject-matter for works of fiction and for critical articles.

That this urge toward candor came into conflict with official efforts to contain it within defined boundaries is not surprising, and it was this struggle between the quest for truth and the desire for order which eventually culminated in the victory of the latter after the Hungarian Revolution.

The political thaw in literature made its impact in a number of ways. The most immediate effect of Khrushchev's speech, at least in *Novy Mir*, was the implicit rehabilitation of certain writers who either had been purged or had at least disappeared from print for many years. This rehabilitation took two forms: the names of some of these authors once again appeared in articles of literary criticism and, in a number of cases, works of the authors themselves began to be published.

Again, the later thaw influenced the actual subject-matter of fiction. Themes of the earlier period were not abandoned. On the contrary, the orientation towards material welfare, the emphasis on the 'trifles of life', the concern with man's private existence, human emotions, individual experience still occupied a central place. But beyond the economic focus there came an increasing emphasis on moral and political issues.

The discussion of the bureaucracy and of the fundamental problems inherent in bureaucratic management which became a hallmark of the literature of 1956 can be seen as a direct outgrowth of the political rethinking inspired by the 20th Party Congress. The exposure of Stalinist injustices, of the arbitrary measures taken against segments of the population, stimulated a sharp introspection and an obliquely expressed desire that history not repeat itself. The level at which the average citizen was confronted with arbitrariness was in his relationship with the bureaucracy. It was here that the national catastrophe was brought to the plane of everyday life and thus the misery of numberless victims of the purges could symbolically be equated with the injustice inflicted by the bureaucrat on the ordinary citizen. The problem of the bureaucracy, combined with dilemmas of personal honor and integrity, recurred in a number of works in 1956 and became a subject of sharp public discussion.

Clearly, moral dilemmas and individual decency were not new themes in Soviet literature. But the frequency and the frankness with which they were discussed now were characteristic of this second phase of the thaw.

Items of non-fiction also reflected the new political atmosphere. In a number of articles of literary criticism the names of rehabilitated writers now began to appear. Beyond this, literary critics took up themes of the 20th Party Congress. Thus, during 1956 the cult of personality, abuses of nationality policy under Stalin and the oppressive demands made on writers in the Stalin era were all discussed. It was now (for almost the first time) that mention of the purges was made in both fiction and non-fiction.[1]

It was a period of extraordinary vitality. Great hopes had been inspired by the 20th Congress and were nurtured in the ensuing months by rehabilitations and other liberalizing measures. It was a time for pulling manuscripts out of the drawer and for sitting down and writing what might have been unthinkable only months before. Timing was of the essence. Some daring items were published and fortuitously ignored by the critics. Others published too late in the year were attacked for mere innuendoes. The entire period of relaxation was, in fact, sandwiched into a six-month span, and (after-effects apart) the outburst of liberal response to the 20th Party Congress was more or less over by early 1957.

Continuing its function as a liberal journal, *Novy Mir* pursued a vigorous role in this second, dynamic, phase of the thaw. The editorial board which saw the journal through this period was not newly appointed to cope with a changed situation – as was the case in late 1953 – but was the board which Simonov had gradually put together after his appointment.[2] Until the spring of 1956 the journal had kept a low profile in the wake of Tvardovsky's dismissal and the becalming aftermath of the Second Writers Congress.

Between November, 1955 and July, 1958, Simonov's board remained constant:

B. N. Agapov   (assistant editor)[3]
S. N. Golubov
A. Yu. Krivitsky   (assistant editor)
B. A. Lavrenev
M. K. Lukonin
A. M. Mar'yamov
E. Uspenskaya
K. A. Fedin

Of these, two men are associated personally with Simonov. His assistant editors, Krivitsky and Agapov, had served with him in his various editorial posts and had followed him from board to board. They had been on the *Novy Mir* board when he had been editor-in-chief before Tvardovsky's arrival in March, 1950 and had left with him. Subsequently, they had served on his board when he was editor-in-chief of *Literaturnaya Gazeta* until August 27, 1953.[4]

Svirsky gave the following thumbnail portrait of Krivitsky:

Krivitsky was Simonov's deputy; they used to call him, 'Simonov's back door'. When Simonov didn't feel like playing some dirty trick, then Krivitsky did it for him. Simonov promised, Krivitsky refused. Simonov accepted material, Krivitsky threw it out. He is really a repulsive figure, a sort of Jewish antisemite, a friend of Sergei Vasil'ev, the Black Hundred poet...The fact that Krivitsky worked with Simonov for a long time says a lot not about *Novy Mir*, not about Krivitsky, but about Simonov. Simonov always had two sides to him and on the one side there was Krivitsky.[5]

Of the remaining members of Simonov's board, Lavrenev and Golubov were remembered by Tvardovsky in his article on *Novy Mir*'s fortieth anniversary in 1965.[6] He credited them with having given their utmost to *Novy Mir* until their deaths,[7] preparing manuscripts for publication, corresponding with authors, drawing up the plan for the journal. Neither of them was a Party member;

both were active writers.[8] They were to remain on the board after Simonov left. Mar'yamov, who departed with Simonov in 1958, later returned to the editorial board and stayed with Tvardovsky until his board finally broke up in 1970. Except for Fedin, the remaining members of the board were undistinguished as writers or as literary critics. None of them emerged as personalities during the controversy of 1957.

Unlike the 1953–54 editorial board, which took the initiative, this board seems at first to have drifted with the tide of anti-Stalinism. As a result, at no time were any individual staff members singled out for criticism or dismissed on account of their active part in selecting material to be published in *Novy Mir*. Nor, when the time came, did any individual members of the board itself defend their actions, or the journal, at any of the public meetings where 'errors' were discussed: Simonov alone faced public censure.

The response of *Novy Mir* to the charged political atmosphere did not make itself felt for a few months. Unlike the earlier thaw, when the October plenum came as a culmination of recent developments and the journal's reaction was immediate, the 20th Party Congress was not reflected in *Novy Mir* until after the normal time lag required by the publishing process. The first change of tone came in the May issue; a few innovative items followed in June; the climax was reached in the September and October issues.

In spite of *Novy Mir*'s generally accepted – and deserved – reputation as the best literary journal of the day, the items which were published in these months were not generally of lasting literary value. Works so often described as exciting, daring, innovative were outstanding almost entirely from a political – not a literary – point of view. In the long run they were works of more concern to the political scientist than to the literary critic. This in no way altered their contemporary interest.[9]

The first post-Congress thaw item to be published in *Novy Mir* was not a recent work. On the contrary, it was part of an unfinished novel by Bruno Yasensky which had actually been written in Moscow in 1937.[10] Significant in the publication of Yasensky's work was that nothing of his had appeared since his arrest almost twenty years before. The reappearance of his work was thus tantamount to the rehabilitation of a purged writer. Furthermore, the novel was prefaced by Yasensky's wife, who wrote that her husband had worked on part one of the novel and that his 'arrest caused by the slander of provocateurs had cut short his work'. She was quite explicit in stating that she had tried to reconstruct those chapters which should have completed the book and which, 'unfortunately, were not saved'. This was a reference to the seizure of manuscripts by the secret police.[11]

The novel itself, an anti-fascist work partly set in Germany, was made more interesting by its foreword and the very fact of its publication. The four-line poem with which Yasensky began it was equally valid for the thirties and the fifties:

Do not fear enemies – at worst they can kill you.
Do not fear friends – at worst they can betray you.
Fear the indifferent – they do not kill and do not betray,
But only with their silent approval do treachery and murder exist on earth.

This *de facto* rehabilitation of Yasensky was followed by the appearance of a number of poems by poets who had been out of favor or purged. Some innocuous poems of Lev Kvitko, translated from Yiddish, were the first by the poet to be published since the forties.[12] With the publication of some Yiddish poems (in Russian translation) of Vergelis in 1955,[13] *Novy Mir* had already been the first journal to publish Yiddish poets since the anti-cosmopolitan drive seven years before. Simonov's pangs of conscience with regard to his own role in this, coupled with official permission, may have led him to be the first to bring back the Yiddish poets, many posthumously. In October another Yiddish poet, Perets Markish, was published in *Novy Mir*.[14] The poems, written in 1947 and 1948 by the poet who was soon to perish on Stalin's orders, were published without comment.

The June and October issues of *Novy Mir* contained poems by Nikolai Zabolotsky.[15] Zabolotsky was one of the older generation of poets who had returned from prison. He was to die a few years later of heart disease, a result of his imprisonment.[16]

There were other poets whose works were published in *Novy Mir* at this time who, if they had not been on a black list, had certainly been on a grey one. Pasternak, for example, had some Georgian poems in translation in the July issue of the journal,[17] and his own poem in the October issue.[18] Anna Akhmatova was one of the translators of Markish's poems.[19] There was a small item by Viktor Shklovsky in the June issue.[20]

7   Vladimir Dudintsev, author of *Not by Bread Alone*
(reproduced by courtesy of Novosti)

8 D. Granin, photographed the year before the publication of 'A Personal Opinion'

While the *de facto* rehabilitation of numerous writers and poets was one of the most significant by-products of the later thaw, it was in works of fiction that the Soviet reader found the most profound expression of the disillusionment and aspirations which had been aroused by the 20th Congress. Eschewing the most sensitive subjects – the purges and the camps – as central themes, writers in 1956 centered on the subject of the bureaucracy. Superficially this seemed innocuous enough, but in fact it turned out to be explosive. The intense feeling of grievance of the individual against the bureaucratic machine was expressed repeatedly at this time. And later it was these works of fiction dealing with the bureaucracy and, in general, with the inhuman aspects of ordinary Soviet society, which received the harshest criticism.

The most famous work dealing with Soviet bureaucratic injustice and, indeed, the single best-known work to be published inside

Russia during this period of the thaw, was Vladimir Dudintsev's *Ne khlebom edinym* (Not by Bread Alone). It was published in *Novy Mir* late in the summer of 1956.[21] The book deals with the struggle of a lone inventor to gain recognition and acceptance of his invention, which he is certain is preferable to the industrial method in use. As the reader never doubts the superiority of Lopatkin's invention, he regards with disbelief – and eventually bitterness – the tactics of evasion used by the various officials approached. It is only through the efforts of one sterling character – a single exception in the bureaucratic jungle which Dudintsev describes – that the new machine is eventually accepted. But this is only after various tragic events which culminate in Lopatkin's imprisonment. Nor does the book end with the just punishment of all the villains. On the contrary, most of them are still entrenched, and some have even received promotion. Lopatkin, though he has the satisfaction of seeing the final victory of his invention, foresees the possibility of future struggles, perhaps this time on the political level.[22]

The book, like so many best-sellers all over the world, has limited literary merit, but it proved to be enormously popular in the Soviet Union. The topicality of the subject as well as the frank way in which it was handled attracted a large number of readers. Dudintsev had diplomatically set the novel's action in the recent, Stalinist, past, but this did not detract from its relevance for his readers in 1956. Nor did it later deceive his critics.

Lopatkin's first and constant enemy, Drozdov, came to symbolize all that was bad in the bureaucratic hierarchy, and at various conferences and discussions on literature and on production there were so many references to the Drozdovs of Russia that 'Drozdov' came to be synonymous with extreme bureaucratism.[23] A number of works by different authors involving similar situations, fictitious or real, appeared in 1956, thus reinforcing the impression that the problem raised in *Not by Bread Alone* was widespread and familiar. For example, in the June issue of *Novy Mir* there was a book review by D. Granin of the American writer Mitchell Wilson's recent novel *My Brother, My Enemy*. What is notable in the review is Granin's allusion to the kind of situation in Soviet – and American – life of which Wilson wrote and which Dudintsev was soon to describe.

To a Soviet engineer or scholar the absence of a conscious grasp of the social aim of his work is deeply alien. In our science there exists a bitter struggle with greed, ignorance, routine; there are people whose discoveries were kept

secret for years, but in the very worst cases the Soviet scholar knows that
he is fighting in the name of a great goal. The conscious feeling of
responsibility to the people, the only master of his talent, helps him.[24]
Indeed, Dudintsev's theme became a leitmotiv of the middle fifties.
Thus, Granin's 'Sobstvennoe mnenie' (A Personal Opinion), a
poignant story, again published in Novy Mir, likewise takes place in
a scientific milieu, and stresses the effect of position on one's own
moral standards.[25] A young inventor struggling to gain acceptance
for his invention is persistently put off by his superior. The story is
less about the young inventor's failure than about the personal
tragedy of his superior, Minaev, who is unable to respond to his own
conscience and discovers that he no longer holds any personal
convictions by which he can live. In this, Granin succeeded in delving
deeper than Dudintsev. Granin presented a 'negative' character who
is introspective and whom, in fact, one ends by pitying. The
administrator, too, thus becomes a victim of the system and, trapped
in his upward momentum, is unable – or lacks the courage – to act
according to ordinary tenets of human decency. While this is a
personal tragedy, it is predicated on the system within which Minaev
lives. The situation is in no way portrayed as unique. Furthermore,
in presenting retrospective glimpses of Minaev in his youth as a
parallel to the young inventor in his enthusiasm and innocence,
Granin implies that the system dehumanizes some of the best and
brightest young men in the course of their upward climb. Whereas
Dudintsev's novel ends on the buoyant note of the final acceptance
of Lopatkin's invention, Granin's little story is gray and leaves the
reader with a feeling of helplessness.

Preceding these two works by several months was Tendryakov's
'Pot-Holes', a story which revolved around the same general theme.
It was reviewed in a revealing article in Novy Mir in September.[26]
The reviewer, Yu. Kapusto, briefly retold the story, which concerned
the victim of a road accident who was brought to a first-aid station.
There the decision was made that he be transported for surgery to
a hospital thirty kilometers away. Knyazhev, director of the local
Machine Tractor Station, generously and with great effort helped to
carry the victim to the first-aid station. But he subsequently refused,
when sitting behind his desk at the MTS, to lend a tractor for the
trip to the hospital, because the tractor was needed for farming. In
the end, the man died.

In her review, Kapusto emphasizes Tendryakov's contrast between

Knyazhev the private person, humane and helpful, and Knyazhev the MTS director, the bureaucrat. As an individual he is a comrade and has a feeling of collectivism, of social conscience; as a bureaucrat he feels no personal responsibility. While citing the cult of personality and the lack of genuine criticism and self-criticism as causes of this bureaucratic approach, Kapusto does not stop here. The problems of bureaucracy plaguing the Soviet Union have deep implications and far-reaching repercussions which, she says, the story brings to light.

...in a socialist system 'bureaucratism' is not only less tolerable than anywhere else but – we have to state this quite frankly – is more dangerous than anywhere else, because even if Knyazhev as a private person is able to do good from time to time, the scope for him in this respect is limited. We have no private property. All material goods produced by the community belong to the community itself, but it makes use of them through the agency of its state administrative apparatus. The bureaucrat who occupies a post in the state apparatus places himself between the community and its own material means. This explains the significance of the fight waged by the party against bureaucratism. But the party has by now condemned the phenomena which lead to the appearance of people like...Knyazhev. How is it then that Knyazhev remains unchanged? The reason is that he accepts the policies of our party in a formal sense only.

Tendryakov's story is a warning. It shows how much we have yet to do, how tenacious bureaucratism still is, how from time to time it is able to bureaucratize even the battle with bureaucratism.

At least implied in this remarkable passage was the idea that with socialism – the nationalization of the means of production – man's cruelty to man could actually increase. Kapusto can thus be seen to be exposing the impact of Stalin's doctrine – condemned specifically by Khrushchev at the 20th Party Congress[27] – that the class war grows more violent the stronger socialism becomes.*

---

* For example, Khrushchev said, 'when socialism in our country was fundamentally constructed, when the exploiting classes were generally liquidated, when the Soviet social structure had radically changed, when the social basis for political movements and groups hostile to the Party had violently contracted...then the repression directed against them began'.

In the passage quoted in the text, Kapusto was clearly referring to the 20th Party Congress, and her condemnation of bureaucratism was almost certainly meant to cover the major political abuses of the Stalinist regime. It is interesting to note that Bukharin in his famous article 'The Theory of Unorganized Economics', published on June 30, 1929 in *Pravda*, formulated his attack on Stalin as an attack on bureaucracy. See George Katkov, *The Trial of Bukharin* (New York: Stein and Day, 1970), p. 62.

This concern with the bureaucracy was only one aspect of the growing attention paid to the entire question of personal convictions, of moral fiber – be it on the part of the bureaucrat, be it in the attitude of the individual to his personal life, to the collective, to comrades victimized by the system. The last facet of the question, the problem of how the individual is to act morally in a virtually amoral society – as in the time of the purges – was explored in depth years later, in *samizdat* works.

In her second book, *Hope Abandoned*, Nadezhda Mandelstam speaks of the complete subversion of the individual under these conditions, of the loss of self. But it was now, in the middle and late fifties, that the Soviet writer, having survived the purges, the war, and Zhdanovism, began once again to seek the self in his writing, to look into the emotional complexities of life, unrelated to political contingencies, to determine moral questions on a strictly personal level.

Pauir Sevak's poem, '*Nelegky razgovor*' (A Difficult Discussion), which appeared in the June issue of *Novy Mir*, dealt with the condemnation by the collective of an illicit romance.[28] In the poem the 'I' is in love with a young married woman, mother of a small boy. Although he was chastised at a public meeting, and has promised to stop loving her, the poet confesses to the reader that there is a truth reserved for public meetings, and that he loves her still. She eventually leaves her husband and brings her child to live with her lover.

Although the press ignored this poem, *Novy Mir* itself published a reader's attack on it a few months later, accompanied by *Novy Mir*'s own reply, defending the poem, written by Valeriya Gerasimova.[29] In their own prefatory note the journal's editors commented that the critic's attack showed 'a tendency to treat a work of art as a mere record of events and utterances, which ignores the complexity, poignancy and individual nature of man's experiences which are the very subject of poetry'. Here they were reinforcing a trend in liberal theory which had been developing over the previous four years.

Semen Kirsanov's poem, '*Sem' dnei nedeli*' (Seven Days of the Week), written in the period from May to July, 1956 and published in *Novy Mir* in September, certainly belongs to the 'year of protest'.[30] On various levels Kirsanov registers complaints against the society in which he lives. On the most basic level, he is reiterating the theme of Dudintsev's novel: an inventor brings his invention to the authorities and, although it is a good – and needed – one, it is rejected. He later discovers that someone else's invention, which is greatly inferior, has been accepted instead. However, the poem is wider in scope than this.

The setting is that of a fantasy world, with walls which open to the touch and a symbolic Country which appears in the heavens. Yet it has enough of a familiar character – the Institutes, Sections, Committees – to be recognizable to the Soviet reader as his own milieu.

The poet is trying to create a heart which will respond as hearts are meant to. In his opening lines he asks the Country to 'accept in your kind hands a complaint against those whose hearts are stone' – clearly a reference to bureaucrats. The heart sought has two aspects. It is a physical heart which beats, registers on the cardiogram, and will save the poet's dying friend. It is also a metaphysical heart, that part of the human being which responds to emotional stimuli, which is the center of the passions. It is the latter aspect of the heart which is central to the poem.

> Here is the new-model heart
> for quick, future weeks!
> For connections on earth
> It will serve us
>   like a relay.
> As with a wire filament
> you can link to others
> your emotion
>   joy,
>   anguish,
> love![31]

The inventor speaks of the importance of the heart he has created.

> Such a heart is awaited everywhere,
> they are waiting in the *ispolkom* and in the court.
> Without the heart
>   you see it is forbidden
> To sit in judgment.[32]

Kirsanov assures us that this heart will never let you down.

But although the Country seems ready to accept this marvelous invention, a commission intervenes and destroys it. Such hearts, they say, are not needed. What the market calls for are 'useful hearts, like iron locks, uncomplicated, convenient, capable of performing well':

Blacken? Blacken!
Value? Value!
Destroy? Destroy!
Nurture? Nurture!
Growl? Growl!
Keep silent? Keep silent!
Ruin? Ruin!
Love? Love!
And no cardiograms,
But to set things to rights –
                    two hundred grams![33]

In a grotesque parody of the poet's invention, the officials market hearts in the local department store. But these are merely cheap tawdry hearts, brightly colored, decorative, but without the function the poet had intended.

A lie in the form of a heart was impudently offered,
  but the public
              was taken in by the fraud.[34]

The poet, in the concluding lines, addresses the Country and demands that it drive out deceit and sham.

Kirsanov, in this poem, was calling for a return to those fundamental human emotions, to a straightforward, humane approach without which people cannot function. In using the image of the dying friend he presented an implied analogy to the country itself, which likewise was dying for want of a new heart.

Kirsanov, who was a well-established poet in the Soviet Union at the time of the publication of 'Seven Days of the Week', had a solid reputation and a long list of published works. But his poem shook the circles of authority and was one of the items under heaviest attack in 1957.[35]

Various other works contained sections, or paragraphs, related to the theme of conscience, personal morals and genuine emotions.[36] But in none of them was this theme so central to the whole as in the works discussed above.

The inability of Soviet authors to discuss many of the most immediate and important facets of Soviet life had characterized Russian literature since the thirties. The upheavals of the thirties and late forties, the injustices perpetrated by the system, the enormous sense of loss and frustration and fear had been taboo subjects for decades.

Thus the mention of the camps, of the purges, of rehabilitated writers had a traumatic and cathartic effect. Seen from the vantage point of the eighties, after the publication abroad of works by Solzhenitsyn, Nadezhda Mandelstam, Marchenko, Grossman and Ginzburg, these early references seem timid. But at the time they had a revelationary impact.

The brief statement about Yasensky's fate written by his wife was an early reference to the purges. The following month, in S. Zalygin's 'Witnesses', a cautious mention of the purges was made again.[37]

Dudintsev himself played a prominent part in introducing the subject of unjust imprisonment into the Soviet novel in the fifties. In fact, the facet of Dudintsev's book which Zhores Medvedev considered most startling was not the all-out attack on the bureaucracy, but the episode of Lopatkin's imprisonment.

The finest pages of Dudintsev's splendid *Not by Bread Alone* are those which describe the hero's arrest and 'court martial', a glaring example of senseless arbitrariness.[38]

The purges were central to some of the poems published in *Novy Mir* by Ol'ga Berggol'ts in a fine collection entitled 'Poems from Diaries', which she had written between 1938 and 1956. Berggol'ts, a well-known poet, had also distinguished herself in 1953 as a defender of the rights of writers.[39]

It is surprising that none of these poems was ever attacked in the Soviet press and that the poems were hardly discussed in Western commentaries, then or later. For this reason, a few of them will be reproduced here in full.

The first poem in the cycle is dated 1938 and entitled '*Ispytanie*' (The Test).[40]

> ...And again there will be strength enough
> to see and learn
> that everything you loved
> will begin to torment you.
> And a friend will suddenly appear
> before you in a new guise
> and will slander [you]
> and another will turn his back on you.
> And they will start tempting,
> they will command: Renounce!
> And the heart will writhe
> in terror and grief.

9 Ol′ga Berggol′ts, poet and author of 'Poems and Diaries'

> And again there will be strength enough
> to repeat one thing only in answer
> – I am not renouncing
> everything I lived by, no!
> And again there will be strength enough
> remembering these days
> to cry to everything you loved,
> Come back! Give back!

Here Berggol'ts is dealing directly and courageously with the moral problem of retaining one's own integrity under enormous pressure. The poem provides an unusually straightforward treatment of a problem of great urgency to the Soviet intellectual. And it is a unique example even in an outspoken period.

A second poem dealing with the purges, but dated 1955, treats not the moral problem but the physical fact of the camps and the return of friends after many years' absence. Entitled '*Tot god*' (That Year), it celebrates the post-Stalin exodus from the camps.[41]

> And I recalled my whole life,
> and my life recalled everything
> in that year when from the bottom of the seas,
>   from the canals,
> suddenly friends began to return.
>
> Why hide it – few returned.
> Seventeen years is seventeen years after all.
> But first those who returned went
> to get back their old Party card.
>
> I will add not a sound to this,
> not even a sigh: we live anew.
> Well, what else? Comrade, give me your hand!
> How good we two are together again.

Berggol'ts' poem is distinctive in that she took as a central theme a subject which was foremost in people's minds, yet thus far scarcely mentioned in contemporary Soviet literature. Herself a Party member, she emphasized that those so severely punished were now even retrieving their Party cards, an indication of their innocence. In the poem they are 'rehabilitated' on both an official and a personal level.

One last poem in the group which deserves special attention was written in 1949 and is entitled '*Otvet*' (The Reply).[42] It is an impassioned plea for complete fidelity to one's ideals, uncorrupted by considerations of outside demands or any fear of the consequences. The poem was written in a dark period for Soviet intellectuals, at the time of the attack on bourgeois nationalism, the arrest of writers and a nadir in the quality of literary publication. It is an excellent example of a work obviously 'written for the drawer' but which

finally saw the light of day through a judicious exploitation of
changing publication policy. It was ignored by the critics.

> Friends repeat: All means are good
> in order to save from malice and disaster
> even a part of the tragedy,
>   even a part of the soul. . .
> But who said that I am divisible into parts?
>
> And how can I conceal – by half – my passion,
> so that it does not cease to be passion?
> How to give only a part of myself at the behest of the people
> when a whole life would be too little?
>
> No, if there is pain – then the whole heart is in anguish,
> or if joy – then it is burning before all.
> And it is not fear which commands it to be open
> But its own freedom which is stronger than all else.
>
> Thus I desire,
>   thus I believe,
>   thus I love.
> Do not show your paltry concern.
> I would not exchange even my ruin
> for your Philistine happiness.

A number of articles of literary criticism appearing in *Novy Mir*
in 1956 also significantly registered the liberalized atmosphere of the
post-20th Congress months. In many ways the most interesting – and
startling – was the first, which was written by the editor of *Novy Mir*
himself and published in June. Simonov's article was on Aleksandr
Fadeev, who had recently committed suicide.[43]

The story of Fadeev's rewriting of *The Young Guard* is well known.
The novel, which received the Stalin Prize for literature in 1946, was
attacked in the following year by *Pravda* and *Kul'tura i Zhizn'*.
According to the criticism, the plot, which centered on the early war
years in Krasnodon and the heroic part played by young Komsomol
members, gave an impression of weakness and chaos in the Soviet
ranks at the beginning of the war and did not portray the exemplary
role of the Communist Party in the struggle against the fascist enemy.
Fadeev, who was the secretary of the Writers Union and a powerful
figure in the literary world, accepted the criticism and proceeded to
rewrite his novel, which was published, in revised form, a few years

later. It was this which Simonov discussed in his June, 1956 article. He took the view – original in Soviet criticism – that the novel as rewritten was not as good as the first version,[44] and he went on to question the very practice of asking authors to rewrite their books. Simonov specifically stated that it was the right of the author himself to decide whether or not criticism of his work was correct. He took an outspoken stand.

...now, when Fadeev's literary work and life are at an end, recognizing all the value of the splendid new pages of the second edition of the novel *The Young Guard*, I would like to say that his first edition did not merit the criticism it received. Fadeev was reproached for the fact that the first edition of his novel did not sufficiently show the educational role of the Party, that in it youth was shown to be cut off from the Party underground, left to itself. There is no point now in arguing over the documentation of history in Krasnodon, for Fadeev's novel is a novel and not a historic chronicle.[45]

The points Simonov made here are of political as well as literary significance. He not only declared that it must be the author's decision whether his work should stand as written but also left open the historiographical question of whether or not the Party had played a leading role in the events depicted by Fadeev. By the time Simonov wrote the article numerous questions had already been raised about the preparedness of the Soviet Union for the Nazi invasion, but the leading role of the Party remained a given not to be questioned openly. Fadeev, basing himself on local documents for the original version of the novel, had portrayed young people as virtually working on their own, without the close supervision and direction of Party leaders. Simonov tacitly rehabilitated this – the original – interpretation. Moreover, in stating that Fadeev's work was a novel – a work of art with its own aesthetic rules – Simonov was in fact undermining a tenet of socialist realism: that in his work the writer must elevate and enhance the role of the Party.

Undoubtedly, in writing this article Simonov had been deeply affected by Fadeev's recent suicide. In it there is a palpable feeling of sympathy for the author who had been forced to rewrite an entire novel. But while in the summer of 1956 such an article was publishable, this did not prevent it from being fiercely attacked later.

A major article on the literary problems inherited from the Stalin period was that by S. Shtut, published in the September issue of *Novy Mir*.[46] Shtut was particularly concerned with what she called 'the blank spaces' in Soviet literature.

The appearance of blank spaces in our literary scholarship had many and varied causes. A great number of them were the result of the devastation caused to literature by the cult of personality and its consequences. And these are not just the books of M. Kol´tsov, I. Babel, B. Yasensky – writers physically snatched away from the literary ranks; and not just books of writers safely hailed now but for a long time shut away – without sufficient basis – in a closed treasure house; it is also those books (*Duma pro Opanasa* of E. Bagritsky, the novels of I. Ilf and E. Petrov) which, not subject to direct administrative persecution, underwent an extremely real ideological ban.

The very list of these works, well known to the reader and dearly loved by him, speaks for itself. It is not necessary to worry about the fate of such 'blank spaces': they will very soon...be filled...[47]

In her article, Shtut discussed the weaknesses of a school of literary criticism in which too much emphasis was placed on the Bubennovs and too little on other writers: Prishvin, Grossman, Martynov, Kaverin. She blamed the cult of personality for having dried up not only the writer but the scholar. The entire system of literary prizes, of predetermined analyses and evaluations, of aesthetic norms 'from above', continually removed from the researcher his personal, subjective connection with literature. Thus, the lack of faith in the creative energy of the researcher fettered his powers and, more than anything else, hindered the art of literary criticism.[48]

The general line of Shtut's article was followed up and even extended later in the year by A. Metchenko, a Moscow University professor.[49] His article was published after the Hungarian uprising when, in fact, the reaction against liberal utterances was already to be felt.[50] He began by stating some of the problems of Soviet literature.

The scholarly approach to the history of Soviet literature suffered greatly from the fact that a huge quantity of books, journals, almanacs, newspapers, not to speak of archives, were to be found under seven locks...

Today the situation has somewhat improved in this connection, but the routine, the bureaucracy, the system of playing safe still make themselves felt at every turn.[51]

Metchenko questioned the practice – still in use – of omitting selected pieces from volumes of collected works. This led to sterility. Why, for example, in the latest collection of Gorky's works was his essay on Leonid Andreev omitted?

They say that such arbitrariness was connected with the cult of personality. But now when a struggle is being waged against the consequences of the cult of personality, new variants of 'improved history' can be traced which, in fact, as always in such cases, lead to a distortion of history.[52]

Metchenko expressed himself even more militantly than had Shtut. He called for the restoration not just of the civil rights but of the 'author's rights' of Vesely, Babel, Gerasimov, Kirillov, Kirshon and other poets, dramatists and prose writers who had been unjustly removed from literary history.[53] He further urged that the works of various writers from the early history of Soviet socialism be made available to Soviet readers. He would like to examine the history of the literary groups flourishing between 1917 and 1932, examine the Proletcult poems, appreciate the writings of the Serapion Brothers whose fiction, he wrote, was good, even if their literary criticism was apolitical.

Outspoken as this article was, it was ignored by the critics even during the most vociferous period of the campaign against *Novy Mir*.[54] In Soviet literary history it has happened that the most 'offensive' material somehow escapes censure while fairly harmless texts arouse violent outbursts.

The last critical article of interest to appear in *Novy Mir* in 1956 was Konstantin Simonov's 'Literary Notes', published in the same issue as Metchenko's.[55] Simonov's December article was written in the same spirit as that of the previous June, but is on a far more personal level and is filled with a sense of guilt.

In the first section of the article Simonov surveyed post-war Soviet literature. Here his central point was that, in blaming Stalin's cult of personality for the low ebb which literature had reached, critics were oversimplifying the problem. The obvious consequence of the cult of personality, wrote Simonov, had indeed appeared in his own as well as others' works – the direct, uncritical glorification of Stalin. But if this were the only shortcoming in recent literature it could be overcome simply by deleting all praise of Stalin. What was left would be literary productions of a high calibre.[56]

But the more invidious influence of the Stalin period was seen in an excess of embellishment: the wish was taken for the fact. The cult of infallibility had created an official atmosphere in which much was said of success and little of failure. Thus, in postwar books, talent, when coupled with untruth, had been debased. Literature presented not an out-and-out lie about postwar life, but, certainly, a half-truth.[57] In order to escape having to write about contemporary life and its conflicts, complained Simonov, some writers delved into history or

wrote about life in other countries. This point, it will be recalled, had
already been made in Stalin's time, in 1952, by Virta.[58]
    In part two of his article Simonov returned to the theme he had
discussed in June: Fadeev's rewriting of *The Young Guard*. This time
he singled out one of the principal articles which had demanded
revisions: 'The Young Guard, on the State of our Theater'.[59]
Although Simonov still defended some of the points made in the 1947
article, he declared that the main thrust had been wrong and
proceeded to discuss it in detail. The criticism, he said, had denied
the facts – so well researched by Fadeev – of what had actually
happened in the anti-Nazi underground movement.[60] It was well
known – and to Fadeev himself – Simonov now declared, that Stalin
had directly given the order for this article.[61]
    In summarizing the negative significance of the 1947 article
Simonov made two points. First, the criticism of *The Young Guard*
had presented a series of normative demands concerning not only this
novel but literature in general: 'The version that the beginning of
the war and the evacuation had an organized character led to a
countless number of distortions of the historic truth in many
works.'[62] Many writers who had seen the war with their own eyes
had had to refuse to write first-hand accounts and had fallen back
on other themes which to them were of marginal interest.
    On a more personal note, Simonov suggested that the attack had
placed Fadeev in an extremely difficult position. He not only had to
rewrite his novel but was also burdened by the knowledge that Stalin,
in whom he believed, felt that he had erred as an artist. Further, the
four years spent on rewriting the novel meant that other works which
Fadeev might have created were never finished. Wouldn't the readers
have preferred – rather than two versions of *The Young Guard* on his
shelf – to have had, for example, the completion of the epic *The Last
of the Udeg*? 'The fate of literature', Simonov continued, 'depends
on the fate of the artists and it is our collective responsibility always
and under all circumstances to remember this.'[63]
    Simonov then proceeded to the field of drama. Here he discussed
his own responsibility for the attack on the 'cosmopolitan' theater
critics. A whole group of writers and critics, who certainly could not
have been accused of being unpatriotic, had been unable, he asserted,
to get work as a result of the campaign.[64]
    Simonov cited the *Pravda* article from January, 1949 that had set
the tone of the criticism.[65] The article had demanded that Soviet

writers emphasize the achievements of the regime. Writers describing its shortcomings or the shadier side of life had been reproached for a lack of patriotism. Critics pointing out the imperfections of Soviet drama had been called anti-patriots and accused of conscious premeditated group activity directed against Soviet literature. It was well known in literary circles, said Simonov, that the ideas in this article were Stalin's.

The then-leaders of the Writers Union, including the author of these lines, and a whole series of writers and critics did not find the courage in themselves to make at least an attempt to show the one-sidedness and incorrectness of this article... On the contrary, they floated with the tide. In their speeches (and these included my statement at the Moscow meeting of dramatists and my speech to the *aktiv* of the film workers) they not only defended the correctness of everything said in the article, but greatly increased its negative significance by expressing numerous quite personal, grossly unjust evaluations of the activity of our theater critics.[66]

This self-criticism is summed up at the end of the article in Simonov's plea that writers not ignore their own part in Soviet literary history.

In speaking about the history of postwar literature, we writers should not merely emphasize those questions where we *personally* were less at fault, while passing over those questions where we *personally* made greater and worse mistakes. It seems to me that our collective discussion of the problems of our postwar literary history should at the same time involve a discussion of each individual with his own self, a discussion of one's own mistakes and errors, of one's own lack of ideological firmness in those cases where it revealed itself. As concerns myself, I personally in no way intend to detach myself from all those mistakes I have described in this article, in many of which I was in some measure or other involved.[67]

Looking back at the issues of *Novy Mir* published under the influence of the 20th Party Congress, we see that a number of the bold literary and political statements in the journal were probably selected in response to the demands of Simonov's own conscience. Both of his critical articles as well as his publication of the purged Yiddish poets seem to have been attempts to atone in part for his own role in the disasters which befell the 'cosmopolitans' and Fadeev.[68]

As in the previous phase of the thaw, the pages of *Novy Mir* were not entirely given over to an expression of liberalism. Various articles urging restraint continued to be published. Furthermore, the discussion of literary problems, even in outspoken articles, was not given full range. Although more basic analyses of the fundamentals of socialist realism were certainly being written at this time, they did not appear in *Novy Mir* or other journals, but were assigned to the drawer.[69]

The political leaders always had an equivocal attitude towards de-Stalinization, and as a result the relaxation process in literature developed unevenly. The old tensions remained, as they had in the first upsurge of 1953–54. It was simply a question of whose voice would eventually prevail. Ultimately, everything, as always, would be reduced to politics.

The official reaction to the 1956 thaw proved, when it came, to be remarkably similar to the pattern set in the two attacks on *Novy Mir* which had preceded it.[70] In each case the heterodox items in the journal had been sandwiched into a period of six or, at most, seven months: this seems to have been the longest extent of 'liberal' toleration which the system would sustain.

The internal Soviet reaction to the Hungarian uprising came swiftly. Whereas the thaw resulting from the 20th Party Congress had made itself felt gradually, the new 'freeze' was effected rapidly.[71] Thus, while two articles of interest still appeared in the December issue of *Novy Mir* – those of Metchenko and Simonov – nothing of this nature was to be found in the issue of January, 1957. The invasion of Hungary proved to be the prelude to a rapid acceleration of attacks on the journal.

As in the preceding cases, *Novy Mir* was criticized for a variety of often unconnected reasons, and, like Tvardovsky, Simonov was held responsible for his journal's faulty policy. This time there was no reference to a 'series' as there had been in 1954. What was unique in this campaign was that it lasted for so long. In 1954, the attack went on for approximately five months and had actually petered out before the change of the editorial board.[72] This time the campaign lasted for about a year. During this period there were critical articles, meetings, apologies, and then renewed criticism.

Of the *Novy Mir* articles and fictional works of 1956, that which was criticized the most was Dudintsev's *Not by Bread Alone*. After this came Granin's 'A Personal Opinion' and Kirsanov's 'Seven Days of the Week', which were attacked in approximately equal degree. Simonov was also singled out, both as author of his own two articles of literary criticism and as the editor responsible for the journal. However, the brunt of the assault was borne by the journal itself.

Besides the major works, a number of other items were singled out, either in general articles or in individual reviews. Thus, Zalygin's story was criticized twice,[73] Shtut's article was criticized once[74] and other articles which have not been described here were mentioned on single occasions.[75] Other *Novy Mir* items which might have been attacked were not: Sevak's poem, Metchenko's article, Kapusto's review, Berggol'ts' poems.[76]

Characteristic of the year 1956 – prior to the Hungarian invasion – was the broader spectrum of opinions on literary works. Thus, Dudintsev's novel was praised in *Trud* and at a public discussion late in October,[77] while Granin's story came under assault in a letter published in *Partiinaya Zhizn'* in September.[78] Only after the clampdown was there a return to a more unified attitude towards literary works.

One by-product of the post-Congress thaw was that, at least in the early months, authors under attack not only refused to admit their 'guilt', but even fought back. On two occasions, for example, at a two-day plenary session of the board of the Moscow branch of the Writers Union in March, 1957, Dudintsev defended himself articulately.[79] In a deeply personal speech, published in *Literaturnaya Gazeta*, Dudintsev spoke of the reasons for his writing *Not by Bread Alone*. He was tired of the lies which had been perpetrated for so long in the Soviet Union, and of the harm the lies had done. As an example, he told of his profound shock during the Second World War when he had seen the supposedly invincible Soviet aircraft shot down by German Messerschmitts, inferior in number.

The second time that Dudintsev spoke at the meeting he expressed his doubt as to whether truly creative discussion could ever really take place.

I think that we might be allowed, like people learning to swim, to try to swim on our own, to take our own chances of drowning. But, alas, I always feel a halter, like the harness by which children are sometimes supported. And it keeps me from swimming.[80]

By May, however, at the plenary session of the board of the Writers Union, every speaker spoke out against Dudintsev, Granin and Kirsanov, as well as against the editorial board of *Novy Mir* and *Literaturnaya Moskva*.[81] Those who differed chose to express their dissent by remaining silent. An example of this was Valentin Ovechkin who, while not criticizing specific points of the secretariat's report, made it clear that he could not speak in favor of it. It was at this meeting that Surkov spoke in language reminiscent of the very worst periods of repression. After speaking of Dudintsev, Granin and Yashin (whose 'Levers' had been published in the second volume of *Literaturnaya Moskva*), he referred to the seeds of discontent sown in some of the satellite countries.

Looking at the hue and cry that has been going on in recent times in certain literary circles of Poland, Hungary and Yugoslavia under the widely proclaimed slogans of fighting routine and stagnation, under the slogans of innovation, one cannot but note that all these adept innovators face toward the past, toward the rubbish dump of world culture, in which the offal of all kinds of 'isms' from fifty or sixty years ago has long lain fetid and rotted, rejected by history.[82]

This language was not unique during the period of reaction. An article that appeared in *Ogonek* at the beginning of February attacked Kirsanov's poem in equally vulgar terms.[83]

Also typical of the attacks in this period was the repeated mention of the Zhdanov decree on the magazines *Zvezda* and *Leningrad*. The symbolic import of this could not have been lost on readers. It came as a clear sign of the change of atmosphere then pervading Russia. An attack on Granin which had already appeared in *Partiinaya Zhizn'* in December, 1956 made use of the Zhdanov decrees in establishing the 'correct' position.

The Communist Party and its Central Committee have repeatedly pointed out – in documents known to everyone (the 1925 resolution 'On Party Policy in the Sphere of Literature', in the 1946 decision 'Concerning the Magazines *Zvezda* and *Leningrad*', etc.) – the need to give every possible support to writers whose work contributes to the Soviet people's struggle for communism, to help overcome shortcomings and defects in literature through principled Party criticism and to fight decisively and uncompromisingly against all attempts to lead Soviet literature from the correct path of helping to build a communist society with their pens.[84]

It is a sign of just how far Soviet literary criticism had (or had not) progressed since the death of Stalin to see with what ease the old formulas and techniques were put to use.

In other ways also the old forms were adhered to. Apologies and recantations were still expected, and, sooner or later, were produced. Perhaps one sign of moderation, however, is the length of time that it took some of the authors to make their modest apologies. (It should be remembered, though, that in 1953 no apologies had been made by Vasily Grossman or Emanuil Kazakevich.)

Simonov made the first and the most repeated apologies. Some were made on his own behalf, others in the form of an attack on Dudintsev. He expressed his contriteness more often than any of the other writers under attack.

At the May session of the board of the Writers Union Kirsanov, too, admitted that he had acted wrongly. According to the report, 'the non-Party writer S. Kirsanov took a serious view of the criticism of his poem "Seven Days of the Week" and announced that he was undertaking a fundamental revision of his work'.[85]

Dudintsev, who had defended himself defiantly at the March meeting, was reported in June still to be holding out.[86] After nearly a year of pressure to apologize for the 'mistakes' made in his novel, Dudintsev finally succumbed, according to a single report in the newspaper *Vechernyaya Moskva* in December, 1957.[87] In an article on a meeting of the prose section of the Moscow branch of the Writers Union, Dudintsev was reported to have admitted that the critical reactions of the Soviet public to his *Not by Bread Alone* were entirely correct and justified. His moderate apology came months after critical interest had subsided.

Only Granin appears to have refused to apologize. He was not even reported to have taken part in the earlier meetings. The only Party member of the three *Novy Mir* contributors, Granin did not bow to criticism, and indeed defended himself, apparently without any great harm to his career.[88] For example, an article in February, 1957 reported him as having been elected Assistant Responsible Secretary in the Leningrad branch of the Writers Union.[89] This was at the height of the attacks upon him and upon Dudintsev.

In spite of his continued apologies, the criticism of Simonov lasted for a long time, although it changed somewhat in character. In the beginning, it had centered on Simonov, the editor of *Novy Mir*. Later this criticism dissipated into a variety of comments, largely focusing on a series of stories he published in the journal *Moskva* in 1957.[90]

Simonov stands out as an interesting – if not entirely admirable – personality in Soviet literary history. He had the reputation of knowing how to trim his sails with the wind. Instinctively, one feels that his tendencies, given their natural bent, were towards the 'liberal' rather than the repressive in literary policy. Were he fundamentally a conservative by conviction it would be hard to

explain his eagerness to publish what he did after the 20th Party
Congress. A man of little nerve, he chose to take his chances when
he felt it was relatively safe. And, indeed, as a result of his direction,
the tone of the thaw was set by *Novy Mir* in the summer and autumn
of 1956.

Simonov's sense of timing, however, was not always the best. His
publication in *Novy Mir* of the article on the anti-cosmopolitan
campaign in December, 1956 is a case in point. Furthermore, in an
interview published in mid January, 1957, he promised that works
by Kirsanov and Dudintsev would be published in *Novy Mir* during
the coming year.[91] At that very moment, both writers were under
intense attack. Indeed, the assault on Dudintsev had begun some
months earlier. Unless the interview had taken place long before, it
is difficult to understand Simonov's statement. His courageous
publishing policy had already been abandoned with the start of
1957.[92]

Again, together with his apologetic article in the March issue of
Novy Mir, Simonov also chose to publish – in the April, 1957 issue
of *Moskva* – a war-time story which contained a controversial
description of a victim of the purges. This description was quoted
in a critical article attacking him the following July.[93]

Baburov was not a physical coward. During the Civil War he had fought
in battles and was awarded inscribed side arms for bravery, but in 1937 he
was suddenly arrested in Kerch, where he was serving as the city military
commissar. That was the same wave of arrests in 1937 that many remembered
willy-nilly now during the war... When they arrested Baburov and demanded
that he admit his participation in some sort of monstrous plot, of which he
had not the slightest idea, he became frightened and he remained a frightened
man all the rest of his life. And when, after two years, he was released from
prison and told he was not guilty of anything, he was tall and healthy-looking,
but he was suffering from the most terrible of human diseases – he was afraid
of his own acts.[94]

The excerpt illustrates the difficulty of analyzing Simonov.

Solzhenitsyn's Galakhov, in *The First Circle*, is generally accepted
to be a portrayal of Simonov – in his thirties at the time of the novel,
a famous war correspondent, popular poet, playwright, novelist,
winner of numerous prizes. Solzhenitsyn describes the plight of
Galakhov and other writers like him.

Of course, they couldn't write much of the truth. But they consoled
themselves with the thought that some day things would change, and then
they would return to these times and these events, and record them

truthfully, revising and reprinting their old books. Right now they must concentrate on that quarter, eighth, sixteenth – oh, all right, that thirty-second – part of the truth that was possible. Even that little bit was better than nothing.

But what oppressed Galakhov was that it was getting harder and harder to write each new page. He made himself write on a schedule...

Whenever he began some big new work, he would be fired up, he would swear to his friends and to himself that this time he would not make any concessions to anyone, this time he would write a real book. For the first few pages he would work away with enthusiasm. But soon he would notice that he was not writing alone; that the presence of the person he was writing for always loomed over him; that he was involuntarily rereading every paragraph with that person's eyes. That person was not the reader, fellow man, or friend; not even the critical fraternity in general – it was always that most important critic, the celebrated Zhabov...

So, paragraph after paragraph, Galakhov would try to anticipate Zhabov's objections and adapt himself to them; and the book would roll out, duller and duller, falling obediently into place.[95]

The same pliant Simonov, who in the late forties attacked the 'cosmopolitan' critics and in the fifties regretted it, who first demanded that Fadeev rewrite *The Young Guard* and later insisted that the first version was the better one, initially praised Solzhenitsyn's 'One Day in the Life of Ivan Denisovich', and later – in 1974 – attacked him in the press.[96]

Novy Mir was not the only publication criticized for its policy during the post-20th Party Congress months in 1956: although it received the brunt of the attack, the literary almanac, *Literaturnaya Moskva*, was also severely criticized. In fact, most of the handful of titles which symbolize the 1956 thaw were published either in *Novy Mir* or in the second volume of *Literaturnaya Moskva*. Kron's 'Writer's Notes', Yashin's 'Levers' and Ehrenburg's 'The Poetry of Marina Tsvetaeva' were typical of those thaw items which appeared in the almanac.

The almanac had been collected in 1956 and was submitted for publication at the beginning of October. At the end of November the manuscript was approved for printing, so that the book actually appeared after the events in Hungary. It contained stories, poems, reminiscences, literary criticism and even a novel in its 800 pages. Among its contributors were some outcasts, such as Yury Olesha, as well as some Soviet writers of unquestionable reputation, such as Fadeev and Surkov. In general it reflected the pre-Hungary atmosphere. Many of the themes found in the almanac were similar to those in *Novy Mir* that had been attacked.[97] That there was a connection between *Novy Mir* and the almanac was assumed by some of their critics, and much of the criticism in articles and speeches coupled them.

Many of the writers represented in *Literaturnaya Moskva* were *Novy Mir* contributors, both before and after 1956: Yashin, Marshak, Vanshenkin, Kirsanov, Zabolotsky, Dorosh, Shcheglov. The editors, too, had connections with *Novy Mir*: Bek had published his latest novel there, Tendryakov his stories; Kazakevich's 'Heart of a Friend' had been printed in the journal and his most recent novel had been well reviewed in the September 1956 issue.[98] Others associated with *Novy Mir*, including Simonov, Tvardovsky and Chukovsky, had contributed to the first volume of *Literaturnaya Moskva*.

Although it is doubtful whether *Novy Mir* as a journal took an active organizing role in the literary almanac, it is certainly clear that a circle of more liberal writers had formed and that the feeling of isolation felt by creative people under Stalin had come to an end. *Literaturnaya Moskva* was one product of this more communal spirit of like-minded people. These writers had a sense of solidarity which was expressed in the support they sometimes gave in print or at meetings to those under attack.

A noteworthy example of this interrelationship and sense of solidarity is the case of *Moskovsky Literator*, the information bulletin of the Moscow writers organization.[99] Its editor in 1956–57 – until he was fired – was V. A. Rudny. Rudny was also on the editorial board of *Literaturnaya Moskva* II and was one of those under heavy attack during 1957. Aside from his role in the almanac, Rudny had defended recent literary *bêtes noires* in his information bulletin and at meetings. In fact, he was one of the first – and only ones – to receive actual punishment for his participation in the literary activities of 1956–57.

A reference to the interrelationships in literature was made in an editorial in *Literaturnaya Gazeta* in May, 1957. In it *Moskovsky Literator*, *Literaturnaya Moskva* and *Novy Mir* are all linked together:

As is known, in the journal *Novy Mir*, the almanac *Literaturnaya Moskva* and the newspaper *Moskovsky Literator* there appeared works, articles and statements which were contrary to the main direction of contemporary Soviet literature. In a series of meetings in Moscow, and in particular at the recent plenum of the board of the Moscow section of the Writers Union, several writers tried to create the impression that the writing masses follow them. They tried to present as the newest word in our literature V. Dudintsev's *Not by Bread Alone*, A. Yashin's story 'Levers', and other works similar to these which describe Soviet reality in a distorted way.[100]

At the plenum itself, Rudny was attacked by E. Dolmatovsky for the role he had played as editor of both the almanac and the paper.

The presidium of the Moscow writers organization has been very afraid of engaging in administrative interference. But evidently we shall have to interfere in the work of the editorial board of *Literaturnaya Moskva*. Sometimes it is necessary to be severe. We put up with the fact that the house organ, *Moskovsky Literator*, published, under a guise of objectivity, materials that muddied the waters in our organization, and then we took heart and fired the editor, Rudny.[101]

The following month, a meeting of the Moscow Communist writers approved a decision of the Party committee of the Moscow branch of the Writers Union to expel Rudny from its ranks.[102]

Rudny was singled out as a leader of the 'unhealthy' tendencies which had been apparent in literature in the second half of 1956. Indeed, the furor over Rudny's role and over the biased character of the house organ of the Moscow writers organization was symptomatic of the rationale behind the decision in the summer of 1957 to set up a Writers Union of the RSFSR which would offset the stronghold of the Moscow writers.

In the previous campaigns against *Novy Mir*, the journal had held an isolated position, but in 1957 a number of other journals were also under attack for a variety of reasons. In fact, by the time *Novy Mir* finally made its formal apology, other journals – *Moskva* and *Molodaya Gvardiya* – were clearly subject to far and away the greatest volume of criticism. *Novy Mir*, still suffering from the shock of the onslaught which had begun in the autumn of 1956, had produced nothing new worthy of criticism.

5

The return of Tvardovsky

> ...later, after many years have passed,
> It will be you again who will lecture me:
> Where were you, poet? What did you see?
>
> Aleksandr Tvardovsky, *Novy Mir*, July, 1958

In July, 1958, *Novy Mir* was published under the editorship of a new board.[1] Konstantin Simonov lost the post which he had held for four years and Aleksandr Tvardovsky, who had been replaced by Simonov in 1954, returned as editor-in-chief. This event did not involve merely the journal's domestic politics culminating in a routine change. It was integrally related to literary–political developments which can be traced back to the 20th Party Congress.

There are a number of inter-related theses which have tended to form the framework for Western analyses of literary politics in the Soviet Union in the period 1956 to 1958 in general, and Simonov's dismissal in particular. It has been widely assumed that much responsibility for the atmosphere of greater creative latitude which writers enjoyed after the 20th Party Congress lay with Shepilov; that Khrushchev, having finally ousted his opponents in June, 1957, then turned to the field of literature and acted to impose discipline on the liberal writers; that, concomitant with this, the turning-point at which the Party laid down its hard line, finally and firmly, came in July, 1957 in an editorial in *Kommunist*; and that following these developments Simonov was dismissed for his erroneous post-Congress editorial policy.

A re-examination of the events preceding the board change indicates the weaknesses of this interpretation. It is the purpose of this chapter to reconsider the accepted theses and evaluate Khrushchev's literary policy at the time and its effect on *Novy Mir*.

Too many aspects of the question of Simonov's removal are left without adequate explanation if one accepts the usual rationale: that Simonov's rash publication of Dudintsev's *Not by Bread Alone* led to his dismissal.[2] The timing, for example, gives rise to a legitimate question: even if the authorities had chosen to pause between the public attacks on Simonov and his removal, would they have waited as long as they did? *Not by Bread Alone* was published in August, September and October, 1956. It was harshly criticized shortly after its publication and for several months thereafter,[3] but the attack was, to all intents and purposes, over by the summer of 1957, by which time Simonov had apologized more than once.[4] The official apology of *Novy Mir* itself, which might conceivably have been published concurrently with a change of the editorial board, was already in print in the autumn of 1957, nine months before Simonov's dismissal.[5] Even after the very last mention of *Novy Mir*'s heterodox publication policy of 1956 had appeared, there was still a lapse of over four months.[6] This chronology casts doubt on the argument that *Not by Bread Alone* was the main – or only – cause of Simonov's ousting. Similarly, the publication in *Novy Mir* of the works of Granin, Kirsanov and Simonov himself, though arousing virulent criticism in the Soviet press, does not provide a likelier motive if only because the attacks upon them closely followed those on Dudintsev's novel.

Furthermore, if the reason for removing Simonov from office was his overly 'liberal' publishing policy, then why would Tvardovsky – of all Soviet editors – have been chosen to replace him? Surely it would have made more sense in those circumstances to choose some literary figure of a conservative bent who would be certain to restore 'order'. These facts provide a legitimate basis for re-questioning the motivation for Simonov's removal as editor of *Novy Mir*.

The number of innovative items appearing in *Novy Mir* in 1956 reached its peak in September and October and dropped sharply by December. The post-Hungary period witnessed the same pattern as in earlier campaigns against the journal: attacks on individual items for a variety of reasons, vilification of the editor or editorial board, and characterization of the journal as a vehicle of ideologically noxious material. This phase was unusually prolonged – particularly in light of the fact that the journal had clearly changed its publishing policy. Thus, Dudintsev's novel was still being attacked in Khrushchev's published statement in August, 1957 and by Surkov in December.[7] Despite the repeated apologies the campaign went on, as if there were uncertainty as to the appropriate end to such an attack in the post-Stalin, post-Congress days.

This is not to say that the literary situation was ever homogeneous. It was possible, even during months of enthusiastic innovation – as in the late summer and early autumn of 1956 – to witness carping criticism of a type identical with that of the late 1940s and early 1950s. Nor did the crushing of the Hungarian Revolution by Soviet forces signal total regression in terms of literary debate inside Russia. Some of the staunchest defense of the previous – 'emancipated' – publication policy was heard at the March meeting of writers in Moscow in 1957.[8]

Nevertheless, a brief look at literary publications early in 1957 suffices to show that by then the period of relaxed literary policy had, to all intents and purposes, come to an end. However, the question of when the Party itself publicly stated its position and set down its hard line *vis-à-vis* the intelligentsia has not been adequately examined. Harold Swayze has suggested that an editorial in *Kommunist* in July, 1957 marked 'the turning point' in the drive for ideological orthodoxy, that it 'vigorously reaffirmed party control in the arts'.[9] This would corroborate the theory – to be discussed below – that after his victory over the anti-Party group in June, Khrushchev turned to the arts and established his firm control. But there seem to be no grounds for seeing the 'turning point' so late in the day. The Party position had clearly been stated much earlier and a strong case for Party control can already be seen in an editorial in the February issue of *Kommunist*.

As the official journal of the Central Committee of the Communist Party, *Kommunist* can be regarded as a reliable source of official policy. The February editorial was an outspokenly repressive statement. Ironically, this editorial was singled out by Conquest as an illustration of the 'liberal' line expressed while Shepilov was still in favor.[10] The paragraph which he cites appears to deny Party surveillance (*opeka*) over literature:

Our enemies slander us in asserting that in the Soviet Union the Party established 'supervision' over literature and art. But that is the nature of enemies, to use every weapon against us; as we see, they do not disdain to use dirty slander. However, the actual fact is that Leninist principles of leadership in the sphere of literature and art are directed specifically against any 'supervision', against interference in the process of artistic creation.[11]

Although, read alone, this seems to be an affirmation of the more liberated literary developments of the summer and autumn months of 1956, the article as a whole presented a very different picture. The statement immediately following this paragraph greatly modified its thrust:

Of course, the consequences of the cult of personality could not but be reflected in literature and art. In the period of the cult of personality of J. V. Stalin, there were elements of administrative excess [*administrirovanie*] and groundlessly sharp criticism, etc. But was this fundamental, as they try to present it? Exaggerations are exaggerations, but the basic direction in the leadership of literature and art in that period consisted of the implementation of Marxist–Leninist principles in this sphere. It is expressed in the well-known resolutions of the Party Central Committee of 1946–1948 on questions of literature and art.[12]

The rest of the article not only presented a very strong defense of the notorious Zhdanov decrees, but made the ominous assertion that the literary scene of 1956 was parallel to that of 1946:

However, can it be said that the publication of ideologically questionable works, such as took place in 1946, is not being repeated today? Unfortunately, it is impossible to say so. The facts show that there is sometimes insufficient responsibility and principle. This is particularly true of the journal *Novy Mir*...The example of *Novy Mir* shows that the resolution of the Central Committee 'On the Journals *Zvezda* and *Leningrad*', in part directed against the publication of ideologically bankrupt, harmful works, is still being implemented inadequately, and not by every journal.[13]

The length and content of such an editorial in *Kommunist*, constituting, as it did, a reaffirmation of the principles set out by the Central Committee ten years before during one of the darkest periods of Soviet literature, leave no doubt but that this was a major Party statement intended to put an end to the fledgling experimentation and daring of the previous months. Taken together with the concurrent and undeniable change in literary publication policy, this very strongly worded statement from the Party establishes the fact that the 'turning point' came not in the summer of 1957, but during the previous winter.

The possible role of Shepilov himself in the publication of this document is difficult to ascertain.[14] However, some intelligent guesswork might clarify his general role in 'liberalizing' literary politics following the 20th Party Congress. Each Secretary of the Central Committee had a particular field of competence and Shepilov was the member of the Secretariat in charge of culture. This meant that he was the liaison between the Presidium and the Party's Department of Culture, headed at that time by Dmitry Alekseevich Polikarpov.[15]

However, it would be naïve to assume that because of his position Shepilov's personal tastes alone governed the more relaxed literary atmosphere during the latter part of 1956. Clearly, the policy in literature was a reflection of the political revelations which were made at the 20th Party Congress by the decision of the top Party leaders, primarily Khrushchev. If, indeed, it was Shepilov who encouraged the aura of permissiveness, he must have done so as a response to clear political signals.

In November, 1956, he temporarily left his post as Secretary and was replaced as spokesman in the cultural field by Molotov. Molotov proceeded to lay down a strong line on the correct application of socialist realism. By February, 1957, when Shepilov returned to the Secretariat and took over the supervision of culture again, the more permissive trend in literature had been reversed, or at least halted. Nothing which took place during the next few months in the field of literature gave any indication that Shepilov tried to alter the new direction of events.

Although Shepilov did not speak at the plenary session of the board of the Writers Union in May, he had made two major addresses a few months previously which give some indication of the 'line' he was following. In March, he had spoken at the Congress of Artists and his speech constituted a fairly standard approach to art in the post-Stalin period.[16] It was neither militantly conservative – he made no mention of the Zhdanov decrees, for example – nor was it notably liberal. He did display impatience with stereotyped criticism of works of art:

Some art scholars greatly simplify the question of the bond between art and politics, between art and life. For example, it would be wrong to regard the mere fact that an artist has chosen a topical theme as incontestable proof of the ties between his creative work and politics, between his work and life. It would be just as wrong and ridiculous to declare a superbly executed landscape as a work divorced from politics or lacking in ideas. (*Applause.*)

It is true that this sort of sentiment was out of keeping with the general trend of literary policy early in 1957, but it was not outrageously so and it dealt, after all, not with literature but with the ailing world of the graphic arts. There had, in fact, been no onslaught by the Party in the field of art as there had been in literature. Indeed, the situation with regard to art was significantly different from that of belles-lettres: the level was akin to the low quality of Soviet drama in the early fifties. Art lagged so far behind the developments which had taken place in literature that, while the authorities were trying to slow down and put a damper on writers, attempts were still being made to bring some life into artistic creation.

Several weeks later Shepilov addressed the Second Congress of Soviet Composers.[17] Urging composers to reflect modern life in their music, Shepilov also called on them to be governed by ideological requirements. Ideology coupled with talent, he said, determines the measure of a work. He paid lip service to the Central Committee decrees of 1946–48, but did not linger on the subject.

What strikes the observer about these Shepilov speeches is not so much what was said, as what was not said. It is true that they soft-pedalled the conservative line which was being followed at the time. They lacked any strong statement about the necessity of *partiinost'* in a work of art or music. They did not strongly assert the importance – and relevance – of the Zhdanov decrees. On the other hand, they were perfectly proper policy statements for a member of the Secretariat to have made and were certainly far from being an outspoken advocation of a more liberal policy *vis-à-vis* the intelligentsia.

Immediately after the announcement of the fall of the anti-Party group,[18] Shepilov was singled out for criticism of his ideological policies. One of the key attacks appeared in the editorial published in *Kommunist* at the end of July.[19] He was accused of having gone too far.

Shepilov, whom the Party now knows to be a factionalist who sided with the anti-Party group of Malenkov, Kaganovich and Molotov, bears a tremendous share of the responsibility for the spread of unsound tendencies among a part of the intelligentsia of the arts. Finding himself in the leadership in the ideological sphere, Shepilov betrayed the trust of the Central Committee. He deviated from the line charted by the 20th Party Congress in questions of literature and the arts and took a liberal position contrary to Leninist principle...Seeking personal popularity, he...tried to implement a platform 'wider' than that of the Party...

Highly indicative of Shepilov's positions are his speeches to the artists and composers congresses. Of course there is much that is correct in these speeches. Obviously! But their general tone is a liberal one.[20]

The editorial then went on to criticize Shepilov for having mentioned the 1946–48 resolutions only in passing, for having discussed the key Leninist principles only minimally, if at all, and for having failed to rebuff 'the demagogues who before the congresses permitted themselves to attack Party guidance and the decisions of the Party Central Committee'.

The attack on Shepilov's literary policies must be seen in the context of Soviet politics in 1956 and 1957. The Soviet conservatives might well have placed the blame for the unrest in the latter part of 1956 squarely on Khrushchev – in foolishly carrying de-Stalinization too far, he had set in motion a wave of rising expectations which had engulfed first the intelligentsia and then entire societies in Eastern Europe. By shifting the blame for the encouragement of intellectual experimentation from himself to one of the Party Secretaries, Khrushchev could thus indirectly relieve himself of much of the responsibility for the entire Eastern European episode. This tie-in of Shepilov with the Hungarian Revolution is made clear in the *Kommunist* editorial.

The events in Hungary have demonstrated the consequences of completely disregarding Leninist adherence to principle in the question of the guidance of literature and art. The liberal attitude displayed toward demagogic elements by the former Party leadership had the result that a section of the writers caused great harm to ideological work in Hungary and contributed to the preparation of the counter-revolutionary uprising.

Shepilov did not draw the necessary conclusions from this sad example and took a conciliatory attitude toward the unhealthy sentiments. As a result, some of the demagogic elements among the art intelligentsia were able to go to the limit.[21]

In this way, the anti-Party group was associated – albeit retroactively – with the Hungarian débâcle, and Shepilov in particular bore the brunt of the attack for the literary–intellectual 'excesses' which signalled trouble in Eastern Europe. The reference to Shepilov is, of course, befogged chronologically. This deliberate ambiguity was used to smudge lines and confuse pre- and post-Hungarian situations. By saying that Shepilov had not drawn the necessary conclusions from the events in Hungary, the editorial implies that, after the Hungarian uprising, Shepilov had carried on a faulty policy in the cultural sphere. But in point of fact, Shepilov was not concerned with cultural affairs from November, 1956 to February, 1957, and after that he does not appear to have engaged in any 'harmful' policy. Given the fact that Shepilov had to be ousted with the anti-Party group because of his involvement with their plans, it is probable that, as he had been associated with the cultural field, it was here that he was used as a scapegoat. In fact, the sudden removal of Shepilov from the cultural sphere produced no reverberations in literary output – or literary policy.

The assumption that the July editorial in *Kommunist* was a turning point which signalled the harsh clamp-down on Soviet writers is thus seen to be erroneous. While it did come out strongly against the anti-Party group – as was natural – the article in February had already dealt a much harsher blow to literature. The fact raises the question of Khrushchev's own role in suppressing the intellectuals. If the Party's strong line had already been expressed in February, then the July issue of *Kommunist* was no more than a continuation of a previously established pattern. Furthermore, Khrushchev's own speeches dealing with culture support neither the allegation that he turned to the arts only when he was confidently in full power, nor that his was a repressive voice.[22] Khrushchev's speeches were made on May 13, 1957, May 19, 1957 and at a meeting of the Party *aktiv* in July, 1957. In other words, two of the talks were given prior to the ousting of the anti-Party group and only one was given afterwards. While the combined speeches, published under the title 'For a Close Tie between Literature and the Life of the People',[23] were published only in August, 1957, two of them actually date from the eve – not the morrow – of Khrushchev's near overthrow.[24]

While it is true that Khrushchev went to some lengths partially to re-establish Stalin's reputation and to defend the long-held basic Party position *vis-à-vis* literature, he was clearly trying to strike a balance between the situation during Stalin's lifetime and what happened after his death. For example, he stated that, 'The Soviet people should equally reject such an essentially slanderous work as Dudintsev's book *Not by Bread Alone* and such cloyingly sweet films as "Unforgettable 1919" and "Kuban Cossacks".' Thus the Party was no more prepared to encourage a return to the lifeless material for so long typical of Soviet literature than they were to accept the ideological heterodoxy of a Dudintsev. Very significant is the fact that Khrushchev did not hark back to the Central Committee resolution on the journals *Zvezda* and *Leningrad* for support, nor, indeed, did he so much as mention it. This represents a definite change from the *Kommunist* editorial of the previous February.

Although publication of the Khrushchev statement had the effect of prolonging – or reviving – the by now dormant campaign against *Novy Mir*, this situation did not last long. The 'mistakes' of *Novy Mir* had already become a dead issue to all intents and purposes and the tardy appearance of Khrushchev's speeches only briefly strengthened the conservative critics' attacks on the journal.

Contradictory as it may at first appear, Khrushchev was clearly seeking a conciliatory position towards Soviet writers. Rather than providing the signal for a worsening of the literary atmosphere, the publication of his speeches intimated a mild return to a more reasonable position. Khrushchev, although not forgetting past 'sins', was in a forgiving mood. 'Any man can make mistakes', he assured the writers, 'but it is necessary to see not only what the man did yesterday, but also what he is capable of doing tomorrow'. Khrushchev mentioned two specific literary figures who were soon to be rewarded for having realized their 'shortcomings and mistakes'.

For example, it is known that the public has criticized certain shortcomings in the work of our remarkable poet, Comrade Tvardovsky, whose contribution to the development of Soviet literature has been widely recognized. Friendly conversations with Comrade Tvardovsky give ground for hope that this master of words will draw the necessary conclusions and will delight readers with excellent new works.[25]

He then went on to speak in a similar vein about Panferov, who had been removed from the editorship of *Oktyabr'* even before Tvardovsky had left *Novy Mir* in 1954. Three months after Khrushchev's views on literature had been published, Panferov was back in the editorial chair of *Oktyabr'*. And although Tvardovsky did not become editor again for nearly a year, he was soon to be once more in the public eye as a poet and literary figure.[26]

The circumstances of Simonov's dismissal and Tvardovsky's return to *Novy Mir* corroborate the view that Khrushchev, far from clamping down on the intellectuals, was trying to establish a satisfactory *modus vivendi* between the writers and the regime. In order to appreciate the full significance of Tvardovsky's return, let us first consider Simonov's editorial policy in the political context of the previous year.

From 1957 to mid 1958 *Novy Mir*'s publication record was decidedly dull. Simonov was frightened. His multiple apologies, the board's admission of culpability, the contents of the journal, all point to the fact that he was no longer willing to take any chances. He had not responded to the hints of moderation which had been observable since the summer of 1957: the abolition of obligatory deliveries from the private holdings of kolkhozniks (published simultaneously with the announcement of the expulsion of the anti-Party group); a new decree easing the income-tax demands on kolkhozniks (September,

1957): the presentation of the Order of the Red Banner to Boris Polevoi (March, 1958), who had only the previous September been accused in *Izvestiya* of being a confederate of Shepilov's.

Another sign of a return to the 'thaw' atmosphere came on May 28, 1958 when the Central Committee promulgated a decree, 'On Rectifying Errors in Evaluation of the Operas "Great Friendship", "Bogdan Khmelnitsky" and "With all One's Heart"'.[27] Asserting that the February 19, 1948 decree on Muradeli's opera had played, on the whole, a positive role, the Central Committee then went on to say that the evaluation of the work of individual composers contained in the decree 'was, in a number of cases, unsubstantiated and unjust'. Numerous composers, including Shostakovich, Prokofiev, and Khachaturian 'were indiscriminately named representatives of the antipopular, formalist, school'.

Despite these various signs, Simonov had nevertheless carried on such a timid publication policy that the journal ceased to be a major source of important literary and political contributions. *Novy Mir* had regressed to the point of a few years back when items of interest were marked, not by the issue, but by the paragraph. One new characteristic of the journal, symptomatic of the dull contents and 'safe' articles which appeared, was the addition of very lack-lustre, non-literary sections.[28] There was, for example, a monthly section called 'Forty Years Ago', which consisted of approximately thirty pages of memoirs and documents from the corresponding month in 1917. Other such sections included over thirty pages devoted to items related to the 140th anniversary of the death of Karl Marx (May, 1958), long, boring travelogues, translations of articles by foreign sympathizers and so on. The effect was to cut out a good number of pages of literary material from the journal and this clearly constituted a policy geared to reduce risk. Indeed, so uninteresting had *Novy Mir* become that there was virtually nothing for which it could be criticized. It is thus not surprising that in the furor which raged during 1957 not a word was added about any new items.

Over the years *Novy Mir* had gained a reputation, both in the Soviet Union and abroad, of being a 'liberal' journal. In its early days it had taken over the publication of the 'fellow travellers' from *Krasnaya Nov'*. Later it had attracted editorial members of *Literaturny Kritik* on to its staff when that publication ceased. Even in Stalinist times, when circumstances had permitted, *Novy Mir* had published whatever it could that was bold and probing. Indeed, it had a particular function in the literary world – it served as a safety valve.[29] Rather than keeping the lid of the boiling pot hermetically sealed, the authorities chose to use the device of the valve, which could be opened from time to time to let off some of the dangerous pressure – and which could always be shut again at will. In this context *Novy Mir* served the purpose well. But once the journal ceased to function in this way it became indistinguishable from other publications – and failed to fulfill its purpose. Thus, at a time when the safety valve was no longer functioning as such, and at a time when general trends seemed to be towards relaxation, Tvardovsky was brought back as editor of *Novy Mir*, and was actually permitted to choose his own editorial board.

Tvardovsky was in many ways the perfect man to edit a journal such as *Novy Mir*. A member of the Communist Party (he later – in 1961 – became an alternate member of the Central Committee), he could be trusted for his innate sense of what the Party demanded. A genuine member of the Soviet intelligentsia and a well-known poet, he had the inclinations and the talent to run a discriminating journal admirably.* The new editorial board which Tvardovsky gathered about him contained men who, for the most part, had been associated with him earlier or were to be attached to him in the coming, more fruitful, years: E. N. Gerasimov, S. N. Golubov, B. G. Zaks, B. A. Lavrenev, V. V. Ovechkin, K. A. Fedin.[30] Of Simonov's board, only Lavrenev and Golubov remained – apart, that is, from Konstantin Fedin, who was the sole survivor from Tvardovsky's editorial board of 1954. In November, Dement'ev was to return as

* In *Bodalsya telenok s dubom*, Aleksandr Solzhenitsyn describes his fluctuating relationship with Tvardovsky throughout the decade of the sixties. In characterizing the editor as he knew him in December, 1961, Solzhenitsyn fastens upon the dual loyalty characteristic of Tvardovsky:

He was devoted to Russian literature, to its holy approach to life. And he only wanted to be like Pushkin and his followers. He would willingly have died of happiness imitating Esenin, considered worthy of Pushkin's fate. But that had been a different century and now everywhere and in everyone – and in no one more than the editor-in-chief – a greater truth was recognized and instilled – the Party truth. Today he could not direct Russian literature or help it without a Party card. But he could not carry his Party card insincerely. And it was just as necessary to him as air that these two truths should not be dichotomized, but should blend...Having initially become enamoured of a manuscript because of the former sentiment, Tvardovsky without fail had to guide it through the latter and only then publish it – as a *Soviet* work.

(A. Solzhenitsyn, *Bodalsia telenok s dubom* (Paris: YMCA Press, 1975), p. 36)

assistant editor (a post which he had held under Tvardovsky in 1953–54), and Tvardovsky thus had an editorial board that was more completely his own than ever before.

The July, 1958 issue of *Novy Mir*, the first under Tvardovsky's renewed editorship, proved to be a far more interesting journal than any for a long time. Articles by some writers who were specifically associated with *Novy Mir* were published in July – by Efim Dorosh, for example, who later became a regular member of Tvardovsky's board of editors. Viktor Nekrasov, who had published his famous *V rodnom gorode* (In One's Home Town) in *Novy Mir* in 1954 (under Simonov's editorship), brought out some lively notes of his impressions of France and Italy (during a stay in 1957) in the same issue.[31] These notes are light-hearted and open-minded, telling of the delights of Paris – the streets, museums, restaurants – in a travelogue free of the propagandistic pomposity which often characterized such reminiscences in the Soviet press.[32]

The most striking piece of literary criticism in the issue was written by Samuil Marshak.[33] The first section of his article, entitled 'On the Talented Reader', dealt with the establishment of a work as a classic.

Individual readers might at times judge books wrongly, but it is the Reader in the great, collective meaning of the term – and in the course of a more or less extended period of time – who always has the last word in the evaluation of a literary work.

It is true that the evaluation of a book, affirmed for a certain period of time, very often changes. Some sort of booth placed nearby can screen a tower standing far off. But early or late we recognize the optical illusion and begin to conceive of literary values on a more correct scale.

Time passes, one generation follows another and each of them evaluates in its own way its literary heritage. And if a writer or a poet maintains his significance and weight in the course of the centuries, then it is explained, not by the fact that they were once counted among the geniuses and classics, or immortalized by monuments raised in their honor, but because the new generations recognize them as valuable and necessary for life.
...The fate of a book is decided by...the reader.[34]

This article, which was continued in the following month's issue, was concerned solely with the craft of writing, the skill of the writer. Not a word was spoken of the importance of content in making a work immortal. Leaving the decision on the value of a literary work strictly to the Reader-at-Large, Marshak eschewed any mention of *narodnost'* or *partiinost'*, of the importance of the typical or the function of the work in the progress of history.

Tvardovsky himself published a number of poems in the first issue he edited.[35] Indeed, these were the first of his poems to be published in *Novy Mir* since the spring of 1954. The poems, written between 1936 and 1958, are brief and cover a multitude of subjects. Towards the end of the series, Tvardovsky makes a remarkable statement in his '*Moim kritikam*' (To my Critics).[36] The poem consists of two stanzas.

> You ever strive to dictate to me,
> To give simple advice
> To have me sing, not hearing, not seeing,
> Only knowing: what's permitted, what's not.
>
> But I can't but reckon
> That later, after many years have passed,
> It will be you again who will lecture me:
> Where were you, poet? What did you see?

The last poem in the series, number 25,[37] reinforces Tvardovsky's deeply felt need for scope as a creative artist.

> The whole essence is in one single creed:
> What I shall say when the right time comes
> I know better than anyone in the world –
> Including the quick and the dead – only I know it.
>
> I could never entrust to anyone else
> To say that word – not for anything.
> Even to Lev Tolstoy – no not even to him.
> He couldn't handle it – though he may be a god
>
> And I a mere mortal. Responsible for myself,
> I strive for one thing in life:
> I wish to speak about that which I know better
> Than anyone in the world. And in the way I want.

That Tvardovsky intended to revitalize *Novy Mir* – and that he deemed this the function for which he had been reinstated – is clear. His first issue, the lines which he himself wrote, point to this fact. That he was not immediately successful is also true. Although he tried to start off with éclat, he was at first unable to maintain the standard he had set himself. In fact, a few months after the board change, virulent attacks on Pasternak began to appear in the Soviet press.[38] Nevertheless, although the Pasternak affair turned out to be an ugly reaffirmation of the worst practices in Soviet literary control, it was a self-contained case which was the outgrowth, not of a new general line in Soviet literary politics, but of a foreign development – namely the Nobel Prize nomination.

Evidence that Tvardovsky anticipated a return of the liberal *Novy Mir* can be found in the statement of projected contents of the 1959 *Novy Mir* which was published in the November and December, 1958 issues. The list of authors whose works *Novy Mir* promised to publish in the following year is a veritable 'who's who' of the *Novy Mir* circle. In the literary criticism section were the names of Galanov, Gudzy, Zhdanov, Dement'ev, Lakshin, Lifshits, Smirnov and Chukovsky, among others.[39] Included among prose contributors were Tendryakov, Lavrenev, Simonov – who was obviously not considered a *persona non grata* – Nagibin, Zalygin, Panova and Marshak. Significant was the promise that Kazakevich – who had run into difficulties earlier for his *Novy Mir* story,[40] and later for his role in editing *Literaturnaya Moskva* – was to publish a new story. Even more noteworthy was the assurance that Part II of Vasily Grossman's *For the Just Cause* was to appear in 1959. Grossman had published virtually nothing since the first part of his novel had appeared in *Novy Mir* in 1952.

As it transpired, neither the Kazakevich story nor the Grossman novel actually appeared in the journal in 1959. However, looking at the projected contents, one is struck by the fact that *Novy Mir* seemed to have come full circle, in terms of editors and contributors. Tvardovsky, the one man whose name had been inextricably linked with *Novy Mir*'s liberal policy, was back as editor, surrounded by his own colleagues, and promising a return of many of the writers, poets and critics who had been associated with *Novy Mir* throughout the fifties, both before Stalin's death and after. He clearly intended to maintain the character of his journal by assuring a continuity of its contributors.[41]

Furthermore, it is significant that Tvardovsky brought back with him an editorial board composed of like-minded men. This group, augmented in the coming months, proved to be the distinctive *Novy Mir* circle which was later to publish many of the outstanding works of the Khrushchev era.

It is thus reasonable to view the *Novy Mir* editorial board change of July, 1958 not as signifying the removal of Konstantin Simonov from his post, but as heralding the return of Aleksandr Tvardovsky and the reinvigoration of *Novy Mir*'s publishing policy after a bland

10   The last editorial board under Tvardovsky, which sat for this photograph in
January, 1970, together with some former members of the board. Standing, left to
right: M. Khitrov, V. Lakshin, E. Dorosh, I. Vinogradov, I. Sats; seated, left to right:
B. Zaks, A. Dement'ev, A. Tvardovsky, A. Kondratovich, A. Mar'yamov

period. The immediate post-Hungary dangers had passed,
Khrushchev was firmly in power, and the temporary tightening of
control over the writers, at its height early in 1957, was being replaced
by a more enlightened policy. Khrushchev's more ebullient (or
'adventurist') approach, coupled with Tvardovsky's drive, enabled
the introduction of a new, vigorous chapter in *Novy Mir*'s publishing
history.

6

The literary process

Now he removed a word, now added,
Crossed out the author's phrase,
Put in his own.
Checkmarks in the margin put,
Himself the *Glav*, himself the *Lit*.

Aleksandr Tvardovsky,
'Terkin in the Other World'

The contents of *Novy Mir*, like that of any Soviet journal, reflected
the interaction of various factors. At the root level, the journal's
policy was influenced by the composition of its editorial board and
staff: decisions regarding what was to be published were initially made
in the editorial offices. But before an issue was finally printed, bound
and despatched to its readers, it would have been subjected to more
than the ordinary editorial give-and-take. 'Bargaining' of various
kinds – in committees or with Party leaders – and the adjustment
of manuscripts to suit ideological demands often preceded the
approval of the censor.

The process by which each individual piece was published followed
varying steps depending on the significance of the manuscript in
question, the political atmosphere at the moment, the personality of
the editor and his powers of leverage. The history of a number of
literary milestones in *Novy Mir* shows that there is no single pattern
leading to successful publication and no guarantee that there will be
no negative repercussions once a given work has appeared in print.
Were the matter of publication policy as cut and dried as might be
expected in a system of government–Party control over literature,
this study would have been far less interesting. Let us look, then, at
the intricacies of publishing *Novy Mir* – first at its internal setup and,
second, at the other factors which come into play.

The internal process

The official leadership of the journal, as printed each month on the last page, consisted of an editor-in-chief – either Simonov or Tvardovsky during the 1950s – and an editorial board of generally seven or eight members, one or two of whom were assistant editors.[1]

All Soviet literary journals are the official organs of the Writers Union,[2] and it is the prerogative of the board of the USSR Writers Union – in practice, of its secretariat – to appoint and dismiss individual members of the editorial board, although this is usually done on the recommendation and with the consent of the journal's editor-in-chief.[3] As the editor of *Novy Mir*, Tvardovsky himself sat on the secretariat of the Writers Union.[4]

The Union did not have the authority to dismiss him as editor-in-chief. The appointment (or dismissal) of a chief editor of a central journal such as *Novy Mir* lay in the hands of the Secretariat or Presidium of the Central Committee of the CPSU.[5] According to Zhores Medvedev, in 1954 Khrushchev personally presided over the meeting of the Secretariat of the Party's Central Committee which decided that Tvardovsky be relieved of his post as editor-in-chief.[6] Staff members and assistants were selected by the editor.

Novy Mir had a number of subdivisions, not all of which appeared in every issue of the journal. These included 'Contemporary Sketches', 'Current Affairs', 'Diaries, Memoirs and Documents', 'Book Reviews', 'Literary Criticism', 'On Foreign Themes' and 'Problems of Science'. Some of these headings corresponded with the departments into which the journal was internally organized. The first section of the journal, which might run anywhere from 50 to 150 pages, was untitled and contained prose works interspersed with poems, including works in translation from both the Soviet republics and abroad.

The internal working departments of the journal consisted of Prose, Poetry, Criticism, Current affairs, Science and Foreign literature. *Novy Mir* was set up so that each department would be headed by one member of the editorial board or staff. Under that editor or staff member there was a corps of staff members.[7] These staff members handled the job of reading manuscripts, initially selecting interesting material and editing. Beyond these staff members there were *ad hoc* readers who sifted through manuscripts sent in for consideration. These people were called upon according to the work

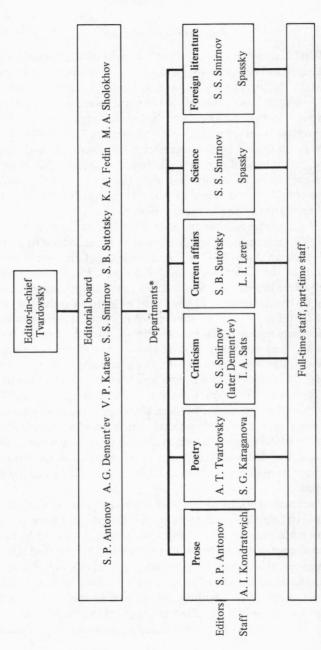

Novy Mir editorial structure, 1953–54

			Editor-in-chief Tvardovsky		

Editorial board

S. P. Antonov A. G. Dement'ev V. P. Kataev S. S. Smirnov S. B. Sutotsky K. A. Fedin M. A. Sholokhov

Departments*

	Prose	**Poetry**	**Criticism**	**Current affairs**	**Science**	**Foreign literature**
Editors	S. P. Antonov	A. T. Tvardovsky	S. S. Smirnov (later Dement'ev)	S. B. Sutotsky	S. S. Smirnov	S. S. Smirnov
Staff	A. I. Kondratovich	S. G. Karaganova	I. A. Sats	L. I. Lerer	Spassky	Spassky

Full-time staff, part-time staff

* This chart is based on the description of *Novy Mir*'s internal structure sent to the author by Igor Sats. However, Boris Zaks, in his interview, differed from Sats in stating that, rather than six separate departments, the journal was divided into four: Prose, Poetry, Criticism and Current affairs. This latter included science materials and was directed by Sutotsky. Foreign literature was handled by other appropriate departments (usually by Lidiya Lerer or Boris Zaks). Zaks noted that he was the staff member who

loads of a given month. They did their reading in their own homes, bringing in material or picking it up at the editorial offices.

The regular staff members – or some of them – were a key factor in running the journal. Not only did they do the necessary editorial work, but some of them were also extremely influential in setting policy. In contrast, as revealed in the criticism voiced during the summer of 1953, a number of the *Novy Mir* editors (as well as those on other journals) were simply figureheads, men whose names appeared on the last page of each issue, but who never participated actively in any editorial work.[8]

The composite impression is that only a small core of senior editors – joined by certain highly influential and active staff members – was significantly involved in running the journal. (The names of the staff members have never been listed, so it is only by chance that they become known.)

I. Sats exemplifies the key position – and confluence of interests with the editor – held by some staff members. He headed the Criticism department under Tvardovsky in the early 1950s and was removed from the staff for his role in publishing the famous articles of Pomerantsev, Lifshits, Abramov and Shcheglov. Sats was later – in the 1960s – to become a member of *Novy Mir*'s editorial board. There is no doubt that, as a staff member, he had been influential in decision-making.[9] There is also no doubt, particularly in view of his later advance, that he was a Tvardovsky man.[10]

Besides the extra readers brought in when necessary, there were various friends and colleagues of the editor-in-chief or board or staff members who participated in an advisory capacity. Mikhail Lifshits, for example, when he was criticized for his adverse influence on *Novy Mir* policy in the summer of 1954, was not a staff member, but was regarded as an 'advisor' – as well as a contributor.[11]

One must imagine the *Novy Mir* editorial offices – at least under Tvardovsky – as not merely the offices and desks of editors and their staff, but also as the meeting place for a fringe of active, interested writers and intellectuals who would drop in to talk, to discuss matters of mutual interest, to bring manuscripts which they considered worthwhile, or just to share the camaraderie.

Above this melee of senior editors, staff members, outside readers, advisors and the '*Novy Mir* circle' was the editor-in-chief. He set the tone. His basic publishing policy – within the guidelines of the Party – was dominant. He chose his colleagues. It is clear in looking at the editorial boards of Simonov and Tvardovsky that each man had a particular coterie with whom he worked effectively and many of whom he selected for himself.[12] His staff reflected his own thinking. His offices were peopled by those attracted to their 'own kind'. As Zhores Medvedev wrote, it was no accident that 'One Day in the Life of Ivan Denisovich' was published in *Novy Mir*, 'for the journal really did bring together the best writers in the country and was not afraid to discuss critical matters pertaining to literature and public life'.[13]

According to Svirsky, Tvardovsky would only employ a reader who shared his views,

> because the internal reviewer determined the potential contents of the journal... And all 15 or 20 readers – internal reviewers – of whom I was one, were people who, as they say, had well-known views, and had demonstrated them more than once and had suffered for them more than once.

Indeed, it would be erroneous to assume that a Soviet journal, given the facts of Soviet literary life, is simply the sum total of the items published in it every month. A journal such as *Novy Mir* very definitely had a character of its own – and represented something special to its reading public.[14] And this character was shaped by the personality of the editor-in-chief.* True, there was probably a reverse effect as well. Just as some public figures grow in stature to suit their high office, so Simonov was probably influenced in the mid fifties to adapt himself to the publishing tradition of the journal he was again editing – and make it a leader in the thaw period.

Besides setting the tone and bringing in his colleagues, the editor-in-chief also exercised considerable influence or leverage. On more than one occasion, the editor's individual resourcefulness was essential for the publication of a controversial manuscript. This was

---

* This was well illustrated in the Svirsky interview, when he discussed his own job at *Novy Mir*, which was the reading of problematic manuscripts sent to the journal. Tvardovsky published only [sic] those people who were ideologically close to himself, and rejected the manuscripts of those people who did not share his ideological aspirations. But it was necessary to refuse these authors somehow. They couldn't be refused in a little three-line note, because these were professional writers, members of the Writers Union. So they took me on to do this difficult task: to give a pure literary critical analysis of rejected works. The works might be at the same time talented and interesting, but they were written in completely the wrong spirit. The difficulty was that it was impossible to talk about the underlying principles for rejecting the manuscript, because this manuscript fully corresponded to Party and government policy, but it did not correspond to Tvardovsky's policy.

true in the case of Ovechkin's 'District Routine'. It was true of Solzhenitsyn's 'One Day in the Life of Ivan Denisovich'. The varying influences, pressures and counter pressures involved will now be discussed.

The system of influence and control

In the Soviet Union there are a multitude of influences and controls operating on differing levels which may affect literary output. These interweave in a complex system which begins with self-censorship – induced by habit or fear for the fate of one's work – and ends with the requisite stamp of the censor.

Thus, the very first limiting factor in literature comes from the author himself. His thinking is governed by the tenets of socialist realism as the only acceptable art form in the Soviet Union. The quality of *partiinost'*, coupled with those of *narodnost'* and *ideinost'*, would be expected to reign supreme in his writing. After forty years of Soviet rule, writers in the nineteen fifties were well steeped in the jargon of socialist realism and knew, as if by second nature, what, in a general way, would and what would not be acceptable. Tvardovsky, in his '*Za dal'yu dal'*', gave an excellent portrayal of the writer who is his own censor.[15]

Once the author has finished his manuscript and handed it in to an editorial office, there is another stage of control. Here the reader, and ultimately the editor himself, judges the work, not only on its literary merits but also on its ideological position.[16] Tvardovsky satirized this editorial function in 'Terkin in the Other World'.

> All asweat,
> His nose followed the lines, left to right;
> Now he removed a word, now added,
> Crossed out the author's phrase,
> Put in his own.
> Checkmarks in the margin put,
> Himself the *Glav*, himself the *Lit*.
> Here he took away the quote-marks,
> There he put them back.
> It seems that when alive he'd warmed a seat
> In a newspaper office.[17]

Thus, two stages of censorship must be passed before any official censoring body looks at the work.[18]

The supreme authority – in terms of ideology and in terms of

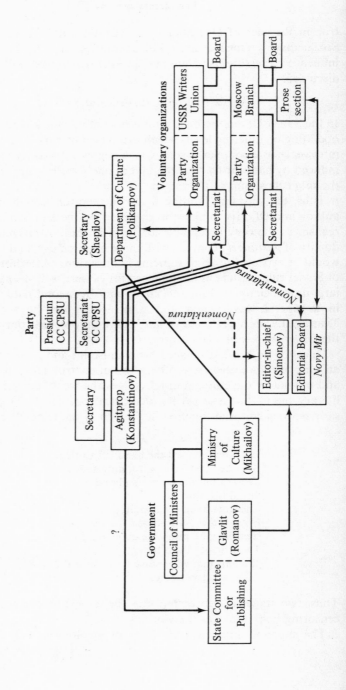

The pattern of literary control and influences, 1957

specific controls – rests with the Communist Party. Official resolutions and a stream of supplementary articles in the press – particularly in *Pravda*, *Kommunist* and *Literaturnaya Gazeta* – lay down the 'main line' to be followed in literature, as in other fields. But beyond these public statements the Party establishes its rule in a variety of ways. The main source of literary control in the Party rests in the Central Committee, which at any given time has a specific organ – designated as a section, department or commission – to deal directly with cultural affairs.

In the nineteen fifties the Party section officially responsible for cultural matters was the Department of Culture. The Department functioned under the aegis of an assigned Secretary of the Central Committee – Shepilov in his time, for example – who was in turn responsible to the Presidium. While major policy decisions would come through the Secretary, the actual running of the Department was in the hands of its chairman.[19] From 1956 to 1962 this was Dmitry Alekseevich Polikarpov, described by Medvedev as 'a man of extremely conservative, Stalinist views'.[20] Polikarpov, who had been in the Party since 1924, became a candidate member of the Central Committee only in 1961. Thus, the head of the Central Committee body dealing with culture did not have the commensurate rank in the Party. He had been a member of the secretariat of the USSR Writers Union on two occasions, had held various other posts, and may be regarded as a professional Party functionary.

Through the Department of Culture, the Central Committee could play an active role in literary affairs. According to Zaks, certain journals regularly sent material there for approval although this was not done by *Novy Mir* (with one or two exceptions). When in doubt, however, Glavlit could send on something of *Novy Mir*'s to the Department. Furthermore, if the journal had committed an error, the editor might receive a phone call from someone at the Department of Culture, though often he would simply read about it in the press. Quite regularly Tvardovsky and one or two of his editors (usually Dement'ev and Kondratovich in the sixties) would be invited along with editors from other journals to hear a lecture from an official spokesman of the Department, often Polikarpov himself, in his time. Polikarpov, or one of his subordinates, would then evaluate the works printed in the journals, often launching a vigorous attack. 'There would also be someone from the newspapers,' said Zaks, 'and they would pick up [the criticism] and write an article, expressing not their own opinion, but [that of the Department of Culture].'[21]

During the early sixties when Khrushchev actively expressed his interest in literary affairs, the Department of Culture was superseded by the Commission on Ideology, which was itself part of the Central Committee complex. The chairman of this Commission was Leonid Fedorovich Il'ichev, who was a member of the Secretariat of the Central Committee from 1961 to 1965. (His chairmanship of the Commission was within this period.) Il'ichev had been on the editorial board – and editor-in-chief – of *Izvestiya* and *Pravda* and was later on the board of *Kommunist*. He was also active in the fifties in other fields (in the Ministry of Foreign Affairs and the Department of Agitation and Propaganda, in particular) and often accompanied Khrushchev on his trips abroad between 1956 and 1963. Il'ichev was obviously a more visible type than Polikarpov – and of higher rank – and it is possible that Khrushchev felt the need for this kind of personality in the cultural field in the early sixties. Polikarpov remained in the sphere of culture – as deputy chief of the Ideological Section of the Commission – while Il'ichev held sway.

The Commission was a unique – and brief – departure from the ordinary setup of departments within the Central Committee. Coming as part of Khrushchev's general policy of removing functionaries and bringing in new people, it thus had as its official head the Party Secretary, who would previously have been in the background, above the *apparatchik* Department chairman.

Looking at the dates one can see how flexible the system could be as it adapted to shifting needs of the moment.[22] In appointing Il'ichev to head the Commission on Ideology in November, 1962, Khrushchev was probably trying to demonstrate his own ability to cope with the political problems which followed the Cuban missile crisis, an ability to 'clamp down' without being pushed into a corner by more conservative colleagues.* Il'ichev was a successful spokesman in the

---

* A plenary session of the Central Committee of the CPSU set up the Commission on Ideology and its Ideological Section (both headed by Il'ichev) on November 19, 1962. Priscilla Johnson suggests that these agencies were designed to be relatively modest in size and scope: 'Streamlining the entire Party apparatus into parallel industrial and agricultural units, the reform [announced by the Central Committee on November 19, 1962] drastically reduced the power of the Party's agencies for ideological and political control' (*Khrushchev and the Arts*, p. 5).

An examination of the membership of the Commission – all of whom, except one, were Central Committee members or candidate members – would negate this view. That authority was taken away from a Stalinist like Polikarpov and placed in the hands of Il'ichev, who had been Stalin's editor of *Pravda*, is true, but the composition of the Commission as compared with the Department which preceded

ideological realm, able to enunciate the Party's position. After Khrushchev's removal from office, the Commission on Ideology disappeared from the listing of sections of the Central Committee, and the Department of Culture returned. The Department chief, until his death in November, 1965, was again Polikarpov.

Over and above the Central committee *apparat*, Khrushchev himself, and other Party leaders, had their own viewpoint in the cultural field and, from time to time, made this felt in either broad ideological terms – as in some of their speeches – or in specific policy – as in the case of the publication of Solzhenitsyn's 'One Day in the Life of Ivan Denisovich', which resulted directly from Khrushchev's personal influence with the Presidium.

A similar instance of the impact of the individual leader on specific literary policy was suggested by Arkady Belinkov, who asserted that Ovechkin's 'District Routine' had been published 'on personal orders from Stalin, who decided what should or should not be published'.[23] Whether or not this is true, we can assume that at least some material is published in Soviet Russia with the direct permission

it – and which consisted of only functionaries, with not a single Central Committee member – was clearly weightier in terms of Party prestige. (The Commission was also larger in size, not smaller.) The timing of the change, coming a few weeks after the Cuban crisis, would also indicate a recognition of the need for greater ideological control – or one with high Party authority – than had been in effect under a Party hack. Members of the Department of Culture in the late fifties were:

Chief	D. A. Polikarpov
Deputy Chief	N. I. Glagolev
Deputy Chief	A. Petrov
Deputy Chief	B. S. Ryurikov
Chief, Arts Sector	B. M. Yarustovsky

Members of the new Commission on Ideology and its Ideological Section:

Chairman	L. F. Il'ichev	Secretariat
	A. I. Adzhubei	Central Committee
	S. P. Pavlov	Central Committee
	A. V. Romanov	Candidate, Central Committee
	P. A. Satyukov	Central Committee
	V. P. Stepanov	Candidate, Central Committee
	A. G. Egorov	
Ideological Section:		
Chief	L. F. Il'ichev	Secretariat
1st Deputy	A. V. Romanov	Candidate, Central Committee
1st Deputy	V. I. Snastin	
Deputies	V. A. Kirillin	Candidate, Central Committee
	D. A. Polikarpov	Candidate, Central Committee
	A. G. Egorov	
Science, Education	N. F. Krasnov	
Mass agitation	M. A. Morozov	

– or at the suggestion – of the leader.* (Belinkov went on to say that
certain books were even permitted to pass the censor so that they
could act as examples of how not to write. He gave Kazakevich's
'Two on the Steppe' as an illustration, adding that this was 'at the
personal request of Stalin in order to show what could be done with
a writer'. Zoshchenko, he said, had felt that this was true of his story
'Adventure with a Monkey'.)[24]

Other influences were also exerted within the Party. One example
of this was recalled by Medvedev in his *Ten Years after Ivan
Denisovich*. In order to reach Khrushchev's ear, Tvardovsky gave the
manuscript of 'One Day in the Life of Ivan Denisovich' to
Khrushchev's personal assistant who dealt with cultural matters,
V. S. Lebedev. 'As personal assistant to Khrushchev', writes
Medvedev, 'Lebedev was to a certain extent independent of the
literature section of the Central Committee's Ideological Commission which was headed by D. Polikarpov...'[25] Lebedev then
read the book to Khrushchev, who proceeded to obtain the approval
of the Presidium for its publication.

We should also include here the important role played by the Party
working at the lower level. Consultation with local officials of the

* An interesting example of Stalin's personal attention to literary affairs was
recounted by Grigory Svirsky in his interview, when talking about S. N. Golubov,
a member of the *Novy Mir* editorial board under Simonov and Tvardovsky:

   Stalin liked one of his books – I don't remember the name of it now – and
   Golubov was told through the Writers Union that he should phone a certain
   number. Golubov phoned. He lived in a *dacha* near Moscow...but he had no
   phone. He phoned from a public telephone...[and] when he said that it was
   Golubov they...connected him with Stalin. Stalin told him for a long time what
   he had liked about his book, but meanwhile the people waiting in line began to
   knock on the door of the phone booth and began tugging at him because how
   long can one keep a public phone to oneself? Then Golubov looked out for a
   minute and said, 'Go away. I'm talking to Stalin.' They all took it as a joke. It's
   bad enough that someone should be talking for at least twenty minutes without
   his telling everybody that he's talking to Stalin! Then they simply broke into the
   phone booth and began dragging him out. Golubov managed to shout into the
   telephone, 'Iosef Vissarionovich, excuse me, but they won't let me talk. I'm
   calling from a phone booth. Can I phone you back?' 'All right', said Iosef
   Vissarionovich.
      That same day the whole little village was astounded to see an enormous
   number of military vehicles...They set up a field telephone in Golubov's *dacha*.
   Golubov phoned Stalin once more and spoke to him. Then the major in charge
   of the operation boldly...took the telephone, rolled up the cable, and left.
   Everything was back to normal.

For another example of Stalin's intervention, see Simonov's statement, above
(ch. 4, p. 97).

obkom, specifically with people whose function is to deal with literary matters, also takes place. Here, too, is give and take, and changes may be suggested, as they are at other stages of the complex pre-publication process.[26]

Thus we can see that a variety of crosscurrents were at work within the Communist Party apparatus itself. Medvedev's example amply illustrates how the editor with initiative could, at times, successfully maneuver within this maze.

There were institutions concerned with cultural affairs in the government hierarchy, too. At the highest level was the Ministry of Culture. This was headed by a full Minister, but his importance and influence *vis-à-vis* that of the head of the Culture Department (or whatever it was called at any given time) varied with the individual. Conquest, for example, has shown how the Minister of Culture was a relatively strong person in cultural affairs when Ponomarenko held the position.[27] He was concurrently candidate member of the Presidium. Nikolai Aleksandrovich Mikhailov, who was Minister of Culture from 1955 to 1960, was not re-elected to the Presidium after Stalin's death, although he remained a member of the Central Committee. He seems to have been of a lesser stature and influence as Minister of Culture. He was very much in the background during the tumult of 1956–57 and, when he did speak, did not do so with the authority and vigor which might have been expected. (This same Mikhailov took over as head of the censor's office, beginning in 1963.)

Official censorship is controlled by a government office popularly known as Glavlit. The full title of this agency is the Chief Administration for the Preservation of State Secrets in the Press. It was established in 1922 and its functions derive from a decree issued by the RSFSR Sovnarkom in June, 1931. The latest decree on state secrets in the Soviet Union, 'On the Drawing up of a List of Items of Information which Constitute State Secrets, the Divulgence of which is Punishable by Law', was issued in April, 1956.[28]

Glavlit's function includes prohibiting 'the issue, publication and distribution of works which...contain agitation and propaganda against the Soviet regime and the dictatorship of the proletariat...'[29] The hierarchy within Glavlit remains obscure. It is headed by an official of importance, but without ministerial status. Under him is a collegium which contains representatives of 'interested author-ities' – presumably the Ministry of Defense and the Secret Police.

Below the Union level, each republic has its own Glavlit, and the political divisions down to the city level all have their own organs of Glavlit to deal with publishing activity – *krailit, oblit, railit* and *gorlit*. Directives are sent out from the top to each section on the lower level.

Viewing the official Glavlit *apparat* as it affects the publishing of a literary journal, we can see a two-stage operation. According to the 1931 law, the Glavlit official at the lowest level is to be found in 'publishing houses, the editorial offices of periodicals, printing establishments, radio broadcasting organizations... '[30] Such a functionary is appointed by Glavlit, but paid by the organization – in this case, the journal – to which he is assigned. However, there is no such official at *Novy Mir*: material is sent over to the Glavlit offices.[31]

The second stage of Glavlit control, or 'subsequent' censorship, comes after the journal has been prepared for publication. According to Article 11 of the 1931 law, copies of the printed work – these would be galley proofs – must be submitted to Glavlit before public release. This is the stage which is signified by the lapse of time in dates printed on the last page of the journal. The first date given ('*Sdano v nabor*') indicates when the journal is handed in and set in type. At this point five copies of the printed work are given to the censor. Compositors do not need the censor's stamp before they begin setting the text in type. Printers do. Thus, the compositor will set any given material and make a few copies – a maximum of ten – on a hand printing machine. This galley is then pasted into a dummy issue of the journal and sent to the censor for official approval. Once approved, the dummy then goes to the printing shop and, after printing, the printed version is checked against the dummy.[32] The date of actual printing after the censor's final approval of the galleys is signified by the second date on the last page ('*Podpisano k pechate*'). The lapse of time between the two dates can vary, as we have seen, from a few weeks to a few months.

On the last page of the journal, in the lower left-hand corner, is the censor's imprint. The imprint, consisting of the letter 'A' and five digits, is different, and progressively higher, in each issue of a given year. The difference in number from issue to issue is not constant. This censor's number, rather than representing the particular person who has given his approval, would seem to be one of a year-long series of numbers each of which was given to a separate item of publication. Thus, *Novy Mir* of October, November and December, 1957 had

Glavlit serial numbers A 06981, A 09360 and A 10514 respectively. In 1958 the January serial number was A 10567, because the censor had approved that issue in December, 1957. By February the number was back to A 00653.[33]

A journal has its own specific censor who goes over its material. According to Grigory Svirsky, from 1953 to 1964, for example, *Novy Mir* had six or seven different Glavlit people working with them, one at a time. The Glavlit censor had at his disposal a *spravochnik*, or directory, containing directives about impermissible subjects. Thus, for example, in the spring of 1962 'places of imprisonment' were still treated as a state secret in the *spravochnik*.[34]

The general impression is that the censors are not people of great intelligence or accomplishment. Regarding the personage of the censor, Belinkov averred that, 'the censor is usually a person of average intellect who does not approach a book from the point of view of one trying to understand its structure, its architecture'.[35] Tvardovsky obviously had a similar opinion of the censor. In a reported conversation between him and Khrushchev, in which Tvardovsky argued the case for doing away with censors, he made the point that editors themselves were more responsible individuals than were censors, since the staff at the censor's office was mainly composed of the less-successful employees of publishing houses.

I mean, you wouldn't give them my job, would you? But why can't I, a member of the Party's Central Committee, a writer and an editor, decide whether or not to publish a particular story or poem? After all, our entire editorial staff discusses it and makes a decision – and then some total stranger from Glavlit, some fool who understands nothing about literature, goes and blue-pencils our decisions.[36]

Tvardovsky publicly scoffed at the typical censor in his poem, 'Terkin in the Other World'.

> 'We're conducting a planned program
> Here with fools,

> 'Studying them thoroughly,
> Their nature, ways and habits.
> We've a special Administration
> To direct the task.

> 'It's busily engaged in shifting
> Fools from job to job.
> Sending them to lower posts,
> Discovering them locally,

'Moving these to here and those to there
– A solid program's all lined up.'
'And what are the results?'
'Naturally, there are all kinds of people.

'Some you ask to move aside
But they won't retire.
These we generally make censors –
With a raise in pay.

'From that job
There's nowhere further to move them.'[37]

A poem which is unacceptable for reasons of literary style is more likely to be rejected by the editor. Belinkov said, 'I know of countless occasions when manuscripts have been destroyed by editors, but I can only count on my fingers the number of cases, all publicized internationally, of direct persecution by the censor.'[38] There is no doubt that the censor does play a part in the publication process and that 'bargaining' and alteration do take place at his instigation, but the main burden of Belinkov's statement is relevant.[39]

The fact is that the chain of literary control is extremely complex and that the actual censor – Glavlit – is only one link of it and must be seen as part of the total system, which includes everything from the top Party leadership to the individual writer sitting at his desk. At each stage there is a possibility of give and take, from the internal dialogue of the author, to the discussions with the editor, all the way up to the possible interference of the Party leaders.

Apart from the Party and the government organs, there is one other official organization which is very powerful in the literary world. This is the Writers Union.[40] In theory every professional writer in the country belongs to the Union as a member of a local chapter. In fact, one of the pressures on the writer is that he can be expelled from the Union for bad behavior – Solzhenitsyn and Pasternak being perhaps the two most famous cases.

The Writers Union is ruled by a board of almost 200 members which in turn is run by the smaller secretariat. There are some forty secretaries, headed by a First Secretary. These secretaries are not all equally active and it is only a small core which wields most of the power in the secretariat and hence in the Writers Union. Surkov, Fadeev and Fedin were among the most active in the Union in the fifties.

The Writers Union is directly under the influence of Communist Party policy, which is channeled – via the Central Committee's Department of Agitation and Propaganda[41] – to the Party *aktiv* within the Union. Central Committee decisions – ranging from such resolves as the Zhdanov decrees to the dismissal of Tvardovsky as editor of *Novy Mir* – are implemented by the Union. But this has been a two-way process. Thus, in practice, much of the real power in literary matters has been in the hands of the literary figures who headed the Union. Belinkov gave an example of this process in the 1960s:

If a book is considered really controversial it is condemned and withdrawn, and if not bad enough to be condemned, the discussion just fades out. The decision is taken by the Union of Writers and the Party Central Committee. I give them this order of precedence because I want to stress again the very important role played by a certain group of people within the Union without whom the Central Committee takes no action. The proceedings are quite informal and intimate; everyone concerned sits around in the office of, say, Suslov or Demichev in the Central Committee building, and it is Surkov, for example, who advises Demichev what to do, not vice versa, because Surkov knows more about it.[42]

Here we see the direct link between the leadership of the Writers Union and the Central Committee – through the latter's Department of Culture, specifically its literature section, which is responsible for contacts with the Union as well as with the editorial boards of magazines and publishing houses.

The Writers Union is officially neither a government nor a Party body. Although the Composers Union and the Artists Union have been under the aegis of the Committee for Affairs on the Arts (attached to the Council of People's Commissars of the USSR) since 1936, the Writers Union has remained outside the Committee.[43] Furthermore, even when the Ministry of Culture was established in 1953, the Writers Union was not listed as one of the organizations under its aegis.[44] But, in spite of this, the Union has not displayed any vigorous independence of viewpoint since its foundation – although there have occasionally been some interesting and heated debates carried on within its walls.

The Writers Union is subdivided into republic and local branches. During certain periods these branches have developed their own particular spirit. This was particularly true of the Leningrad branch (not only in the mid fifties, but in the mid forties as well) and of the

Moscow branch. It was the independence and relative power of the Moscow branch and of its house organ, *Moskovsky Literator*, which brought about the establishment – as a counterweight – of the RSFSR Writers Union in 1957. The general view of the Writers Union as a monolith must, therefore, be modified.[45]

Within the Writers Union and behind the solid façade of its official statements there are – and were, even in the early fifties – discussions and debates of a more heated variety than is generally evidenced in public. We know of these disagreements and differences of opinion over literary works only through allusions to them in the press, and from occasional first-hand reports.[46] Works were often discussed in the narrow confines of the secretariat. A broader forum for literary debate was provided by either open meetings of the Party *aktiv* of the Writers Union or its prose, or creative, sections.[47] In the fifties, the prose section of the Moscow branch provided an active arena for discussion.[48]

The prose section was created to encourage the discussion of new works of literature, to bring in new writers and give them the help of their more experienced colleagues and to bring group influence to bear on a work still in its formative – or at least in its pre-publication – stage. Discussion of a questionable work in the section served as a warning signal to the editor who might be considering publishing it, and to the censor. Furthermore, the very knowledge that his work would be discussed by his colleagues in the prose section could intimidate the writer tempted to go 'too far'. Many a work has undergone modification as a result of the comradely criticism given it within the Writers Union.

The prose sections, however, serve a dual function in practice. They are also used as a forum, a testing place, and an aid in achieving publication. Following discussion, revision, repeated debate and further revisions, a work has progressed much of the way toward publication. By the time it has gone through the prose section, one can assume that the work is suitable for publication. Use of the prose section is not consistent, however: not all works are discussed in the sections, nor is there a set procedure – sometimes a work is presented by the writer, at other times by the editor.

The publication of part one of Grossman's *For the Just Cause* exemplifies one instance in which the prose section – as well as the secretariat – discussed a work of fiction, demanded certain changes and then virtually approved the final product.[49] According to reports, the novel had been under discussion in the Writers Union for years before it was finally published in *Novy Mir* in the late summer of 1952. There seems little doubt that when Tvardovsky published it he felt that he had the backing of the writers' community as represented in the prose section. In reality, of course, it was ruthlessly attacked after publication and whatever support the novel had was not in evidence in the ensuing months.

Another, more recent, example of the use of the prose section can be seen in the unsuccessful attempt on the part of Tvardovsky to publish Solzhenitsyn's *Cancer Ward* in *Novy Mir*. In this case Solzhenitsyn first decided to have the novel discussed in the prose section of the Moscow branch of the Writers Union 'to facilitate the novel's passage through the editorial office of *Novy Mir*'.[50] The leadership agreed to hold an open debate on the novel and, in the autumn of 1966, twenty copies of the typescript were distributed to leading Moscow critics and writers. Later, Tvardovsky went beyond the forum of the prose section and tried to get the permission of the powerful secretariat of the Writers Union to publish the novel in *Novy Mir*. In *Bodalsya telenok s dubom*, Solzhenitsyn describes the meeting of the secretariat on September 22, 1967, where over thirty secretaries and three stenographers were present.[51] According to Medvedev, in October, 1967, the secretariat actually agreed that the editor should sign a contract with Solzhenitsyn. Shortly afterwards, Tvardovsky was authorized by K. V. Voronkov of the Union secretariat to send the typescript of *Cancer Ward* to the typesetters. All of the authorizations to Tvardovsky were given by telephone.[52] Medvedev says that he doubted at the time whether the novel would be published.

An instruction from Voronkov was plainly insufficient. On this occasion too the question of actual publication could only be decided at Politburo or Central Committee Secretariat level. But this was 1967 and Tvardovsky was no longer a member of the Central Committee; nor had he any contacts which would allow him to repeat the experiment of 1962.[53]

Tvardovsky's concern to get even oral encouragement from Voronkov for the publication of *Cancer Ward* exemplifies his reluctance to proceed without some kind of assurance that the work was publishable. He summed up this tactic in his words to Solzhenitsyn: 'I am not used to riding a streetcar without a ticket.'[54]

In the end, a proof of the novel in the dummy of the journal was sent to the Central Committee. But the Committee had been 'disqualified from corporate discussion of the question of publishing *Cancer Ward*'.[55] An instruction was issued that the final decision was to be taken by the secretariat of the Writers Union. But the ruling core of the secretariat – Fedin, Sholokhov, Leonov, Tikhonov, Surkov and Mikhalkov – was firmly opposed to publishing the novel. Thus ended the publication history of *Cancer Ward* inside Soviet Russia. Although it was an unsuccessful bid at publishing, the case amply illustrates the many avenues available to the editor intent on seeing a particular item in print. Clearly, the attempt to exert influence at the very top is much more rarely used – and is not a tool which can be used by every editor.[56] But other techniques are available – and often useful – to the resourceful editor.

Undue emphasis on the office of Glavlit, because of its obvious function of censorship, would be wrong. It is merely one among many forms of literary control and policy-making. One should not forget the importance here – as in so many areas of Soviet life – of the omnipresent KGB. Assigned ultimate responsibility for internal security, it clearly considers that it has a vital stake in what is painted, printed or performed. Indeed, Efim Etkind, in his recent memoir, described the KGB as the highest rung in the publication process. The 'Big House', as it is termed in popular parlance, casts a long shadow.[57]

By the nineteen fifties the writer himself, trained as he had been, was in many ways his own worst enemy. But, anywhere along the line a piece of fiction was likely to be attacked, revised or rejected. The complexity of the literary process – and this involved pitfalls as well as aids – cannot be overemphasized. Individual politicians, as well as individual literary figures, differed about how much literary 'freedom' was to be permitted, and about what was or was not 'harmful'. There were, therefore, varying degrees of 'conservatism' or 'liberalism' to be found even within the same organization: a Polikarpov and a Shepilov were both active in high Party cultural politics at the same time. Nor is it a surprise that a Surkov and a Tvardovsky sat together on the secretariat of the Writers Union – nor that on different issues (even in the same period) both had their way. And it is this variety of views which afforded what opportunities there were to see certain 'questionable' items through publication.

On the other hand, there are no grounds for the belief that there were homogeneous groups in the Party or governmental hierarchies which espoused particular aims and could be counted on regularly to bring pressure to bear in the right places. There was some – but not total – homogeneity in *Novy Mir* itself, but that is where it stopped. Paths which were open to the editor in one instance were closed in another. Each problem-case brought with it its own pitfalls and its own possible solutions. One might more accurately speak of individuals who sometimes allied on a particular issue than of cohesive groups.

7

Conclusions

For that which we could not do – and did not do – we won't be made to answer in the next world. But for that which we could have done and didn't do we will be punished.

Aleksandr Tvardovsky

It has been argued here that the return of Tvardovsky to *Novy Mir* in July, 1958 clearly represented a decision on the part of the rising Khrushchev regime to revitalize the journal. And, indeed, this move did usher in a revised editorial policy which in its boldness was to rival and even surpass the most innovative episodes in the fifties. Even Solzhenitsyn, writing in *Bodalsya telenok s dubom* (The Calf Collided with the Oak), recalls reading twenty back issues of *Novy Mir* during the winter of 1968–69 and feeling that the journal was the best of those published in the Soviet Union.[1]

In many cases, the quality of material published exceeded this rather modest praise. Solzhenitsyn's own pioneering work in *Novy Mir*, '*Odin den' Ivana Denisovicha*' (One Day in the Life of Ivan Denisovich),[2] was followed by other short works of his: '*Zakhar-kalita*' (Zakhar 'Money-Bags'),[3] '*Matrenin dvor*' (Matrena's House),[4] and '*Sluchai na stantsii Krechetovka*' (An Incident at Krechetovka Station).[5] Some excellent works of the *derevenshchiki* came out in *Novy Mir* during the decade.[6] Works of Nekrasov, Trifonov, Panova, Dorosh, Zalygin, as well as Sinyavsky's works of literary criticism, appeared, as did translations from such Western writers as Heinrich Böll and Robert Penn Warren.[7] Among the most remarkable innovations of the sixties was the publication of clearly personal editorials. In them Tvardovsky showed himself to the Soviet public at his most vociferous, as he stated his own philosophy of socialist literature. ('Communist *partiinost'* does not negate but, on the contrary, includes within·itself – necessarily and uncondition-ally – the urge to truth.')*

* '*K shestidesiatiletiiu stat'i V. I. Lenina "Partiinaia organizatsiia i partiinaia liter-atura"*', *NM* 11, 1965, pp. 3–8. In this editorial the following comments were also

The decline of the very active role which *Novy Mir* maintained into the sixties can be dated from the time of the Sinyavsky–Daniel trial early in 1966. The arrest of the two young writers signalled the beginning of a critical period for the Soviet intelligentsia as a whole. But the fact of Sinyavsky's affiliation with *Novy Mir* was clearly a cause for added anxiety on the part of its editors.

None the less, the more passive publication policy of the journal was now accompanied paradoxically by an increasingly crusading spirit behind the scenes. Tvardovsky, for whatever the reasons, was no longer as tractable as he had been, nor was he willing or able to respond to the changing moods of the politicians. The reasons for this are doubtless complex: perhaps he had gone through too many 'thaws' and retractions; perhaps he had simply reached the stage – through long years of experience or age or illness – when he was no longer willing to back down. Perhaps he had become too involved in the opposition personified by Solzhenitsyn. Unquestionably, the ultimate refusal on the part of the authorities to permit publication of *Cancer Ward* played a significant role in his embitterment. Having assured Solzhenitsyn that the novel would be published, having gone out on a limb to defend the work and the author, having offended officials of the literary world,[8] Tvardovsky then found that all his planning, his entreaties and his harangues proved ineffective. The novel was never published in his journal and the author was expelled from the Writers Union. But Tvardovsky rejected any possibility of recouping his own prestige by joining the chorus of denunciation.[9]

In 1967, when two of Tvardovsky's closest *Novy Mir* associates, A. G. Dement'ev and B. G. Zaks, were dismissed from the editorial board by an act of the Central Committee, Tvardovsky considered resigning in protest. But he was persuaded by colleagues and literary bureaucrats to continue at his post.[10] In 1970, though, when it became clear to him that his editorial board would be forced to

made: 'And so freedom of artistic creativity is inseparable from *partiinost'*: the freedom of art is the freedom of truth in art, but the defense of truth is precisely what distinguishes Communist *partiinost'*.' 'Socialist realism – if we are only talking about real socialist realism – does not have and cannot have anything in common with recipes prescribed in advance.' See also, for example, 'Po leninskomu puti', *NM* 4, 1964, pp. 5–12. And see the *NM* 1, 1965 article in which Tvardovsky referred to 'a notorious period in the life of our country...it was paralysing the genuine human memory about the events through which one lived...Not only we, but the generations to come will have cause to regret it...The reader badly needs the full truth about life; he is sickened by evasiveness and hypocrisy' (translated in Labedz, ed., *Solzhenitsyn*, p. 77).

undergo fundamental changes, he finally decided to resign as the editor of the journal of which he was no longer master.

Tvardovsky's departure from *Novy Mir* now was an event in no way similar to his resignation in 1954. In the earlier period, after a lull, the journal continued to occupy a leading position in the publishing field during an increasingly liberalized period. In the 1970s, however, *Novy Mir* was to lose its role as a 'safety valve' in the realm of Soviet literature.

Why should the regime have opted to destroy the safety mechanism which had worked with relative success for decades? Perhaps the changes which had taken place in the Soviet Union in the nineteen sixties provide the most plausible answer. It was during this period, and with increasing volume as the decade proceeded, that the phenomenon of *samizdat* became firmly established as an alternative to legal publication within the USSR. By the time Tvardovsky was driven from office, *samizdat* had become a viable outlet of expression for the liberal and reforming inclinations of the intelligentsia.[11] The disadvantage of this arrangement to the regime is, of course, clear: it has no control over it. In the case of *Novy Mir* there had always been limits within which it was permitted to function as a spokesman of liberal ideas.

But there are also benefits to the regime in the *samizdat* process. The top Party and literary leaders are no longer personally responsible for the production of highly questionable material now that the 'publication' process is not a legal one. They cannot be accused of personally legitimizing heresy. Furthermore, *samizdat* reaches far fewer readers than did the 120,000 monthly copies of the journal.[12] The positive aspect here is clear: the minority of the intensely concerned read what they want (at their own risk); while the more peripheral members of the liberal intellectual community are kept from 'questionable' materials.[13]

More recently, the regime has succeeded in employing another kind of safety valve – the emigration (voluntary and, in some instances, enforced) of the dissidents. In this case it clearly hopes to remove certain forms of pressure permanently.

In the pre-*samizdat* period, *Novy Mir* constantly probed the frontiers of the permissible. It was able to move into spaces of freedom opened up by the power struggles within the political leadership. Inconsistency on the part of the leaders was a fact of life in cultural matters as in other areas of Soviet policy. Whether Malenkov was a true patron of the arts, whether Shepilov had genuinely 'liberal' inclinations in the cultural sphere, whether Khrushchev was sincerely interested in the improvement and unfettering of Soviet literature are not as important as what was actually published in the Soviet Union at a given time within a particular political and sociological context.

From time to time, the journal was used by central figures, and the reverse practice – in which editors sought help from the summit – was also the case. But such direct contacts between the journal and the highest echelons of the Party appear to have been the exception. Rather, the journal may be viewed in the light of the 'family circle' as analyzed by Merle Fainsod in his classic work, *How Russia is Ruled*.[14] These so-called family circles were groups of people working together in the lower echelons of Party or government who banded together for mutual protection from above. In 1952, Malenkov referred to these circles of people, 'who shield one another and who place the interests of their group above those of the Party and state'.[15] Fainsod explained that the often impossible demands made upon functionaries led them to 'seek a degree of independence from control by organizing mutual-protection associations in which they agree informally to refrain from mutual criticism and to cover up for each other's mistakes and deficiencies'.[16]

Novy Mir, although far from the milieu of the Party and government functionaries discussed by Fainsod, can be seen as occupying an analogous position. True, the 'family circle' of *literati* is not the secret one of the lower-echelon bureaucrats, but it is nevertheless a kind of fraternal grouping. *Novy Mir* was the obvious place for the writer of a particular kind of work to have sought encouragement and a forum of expression. Furthermore, the editorial board and staff – with the exception of particular members imposed upon them by the Writers Union – did form a more or less homogeneous group, and one which attracted its own 'circle' of writers, advisors, friends. Although the editorial board, unlike the bureaucrats, was not in a position to deceive anyone with false progress reports, it could try every conceivable method to achieve the publication of a particular piece of writing. These methods might include 'slipping' material past an unsuspecting censor, or conceding certain changes while protecting other parts of a work from the censor's pen. The supportive function of family members could be seen on the various occasions when a *Novy Mir* writer reacted – often in print – to what he considered the unjust treatment one of his colleagues had received at the hands of the literary bureaucracy.

In short, the *Novy Mir* community, rather than fitting into a particular slot within the official setup, was more like a dissenting sect – within the system, but not of it. And the term 'family' is, in fact, peculiarly apt. What appears to have unified *Novy Mir* into a loosely homogeneous body – though by no means an ideologically tight unit – in the decade of the fifties and on into the sixties was a framework of mutually held goals and characteristics.

In his interview, Grigory Svirsky emphasized that the unifying element in Tvardovsky's *Novy Mir* 'family' was less in the political than in the ethical sphere:

I want to warn you against the division so commonly made in the West between liberals and conservatives...In Russia the division is often seen as being of a completely different order: a moral order. There are decent people and those who are ready to adapt...It is very difficult for a writer in Russia to be a decent human being [*poryadochnym*]: to speak the truth, still more to write the truth, still more to print the truth...Therefore, apathetic people who were not bothered by conscience or honesty left Tvardovsky and never came to him, because to be published by him meant to have a shadow cast on one's good name and orthodoxy.

The effect of this *poryadochnost'* – if not its aim – was a liberalizing policy pursued by the journal even within the period covered in chapter 1 – when Stalin was alive. There is no question that certain materials were published in *Novy Mir* because there was a strong feeling that they 'should' be published: Grossman's novel, for example. There was a felt obligation to make available to the public ideas which touched contemporary man deeply. This was a duty which exceeded mere adherence to personal taste.

It would be difficult to establish whether *Novy Mir* could legitimately be said to have had a liberal publishing policy over its entire history. It goes without saying that there were some very slack periods indeed in the journal's history. But in the fifties and sixties the editors, above all Tvardovsky, sought to establish the fact that the *Novy Mir* tradition was essentially pluralistic and open. It was clearly very important to them that the journal be imbued with a special *esprit de corps*, and they eagerly sought to demonstrate that the *Novy Mir* ethos could be traced back to the era of Lunacharsky and Polonsky.

The articles and letters published in *Novy Mir* in 1964–65 on the occasion of its fortieth anniversary were devoted, in large part, to the founding fathers of the journal. This was in marked contrast to the *Bol'shaya entsiklopediya* (the second edition), which ignored the early editorial boards entirely, and to the 1934 *Literaturnaya entsiklopediya*, which omitted all mention of Steklov. An article by Dement'ev and Dikushina, published in January 1965, provided much background material on *Novy Mir*'s beginnings.[17] Letters exchanged between Polonsky and Gorky were published in *Novy Mir* in 1964.[18] These articles and letters not only created an image of *Novy Mir* in the twenties as a vital journal of integrity but, through their statements and omissions, provided some insight into the board's attitude at that moment – the mid 1960s – towards literary policies and the journal's liberal origins.

Time and again in the articles of Dement'ev and Dikushina, of Tvardovsky,[19] of Smirnov,[20] emphasis was placed on the direct connection between the *Novy Mir* of the twenties and the *Novy Mir* of the sixties. The decisiveness and single-mindedness of Skvortsov-Stepanov, for example, in insisting on the publication of certain items – and holding himself accountable to the Party – was clearly being held up as an example which *Novy Mir* in the sixties should emulate. Thus, whether or not an outside observer is willing to concede a continuity in the tradition of *Novy Mir* from the twenties to the fifties and sixties, the key point is that the editors themselves accepted and encouraged this recognition of a liberal tradition – and attempted to conduct their journal in accordance with it.

The 'family group' of *Novy Mir* can thus be seen as unified by certain qualities of liberalism, of *poryadochnost'*, favoring particular styles and subject matter. It functioned with a large measure of success in the fifties and sixties, taking advantage of its place and role within the Soviet system. With the shifting situation created by constant maneuvering among forces at the top of the hierarchy, pockets of flexibility opened from time to time. *Novy Mir* would seize upon these opportunities when offered, exploit them and then retrench when the situation changed once again.

There seems no doubt that *Novy Mir*'s reputation as the leading Soviet literary journal, the quality of many of the works published in its pages, its importance to Russian intellectuals – even before the death of Stalin – can be credited to the personality and leadership of Aleksandr Tvardovsky. Who was this man, who set the tone at *Novy Mir* for nearly two decades?

The question is not easily answered, and in recent years has become the source of much heated dispute among Russian literati. The major work dealing with Tvardovsky as an individual and as an editor is Solzhenitsyn's *Bodalsya telenok s dubom*. The book, which the author classifies as 'Notes of a Literary Life', actually centers on the development of Solzhenitsyn himself as a writer in the Soviet Union and the subsequent tribulations to which he and his works were subjected. But because 'One Day in the Life of Ivan Denisovich' and several short stories were published in *Novy Mir*, his relationship with Tvardovsky becomes a major theme. The analysis is complicated by the nature of the book. It is a memoir, written in several instalments and at different times. As their relationship developed, and as Solzhenitsyn himself passed through the vicissitudes of Soviet literary life, so his feelings about Tvardovsky changed; what we have is the record not of a firm position but of an opinion in flux.[21]

Solzhenitsyn's literary memoir and, in particular, his portrayal of Aleksandr Tvardovsky, aroused vigorous reactions. Responses have appeared in *samizdat* literature, in *émigré* publications in the West, and even in the Italian communist newspaper, *L'Unità*. No Soviet journal or newspaper has thus far published any direct response on the subject, though numerous items about and by Tvardovsky have come out in print in recent years. What kind of composite picture can we put together on the basis of the various reminiscences and statements which are available?

There is general agreement on the essential peasant quality of the man who was the editor of Russia's great literary journal of the fifties and sixties. His origins were, indeed, of the village. His father, who was deported during the campaign against the kulaks, had been a blacksmith. Tvardovsky on various occasions reminisced about his father, *inter alia* once in '*Za dal'yu dal'*' and again in his poem '*Po pravu pamyati*' (By Right of Memory),* which was never published in the Soviet Union.[22]

---

* About the decision of *Novy Mir* to publish '*Po pravu pamyati*' Zaks told the following story. The entire board of *Novy Mir* had been invited to the Zaks' new apartment for a house-warming party. Unlike many poets, Tvardovsky was ordinarily reluctant to read his poetry aloud, and only did so at the *Novy Mir* offices in the course of work. But that night, when everyone was comfortably ensconced in the living room,

> he suddenly took out his briefcase and in a sad voice said: 'Brothers! I just got this back from the typist. May I read it?' And we all called out, 'Read it, of course.' He then read it all, from beginning to end, and then one of them (of them, of course, because I was no longer on the board) said, 'The meeting of the editorial board is open. It is proposed that Tvardovsky's poem be sent to the type-setter.' Everyone cried, 'Yes, yes, yes!' And then Kondratovich wrote '*V nabor*'...They really did hand it in for typesetting, but it never got any further.

V. A. Tvardovskaya felt that Solzhenitsyn misinterpreted as pure self-interest what her father meant in saying, 'What would have happened to me, what would I have been, if the revolution had not taken place?'[23] For Tvardovsky, she explains, his own fate was simply a part of the people's fate.[24]

Solzhenitsyn likened him in appearance to a peasant. He described Tvardovsky walking out to the car to see him off – he had put on a simple pea-jacket and a cap, carried a stick for support, and 'looked very much like a *muzhik* who was perhaps just barely literate'.[25] The car drove off and Tvardovsky remained standing there, 'a *muzhik* with a stick'.

This quality was reflected in various aspects of Tvardovsky's character. Lakshin, for example, referred to Tvardovsky's nervousness in crossing the street. It came from the fact, he said, that Tvardovsky had never gotten used to city life, 'remaining a kind of weak leaven, perplexed before its activity and noise'.[26]

In an unpublished article on Tvardovsky and Solzhenitsyn, Roy Medvedev contrasted Tvardovsky with other important officials who gladly made use of the many comforts available to them as perquisites to their jobs.[27] If Tvardovsky ever had to go home in the official Volga car at his disposal, he wrote, he almost always paid the driver: he found it difficult to take advantage of even such small privileges.* As a matter of principle Tvardovsky did not make use of most of the comforts of *nomenklatura* which he had coming to him. According to Medvedev, his refusal to accept them annoyed other secretaries of the Writers Union and chief editors of other journals.

He loved taking walks and spent much time working in his garden. It would be wrong, wrote Medvedev, to describe Tvardovsky as some kind of magnate who, though descended from peasants, now saw the world through the window of a *nomenklatura* car.[28]

This *muzhik* quality could also be felt in Tvardovsky's literary tastes. Literature should have a meaning for the *narod*, in his view.

* This inclination toward simplicity was applied to Tvardovsky's personal work habits. He never talked about his own work, and loved to say, 'The best things are written on a window sill...and not in a well-furnished apartment.' No one saw him writing at the editorial offices, writes Kondratovich, and people who were with him at the front during the war said that he must have done his writing out in the woods or very early in the morning (Aleksei Kondratovich, 'Uroki Tvardovskogo', *Molodaia Gvardiia* 2, 1979, p. 314). Kondratovich also writes elsewhere of Tvardovsky's lack of interest in material things: 'Things never interested him; things were unnecessary and even less than that' ('Poezdka v Pakhru', *Moskva* 9, 1976, p. 208).

Sinyavsky pointed out that Tvardovsky, especially in the field of poetry, preferred the good classic tradition.[29] He did not identify with the modernists and, apart, perhaps, from Marina Tsvetaeva, did not care for the early twentieth-century poets. He had little liking for the poetry of Mayakovsky or even of Pasternak. True, he published Sinyavsky's brief article on the latter,[30] and helped see through publication of the volume of Pasternak poetry,[31] but he and Sinyavsky had major differences of opinion about him. In private conversations, Tvardovsky revealed his esteem for Marshak, though he thought little of Mandelstam or Voznesensky.*

It was important to Tvardovsky, Sinyavsky said in an interview, that 'One Day in the Life of Ivan Denisovich' was about a *muzhik*, for this and its style appealed to Tvardovsky's populist bent (*narodnicheskaya zhilka*). His partiality to authors who wrote about the simple man was apparent in the numerous works in *Novy Mir* which centered on the kolkhoz – above all, of course, in those of Ovechkin.

Apart from his strong peasant ties, another dominant characteristic was his identification with the Party. Indeed, Solzhenitsyn sees Tvardovsky as having been too much of a good Party man.[32] And Tvardovsky's daughter sees her father and Solzhenitsyn as opposites – with Tvardovsky devoted to the revolutionary tradition: Tvardovsky, for whom Marxism 'was not a simple literary ballast'; Tvardovsky, with his little red book in his breast pocket 'next to his heart'.[33] But for all his strong Party feelings and important literary – and Party – posts, he held his own political ideas which did not necessarily coincide with the current Party line. Lakshin was speaking of Tvardovsky's ideology when he wrote about *Novy Mir*'s position:

Of course, *Novy Mir* agreed with Solzhenitsyn in some things. We also disliked formal-bureaucratic socialism; we defended human truth against the formal; we came with a shudder from the terrors of the Stalinist camp and protested when we could against the refinement of forms of social hypocrisy. But we

---

* Sinyavsky interview. Tvardovsky's proclivity toward literature that the masses could appreciate was probably more the product of his own taste than related to the official requirement of *narodnost'* as one of the traditional demands of socialist realism. In his interview with me, Sinyavsky noted that in Tvardovsky's opinion, a great poet, that is, a classic, must have written at least one work which the people (*narod*) would know (e.g. his own 'Vasily Terkin'). He would say, 'Name a work of Pasternak which the people would know.' For this reason, Sinyavsky felt that *Novy Mir* was far more interesting in its prose than in its poetry. Aleksei Kondratovich also noted Tvardovsky's preference for classical poetry as well as his feeling that *narodnost'* legitimized a work of art (Aleksei Kondratovich, 'Uroki Tvardovskogo', *Molodaia gvardiia* 2, 1979, p. 316).

believed in socialism as a noble idea of justice, in socialism with a human interior, not only a human face. For us the democratic rights of the individual were indisputable. We sought support for our feeling and conviction in the people and, fearing the dissipation and false declamation of this understanding, always valued a feeling in common with the working people. This was simply second nature to Tvardovsky.[34]

Lakshin saw the unique existence of such a *Soviet* journal as a tender shoot of socialist democracy. It did not set a norm, but indicated a direction.

...under Tvardovsky's editorship, *Novy Mir* was for many people in our country a pledge that society could undergo a healthy development – with serious literature, a high level of self-criticism and the unmuffled sound of the popular voice.*

In keeping with his conscientiousness as a Party member, Tvardovsky habitually worked through the various channels that he legally had at his disposal. His unwillingness to work counter to approved lines of command was expressed in his statement to Solzhenitsyn (mentioned before) that he was 'not used to riding a streetcar without a ticket'.[35]

Within the framework of his political ideals, Tvardovsky had a clear concept of what *Novy Mir* should publish. Lakshin summed up Tvardovsky's goal of publishing according to conscience by quoting his statement: 'For that which we could not do – and did not do – we won't be made to answer in the next world. But for that which we could have done and didn't do we will be punished.'[36] Lakshin also pointed out that Tvardovsky had insisted upon writing the introduction to 'One Day in the Life of Ivan Denisovich'. By writing the editorial introduction he was declaring to the whole world that he took responsibility for the appearance of Solzhenitsyn's story, that it was not simply an oversight, but a conscious and important step.[37]

Tvardovsky's daughter emphasized that her father had no ready answers, that he was always open to questions, whether the issue was creativity or life. And the most open question for him

till the last days of his life – was the question of the historic, objective, uncompromising appraisal of the generation to which he himself

* Lakshin, 'Solzhenitsyn', pp. 211–12. Lakshin (who lives in the Soviet Union) then adds that, 'The absence of such a publication still six years after is painfully perceptible, not only in literature but in all facets of our life. Tvardovsky's *Novy Mir* was in no way replaced or compensated for.'

belonged...and whose fate so united in a contradictory way victories and defeats, clarity and blindness, courage and helplessness.[38]

This necessity of facing up to the past was clear not only in Tvardovsky's editorial policy, but in his own writing as well. In his preface to 'One Day in the Life of Ivan Denisovich', Tvardovsky wrote:

Although these events are so recent in point of time, they seem very remote to us. But whatever the past was like, we in the present must not be indifferent to it. Only by going into its consequences fully, courageously, and truthfully can we guarantee a complete and irrevocable break with all those things that cast a shadow over the past.
This stark tale shows once again that today there is no aspect of our life that cannot be dealt with and faithfully described in Soviet literature. Now it is only a question of how much talent the writer brings to it.[39]

Tvardovskaya also pointed out her father's interest in helping new generations to work out their own independence of thinking, a critical consciousness, an ability to be faithful to oneself. He saw in this, she wrote, the only authentic Marxist socialist and democratic continuity, the continuation of development. Memory, for him, was not simply an appeal for retribution and repentance.[40]

Tvardovsky was a man with two vocations: poet and editor. The dichotomy of these roles within the Soviet literary system was made clear by him in his ' *Za dal'yu dal'* '. He nevertheless succeeded in both to an extraordinary degree. As a poet he was endeared to the Russian people at all levels. His Vasily Terkin was the great literary hero of the Second World War. By Tvardovsky's own standard – that of writing poetry on a popular level – he was singularly successful, but even according to general standards of literary criticism he ranks as one of the major Russian poets of the Soviet era.

As an editor his contribution is inestimable, though whether he could have accomplished more remains a source of dispute. There seems no doubt that he was utterly devoted to the journal. It is clear from the episodes described in *Bodalsya telenok s dubom* that one of the major factors guiding Tvardovsky throughout was the fear that the journal would go under as a result of the battle royal over the publication of *Cancer Ward*.[41]

Lakshin also wrote of Tvardovsky's devotion to *Novy Mir*:

He hadn't been in a labor camp: on the contrary, he had been shown kindness and crowned. But he changed in these years, as no one else;

sacrificed to everyone for the sake of the journal, for the sake of the common cause and died morally unvanquished.[42]

Tvardovsky's dedication to the journal extended to its contributors and editors. He defended them when possible, tried to publish his favorite writers even in the face of potential trouble.[43] According to Solzhenitsyn, Tvardovsky could never understand or accept that an author whom he liked might not be approved.[44] Tvardovsky's support of Solzhenitsyn is a case in point. After the meeting of the Ryazan Writers Union (at which Solzhenitsyn was expelled), the *Novy Mir* editorial board sat down to hear the account of the meeting. Afterwards, the board went out, leaving Tvardovsky and Solzhenitsyn to themselves. Tvardovsky ordered tea and biscuits, 'the highest form of *Novy Mir* hospitality'. He himself had not gone to a session of the secretariat of the Writers Union in Moscow as he had felt that to do so then would be contemptible.[45]

Tvardovsky's concern for his journal sometimes overrode personal relationships. At the time of Sinyavsky's arrest, Tvardovsky apparently took fright and withdrew. Although a few official writers attempted to intercede on Sinyavsky's behalf, Tvardovsky did not. Further, at the time of the arrest, an article of Sinyavsky's (called 'In Defense of the Pyramids') on Evtushenko's '*Bratskaya GES*' was ready for publication. While the article clearly could not be published after the arrest, there was a procedure permitting payment for writings that had reached a late stage but ultimately could not be published. But *Novy Mir* did not take the option of forwarding the money to Sinyavsky's wife.[46]

The men who actually worked on the journal with Tvardovsky seem agreed upon the fact that *Novy Mir* was run in a democratic spirit. In contrast, Solzhenitsyn and Svetov see the leadership of the journal as a small aristocratic group which did not deign to have much contact with the staff. Indeed, Solzhenitsyn goes so far as to suggest that Tvardovsky had never been in the offices on the upper floors of the *Novy Mir* building until he went to say good-bye to staff members in February, 1970, and asks why he had never called them together in a meeting.[47]

Lakshin rejects this completely. He claims that they all met often, on business or for pleasure. 'Everyone who worked then at *Novy Mir*', he writes, 'remembers the comradely warmth of those meetings.'[48] He goes on to say that Tvardovsky was always accessible, even to people whom he did not particularly care for, as long as they were involved in bringing out the journal.

Any colleague could go to him at any time when he was in his office, and some of us abused this [practice]. I will say further that *Novy Mir* was generally reproached for its organizational spontaneity and disorder. We did not have regular meetings of the editorial board, as a rule, and did not keep shorthand reports and protocols, but the journal was produced faster, as in the old, 'Nekrasov', times.[49]

In another description of the atmosphere at the *Novy Mir* offices Lakshin writes of the typically informal way in which general editorial business was handled.

The editor came, threw on the table a shabby yellow portfolio, packed tightly with manuscripts that had been read and galleys – and around him would immediately spring up a little heap [*kucha mala*] of editorial board members and staff. They came with their questions, requests...and I don't know of a case when Tvardovsky refused his attention, conversation, good advice. In my time I have been on a number of different editorial boards and such a lack of grandeur, of formal etiquette, and such a simple and...democratic quality I have never seen anywhere.[50]

Consistent with this democratic image, Lakshin rejects Solzhenitsyn's position that Tvardovsky had 'protectors' – Dement'ev, Zaks and Kondratovich – who oversaw what materials came to his attention.[51] And he similarly denies the allegation that no one (except, perhaps, Dement'ev) could object to what Tvardovsky said. Lakshin claims that many people argued with Tvardovsky without jeopardizing their friendship, giving as examples Sats, Zaks, Gerasimov, Kondratovich. Indeed, Lakshin writes that Tvardovsky had the wonderful trait of being able to argue with someone over something and then resume his friendship as if nothing had happened. Several times in their own relationship, the two men had argued; Lakshin would walk out, and it was always Tvardovsky who phoned the next day, as friendly as ever.[52]

According to Lakshin, Tvardovsky had a rule that if they were discussing the publication of a work by one of the editorial or staff members, the board had to agree unanimously before it could be accepted for publication. He did not make an exception of himself when one of his own works was under consideration.[53]

There is general agreement that Tvardovsky, perhaps as a result of the competing demands upon him as an editor, poet and Party man, was complex. Roy Medvedev emphasized the man's strength. 'He always made the impression of an enormous piece of native ore which the storms of past times and the blows of fate had marked but had not broken. He retained his original character unadulterated.'[54]

Whatever his personal feelings, Tvardovsky must have constantly found himself on a high-tension wire and fraternizing with people who might at any time use their power to thwart the aims of the journal. Solzhenitsyn, for example, mentions that, during the time that Tvardovsky was clearing his belongings out of Novy Mir, he went to the Writers Union and had his picture taken, smiling, with the presidium.[55]

A major question has persisted. It presents a moral dilemma that affects any critical analysis one may make of various public and private figures in the Soviet Union. Given his position and his ability, did Tvardovsky accomplish all that he could have done? Solzhenitsyn accuses Tvardovsky of cowardice. One example he cites is that Tvardovsky refused, at the end of September, 1965, to keep a copy of First Circle hidden in the safe, although he was told that it was the last copy.[56] The impression given in Solzhenitsyn's book, generally, is that Tvardovsky did not do enough.[57] Svetov, too, is dubious about the value of what the editors achieved. In making so many compromises, he asks, doesn't one lose everything? Is anything left in the end?[58] This is a fundamental issue, with the most far-ranging existential implications. But in their time, to those who did have the thrill of reading a Tsvetaeva poem, a story of Solzhenitsyn, a review by Shcheglov, literary criticism by Sinyavsky, work by Lifshits, Grossman or Pomerantsev, could there have been any doubt?

A number of writers have defended Tvardovsky and his policies, denying any cowardice on his part. Roy Medvedev, for example, writing specifically about the case of Solzhenitsyn, says that it was Tvardovsky's caution which brought success: 'With other conduct, what might have been lost were not only the story and also the writer's whole archive (as happened with Vasily Grossman), but even the author himself when he was still a Ryazan school teacher.'[59] In his own conversations with Tvardovsky, Medvedev had the impression that Tvardovsky had defended Solzhenitsyn at a risk to himself and his journal, and that he also loved Solzhenitsyn and suffered with him for what he was going through.[60] Lakshin also supports the notion that Tvardovsky spoke independently and strongly to the highest-ranking people. For example, at a meeting of the Secretariat of the Central Committee in 1961, Tvardovsky replied to the then powerful Il´ichev, 'I do not permit anyone to judge my sincerity, not even a Secretary of the Central Committee.'[61] Boris Zaks described the complex relationship that Tvardovsky had with Polikarpov. They addressed each other in the personal, *ty*, form and would shout at each other, swear at one another incredibly. Tvardovsky, said Zaks, could say what he wanted to Polikarpov.

On Solzhenitsyn's statement that Tvardovsky's publishing policy should have been carried out independently of the mood of the higher-ups, Lakshin writes that it is amusing to state that an organ of the Writers Union, coming out in a circulation of 100,000 under the fixed stare of readers from 'above' and 'below', printed at the Izvestiya press, could be independent of everyone and everything.[62] He cites the fact that in the last years trouble with the censors (a 'whole censoring collegium') actually grew, with more and more of the censor's pencil applied to the page. No kind of 'bravery' on the part of the editor would help here, he writes, and it was bad enough that issues came out a month or two late: they might not have come out at all after all the waits, appeals, irate protests (many written by Tvardovsky), had the editors not exchanged the controversial material for something else, often no less serious, thus 'starving the censor out'.[63] The question is different, writes Lakshin: Did *Novy Mir* preserve, with all this dependence, its worth, depth, restraint, honor? His own reply is that, with minor exceptions, the journal fulfilled Tvardovsky's criterion to do whatever could possibly be done.

As a person Tvardovsky seems to have been somewhat shy, reticent, reserved, thereby giving some the impression he was unfriendly or even arrogant. He instinctively defended himself against impudence and familiarity and was not a man to greet others with open arms at first meeting. He did have a sense of humor, but much depended upon his mood. Close friendship was reserved for a small number.

Among those who worked at *Novy Mir* Tvardovsky had a few good friends: Dement´ev, Sats, Lakshin.[64] These were men whom he saw regularly at work and who also visited him at his home, his *dacha*. One of his best friends was Emmanuil Kazakevich – despite their different temperaments: Kazakevich the robust ladies' man; Tvardovsky more introspective. They saw each other frequently, and took long walks together. Kazakevich had, of course, also been a *Novy Mir* contributor.[65]

In more general ways, if Tvardovsky was not universally liked, he appears to have been widely respected, as a poet, as an editor and as a human being.[66] His devotion to the journal and to what he saw as the best in Russian literature; his success in producing what was regarded as the finest Soviet literary journal, and the consistent line he followed from the early fifties through the thaw – to the extent that it was possible – gave him a reputation of decency. This characteristic emerged in many ways. Solzhenitsyn tells, for example, of a visit Tvardovsky made to the Secretariat's Department of Culture. Shaura, once again, asked Tvardovsky to read Solzhenitsyn's 'Feast of the Victors', and Tvardovsky angrily refused, saying that it was against the author's will to have anyone read it. Again, when Lakshin suggested that Solzhenitsyn, to placate the authorities, write an anti-Western article for publication in *Literaturnaya Gazeta* or *Novy Mir*, Tvardovsky answered for Solzhenitsyn, saying that such an action was out of the question.[67]

Lakshin insists that Tvardovsky's decency was so deeply a part of him that even inebriation did not destroy it.

It was striking in him that vodka did not destroy his moral 'I'. Never, even in deepest intoxication, did he confuse moral values, could he groundlessly insult a person emotionally close to him, or be carried away with something which he would not have been carried away with in a sober state.[68]

Tvardovsky surely had regrets over some instances in his past when he, perhaps, did not act with the *poryadochnost'* which was characteristic of him. One case was apparently that of Pasternak. Though poetically he was alien to him, Tvardovsky had pangs of remorse about Pasternak. He felt that he should have done something when Pasternak was driven from the Writers Union.[69]

There is no doubt, as witnessed by friend and critic alike, that Tvardovsky was a heavy drinker. Rumor had it that Tvardovsky had become a serious drinker during the war. According to Lakshin, he also drank heavily during certain periods when *Novy Mir* was in difficulty.[70] Efim Etkind, in an article in *Vremya i my*, briefly considered the question of Tvardovsky's drinking and concurred that it was related to his experiences in Soviet literature. 'Some', he wrote, 'committed suicide – these were the bravest or the weakest. Others sank into hard drinking...it is a form of moral suicide – the social illness of Soviet literature'. Solzhenitsyn, he continued, described the mechanism of Tvardovsky's drinking, but did not analyze its real meaning.[71]

Gradually, being the editor of *Novy Mir* came to be as important to Tvardovsky as being a poet. For him, said one of his colleagues, being editor had already become a second 'I'. 'Furthermore, he himself couldn't exist without the journal...it had already become important to him as a poet. The journal became a kind of tower to which there thronged all kinds of people through whom he received such new, important ideas and impressions.' In the end, the editor was as much influenced by the journal as it was by him.*

In the light of this, and our knowledge of Tvardovsky's last years as editor of *Novy Mir*, it is difficult to avoid the conclusion that a relationship exists between his retirement from the journal in 1970 and his death in 1971. His world had, irretrievably, fallen apart. As Solzhenitsyn has written,

> There are many ways to kill a poet.
> Tvardovsky was killed by those who took away *Novy Mir*.[72]

That the *Novy Mir* 'family' genuinely felt the unity which seemed to characterize it can be seen in an unusual photograph which was taken in February, 1970 just before the editorial board left the offices for the last time. Seated at the table were not only Tvardovsky and his board, but also two others – Zaks and Dement´ev – who had been staunch Tvardovsky men and active members of the board. They had been removed from their position four years before.

In *Bodalsya telenok s dubom*, Solzhenitsyn writes of Tvardovsky's farewell scene at the *Novy Mir* offices during those last days of editorship. Solzhenitsyn was at that time preparing to write his own portrayal of Samsonov's farewell to his troops for the manuscript of *August 1914*,

and the similarity of these scenes...and the strong resemblance of the characters came to me! – that same psychological and national type, that same internal greatness, strength, purity – and the practical helplessness, and the inability to keep pace with the times. And, also – the aristocratic nature, natural in Samsonov, contradictory in Tvardovsky. I began to explain Samsonov through Tvardovsky and vice-versa – and understood each of them better.[73]

---

* Zaks interview. Zaks suggests that Tvardovsky could no longer give up being editor. He says that when Tvardovsky returned to *Novy Mir* (in 1958), he agreed to stay for only five years, but at the end of that period he could not bring himself to leave, both through a sense of civic duty and because he simply could not live without the journal.

Notes

The following abbreviations are used in the notes below: *Lit. Gaz.* for *Literaturnaia Gazeta*, NM for *Novyi Mir* and *CDSP* for *The Current Digest of Soviet Press*.

Introduction

1 For an interesting and thorough discussion of the tradition of the thick journal in the history of Russian literature, see Robert A. Maguire, *Red Virgin Soil: Soviet Literature in the 1920s* (Princeton University Press, 1968), pp. 36–66.
2 The use of the word 'liberal' throughout this study should be understood in its specifically Soviet sense, not in the broader usage of the Western world. 'Liberal' here signifies a spectrum ranging from the daring – again, in the Soviet context – publication of Pomerantsev's essay on sincerity to the concept of what is simply less totally repressive than usual. In other words, any more moderate policy toward writers, though still highly confining and strictly within the bounds of the broad tenets of socialist realism, would constitute a 'liberal' swing. In discussing Soviet literature in an interview in April, 1974, Grigory Svirsky, a Soviet *émigré* then in Israel, used the term *progressivny*. This apparently is the word used to describe themselves by those literary groups in the Soviet Union here termed 'liberal'. (This source will hereafter be referred to as 'Svirsky interview'.)
3 This comment was made to me by Andrei Sinyavsky in a personal interview in Jerusalem, October 24, 1977 (later references to which will be to the 'Sinyavsky interview').

1. Literary policy under Stalin, 1952–1953

1 This chapter originally appeared, in somewhat different form, in *Soviet Studies*, July, 1976, pp. 391–405.
2 See two recent but markedly different articles in *Slavic Review* XXXV, 2 (June, 1976): Jonathan Harris, 'The Origins of the Conflict between Malenkov and Zhdanov: 1939–1941', and Sheila Fitzpatrick, 'Culture and Politics under Stalin: A Reappraisal'.
3 Marshall Shulman, *Stalin's Foreign Policy Reappraised* (Harvard University Press, 1963).

4 This is a theme to which Shulman devoted his book. He points out that in order to find means of dividing their foreign adversaries and maximizing their own influence, 'the Soviet Union reintroduced tactical and ideological formulations that had been associated with earlier periods identified as "Right" in Soviet terminology' (*ibid.* p. 7).

5 *Ibid.* p. 6.

6 A literary review criticized an author who 'writes in only two colors – black and white. Her positive characters are good unto holiness, while from the bad character's very first appearance in the story he is completely unmotivated and a scoundrel' (G. Kalinin, 'Zhurnal i sovremennost'', *Pravda*, February 4, 1952, p. 2).

7 The 'no-conflict theory' held that, as all basic conflicts had been eliminated by years of Soviet rule, literature (when dealing with internal themes) should portray only the struggle between 'good' and 'better'.

8 Here Virta is quoting from Pushkin's *Evgenii Onegin.*

9 *Sovetskoe Iskusstvo*, March 29, 1952, p. 2 (trans. in *CDSP* IV, 11, pp. 6–7).

10 The first significant attack came in a *Pravda* editorial. It discussed the crisis in drama, but cautioned against overcorrecting the situation, and then went on to criticize *Sovetskoe Iskusstvo* for not taking a solid stand on the issue. See 'Preodolet' otstavanie dramaturgii', *Pravda*, April 7, 1952, pp. 2–3.

11 *Pravda*, October 6, 1952, p. 6.

12 I. Pitliar, 'About the "Details" of Life as Handled in Literature – Let Us Discuss Questions of Craftsmanship', *Lit. Gaz.*, January 13, 1953, p. 3 (trans. in *CDSP* V, 14, pp. 13–14).

13 *Sovetskoe Iskusstvo*, March 12, 1952, p. 12.

14 Part I of the novel was published in four instalments from July to October, 1952.

15 See, for example, Sergei L'vov, 'Rozhdenie epopei', *Ogonek* 47, 1952, p. 24. A review which appeared at the beginning of 1953 also expressed admiration for the novel, though not unmitigated praise: B. Galanov, 'Epopeia narodnoi bor'by (O novom romane Vasiliia Grossmana, "Za pravoe delo")', *Molodoi Kommunist* 1, 1953, pp. 117–23.

16 Ilya Ehrenburg, *Post-War Years: 1945–54* (Cleveland and New York: World Publishing Co., 1967), p. 293.

17 *NM* 7, 1952, p. 102. The section within square brackets was omitted from later published editions.

18 *Ibid.* In later editions the lines in square brackets were omitted.

19 'Na lozhnom puti – O romane V. Grossmana, "Za pravoe delo"', *Lit. Gaz.*, February 21, 1953, pp. 3–4. See also A. Lektorskii, 'Roman, iskazhaiushchii obrazy sovetskikh liudei', *Kommunist* 3, 1953, pp. 106–15. Lektorskii wrote: 'He sees the whole history of peoples through the anti-scientific understanding of the idealistic–mechanistic philosophy of "energetics" and the Freudian theory of the dark, subconscious instincts...'

20 Vasilii Grossman, *Forever Flowing* (New York: Harper and Row, 1972).
21 *Lit. Gaz.*, February 21, 1953, p. 3.
22 *Ibid.*
23 Vasilii Grossman, *Za pravoe delo* (Moscow: Voennoe izdatel'stvo, 1955), p. 137.
24 *Ibid.* pp. 139–40.
25 Mikhail Bubennov, 'O romane V. Grossmana "Za pravoe delo"', *Pravda*, February 13, 1953, pp. 3–4.
26 *Ibid.* This criticism echoed the notorious attack on Fadeev's novel *The Young Guard*. The fact is that during the early fifties Fadeev was rewriting the entire novel in order to give credit to the Party leadership, which, according to official doctrine, had been responsible for the war effort in the Krasnodon area. Grossman does not appear to have heeded the warning issued to his colleague.
27 A. Fadeev, 'Nekotorye voprosy raboty Soiuza pisatelei', *Lit. Gaz.*, March 28, 1953, pp. 2–4.
28 See also Marietta Shaginian, 'Korni oshibok', *Izvestiia*, March 26, 1953, pp. 2–3.
29 'O romane V. Grossmana "Za pravoe delo"', *Lit. Gaz.*, March 3, 1953, p. 3. In this letter the editors were also apologizing for other articles the journal had published, which had been severely criticized.
30 Grossman was criticized at least twice for having failed to own up to his errors. See, for example, *Lit. Gaz.*, February 21, 1953, p. 3, which reported that at a meeting held at the *Novy Mir* offices on February 2, 1953, Grossman had responded 'scornfully' to the 'completely justified' criticism made by various literary representatives. See also 'V Soiuze sovetskikh pisatelei', *Lit. Gaz.*, March 28, 1953, p. 3, in which A. Perventsev expressed 'general indignation' that Grossman had not replied to criticism.
31 Ehrenburg, *Post-War Years*, p. 166 (my italics).
32 *Lit. Gaz.*, March 28, 1953, pp. 2–4.
33 Agapov was a Simonov associate who followed him on and off a number of editorial boards – including a return to *Novy Mir* in the middle fifties.
34 The only members remaining from the old board were the well-known writers Valentin Kataev, Konstantin Fedin and Mikhail Sholokhov. But these three members were figure-heads largely and were not active on the journal.
35 Bubennov and Kataev objected to the novel, and Kazhevnikov joined them.
36 See Yehoshua A. Gilboa, *The Black Years of Soviet Jewry 1939–1953*, trans. by Yosef Shachter and Dov Ben-Abba (Boston: Little, Brown, 1971).
37 See Ehrenburg, *Post-War Years*, p. 165.
38 See notes 17 and 18 above.
39 *NM* 9, 1952, pp. 204–21. (Among possible translations are 'District

Routine' and 'The Daily Round in a Rural District'.) Ovechkin's series
continued, in *Novy Mir* and *Pravda*, until 1956.

40 Ovechkin's sketches have been described frequently in Western studies.
See, for example, Harold Swayze, *Political Control of Literature in the
USSR, 1946–1959* (Harvard University Press, 1962), pp. 95–7. Ovechkin's
sketch was partially translated in *Soviet Studies* IV (April, 1953),
pp. 448–66. The subsequent instalments in the series were also translated
or summarized in *Soviet Studies*.

Vera Dunham has considered the nature of Martynov's populism in
an interesting discussion; see her *In Stalin's Time: Middleclass Values
in Soviet Fiction* (New York: Cambridge University Press, 1976),
pp. 231–4.

41 See, for example: Marietta Shaginian, 'Kritika i bibliografiia –
"Raionnye budni"', *Izvestiia*, October 26, 1952, p. 2; 'Shirit' front
boevoi publitsistiki! – V sektsii publitsistiki i nauchno-khudozhestvennoi
literatury Soiuza sovetskikh pisatelei', *Lit. Gaz.*, January 17, 1953, p. 2;
'Chitatel'skaia konferentsiia ob ocherkakh V. Ovechkina', *Lit. Gaz.*,
February 19, 1953, p. 3.

42 A. Tvardovskii, 'Po sluchaiu iubileia', *NM* 1, 1965, pp. 3–18. In an
interview with me in Kauneonga, New York on August 10, 1980, Boris
Zaks, who worked at *Novy Mir* for a total of sixteen years, first on the
staff and then as an editor, recalled Tvardovsky's comments years later
about the timing of the publication of 'District Routine'. Tvardovsky
mentioned the sketch at a meeting and erroneously said that it had come
out in 1953. Upon being corrected later by Zaks, he expressed his own
amazement that such a work should have been published in Stalin's time.
(This source will hereafter be referred to as 'Zaks interview'.)

43 *Ibid.* p. 6.

44 *Survey*, LXIX (October, 1968), pp. 112–21.

45 *Ibid.* p. 113. For further discussion of the innovativeness of Ovechkin's
'District Routine' see B. Platonov, 'Novoe v nashei zhizni i literature',
Zvezda 5, 1954, pp. 160–74, and Gennadii Fish, 'Na perednem krae',
NM 4, 1957, pp. 203–4. Fish wrote:
Already in 1952, in the days preceding the 19th Congress, when the
adverse situation in agriculture, the disastrous condition of many
kolkhozy and kolkhozniki was hidden under the froth of official reports of 'unprecedented' successes – the writer bravely, with precise,
spare lines, showed the true picture of life of one artistically generalized
agricultural region of Central Russia.   (p. 203)

46 Arkady Belinkov even suggested that Stalin himself had called for the
publication of 'District Routine'. See his statement in *The Soviet
Censorship*, Studies on the Soviet Union, XI (N.S.), 2 (Munich: Institute
for the Study of the USSR, 1971), p. 17.
Boris Zaks, however, denies this. As a staff member of *Novy Mir* at
the time, working in the Prose department of the journal, Zaks was the
first to read Ovechkin's sketch, and he passed it on for approval to the

editors, who unanimously accepted it for publication. According to Zaks, the manuscript had been rejected by a number of journals and, for Ovechkin, *Novy Mir* was the last hope. He insists that at no point did the journal send the sketch to higher circles for consideration. Referring to Stalin he said, 'If he read it, then it was only in *Novy Mir*.'

47 See, for example, reports of a conference on Mayakovsky in 'Osnovnye voprosy izucheniia tvorchestva V. V. Maiakovskogo (Soveshchanie v Soiuze sovetskikh pisatelei SSR)', *Lit. Gaz*.: January 22, 1953, p. 3; January 24, p. 3; January 27, p. 3; and January 29, p. 3. What is striking about the record of the meeting is the atmosphere of pro-and-con discussion which seems to have prevailed there. Ognev, for example, who was criticized there a number of times for his *Novy Mir* article and for oral statements he had made, was quoted in *Literaturnaya Gazeta* – both his own statements and his attacks on others present.

48 Sidney Ploss, *Conflict and Decision-Making in Soviet Russia* (Princeton University Press, 1965). Robert Conquest, *Power and Policy in the USSR* (London: Macmillan, 1962).

2. The 'economic thaw'

1 *NM* 6, 1953, p. 76.

2 Professor Maurice Friedberg suggested to me that Tvardovsky is here using a typical Onegin rhyme scheme, with the last line ending in an un-Soviet, Pushkin-like reference to a ball.

3 This reference to verisimilitude is the standard conventional wisdom type of definition of realism.

4 *NM* 6, 1953, p. 76.

5 *Ibid*. pp. 76–7.

6 *Ibid*. p. 77.

7 *Ibid*. The editor here uses the familiar '*ty*' form of 'you' while the writer addresses his travelling companion with the formal '*vy*'.

8 *Ibid*. pp. 77–8.

9 *Ibid*. p. 78.

10 *Ibid*.

11 A. Chivalikhin, 'Vzyskatel'nost' khudozhnika', *Lit. Gaz*., July 11, 1953, p. 3.

12 Vladimir Ognev, 'O grazhdanskom dolge', *Lit. Gaz*., August 20, 1953, p. 3.

13 Mikhail Lifshits, 'Krepostnye mastera', *NM* 9, 1953, pp. 220–6.

14 K. Potapov, *Pravda*, June 1, 1953, p. 2.

15 Iu. Karasev, 'Protiv perestrakhovki v literaturnoi kritike', *Lit. Gaz*., August 22, 1953, p. 1.

16 In a report by B. Lavrenev, published under the title 'Novye p'esy i perspektivy teatral'nogo sezona' (in *Lit. Gaz*., October 22, 1953, pp. 3–4), the author, demanding the presentation of real Soviet man, complains that too many plays center so much on scientific–technical problems, and

the dialogue revolves on such technical language, that in order to understand, 'the spectator must bring along a pocket reference book on the technical and agronomic specializations treated in the play'. Lavrenev was later to be an active member of the *Novy Mir* editorial board.

17 See the discussion of the 14th plenary session of the board of the Soviet Writers Union (pp. 28–30).

18 I. Balakhnenkov, 'Obraztsovo obsluzhivat´ pokupatelei', *Pravda*, June 15, 1953, p. 2.

19 'Retsenzii na veshchi', *Lit. Gaz.*, July 11, 1953, p. 2.

20 One of the 'trifles of life' was the problem of shoe repairs and dressmaking and mending; see 'Vnimanie "melocham" byta!', *Izvestiia*, July 24, 1953, p. 2. Another article contained a complaint from a mailman that he could not get good fruit-flavored ice cream in Odessa; see Ia. Zhukovskii, 'Who Benefits from This? – Concerning So-Called Trifles of Life', *Pravda Ukrainy*, July 25, 1953, p. 3 (trans. in *CDSP* v, 31, pp. 5–6).

21 'O rasshirenii proizvodstva promyshlennykh tovarov shirokogo potrebleniia i uluchshenii ikh kachestva', *Pravda*, October 28, 1953, p. 1–3.

22 For a fascinating discussion of the treatment of the general and the particular in Soviet literature of the 1920s, see Robert A. Maguire, 'Literary Conflicts in the 1920s', *Survey*, Winter, 1972, pp. 98–127.

23 F. Abramov, 'Liudi kolkhoznoi derevni v poslevoennoi proze', *NM* 4, 1954, pp. 210–31.

24 See, for example, N. Belekhova, 'Vdokhnovenie i masterstvo', *Lit. Gaz.*, October 10, 1953, p. 3, one-half page; V. Sukharevich, 'Na komediinom spektakle', *ibid.* October 10, 1953, p. 3, one-quarter page; A. Avastes´ev, 'Na krutakh povortakh', *ibid.* October 15, 1953, p. 2, one-half page; T. Trifonova, 'Drama trebuet deistviia', *ibid.* October 17, 1953, p. 2, one-half page.

25 Conquest, *Power and Policy*, p. 246.

26 *Ibid.* p. 198.

27 Conquest states that

The speech had sounded entirely orthodox at the time [in October, 1952], and its use to justify the new line can be taken to indicate mainly that Malenkov's interest had been sought and probably (in view of the unanimity and of Ponomarenko's presence) obtained for the relaxation. (p. 246)

The Medvedevs ignored this point entirely in their study (Roy and Zhores Medvedev, *Khrushchev: The Years in Power* (London: Oxford University Press, 1977)).

28 Announcement of his replacement was made in *Pravda* and *Izvestiya*, March 16, 1954, p. 2. He was replaced by Georgy Fedorovich Aleksandrov. Conquest suggests that Ponomarenko's departure strengthened the hand of the culture sections of the Party apparatus.

So long as the Minister of Culture was himself a candidate member of the Party Presidium it would be difficult for a secretariat to over-ride him, or do much more than carry on a guerrilla warfare on the cultural issues. His replacement, G. F. Aleksandrov, was inevitably a lower-ranking figure.   (p. 247)

29 A. Fadeev, 'O rabote Soiuza pisatelei', *Lit. Gaz.*, October 29, 1953, p. 3.

30 Il'ia Erenburg, 'O rabote pisatelia', *Znamia* 10, 1953, pp. 160–83. Although this issue was prepared before the statements at the plenum, the publication actually followed it, for the October issue of *Znamya* did not reach the public until November, 1953.

31 *Ibid.* (trans. in *CDSP* v, 52, p. 6).

32 *Znamya* was handed in to the printer on September 24, 1953. The December issue of *Novy Mir* was given to the printer on October 1, 1953. Assuming that Pomerantsev must have written his article weeks before, and that he probably did not have access to the works of *Znamya* prior to their publication, it seems safe to say that the later article was written independently.

33 Aram Khachaturian, 'Concerning Creative Boldness and Inspiration', *Sovetskaia Muzyka*, XI (November, 1953), pp. 7–13 (trans. in *CDSP* v, 45, pp. 3–5). See also D. Shostakovich, 'The Joy of Creative Search', *Sovetskaia Muzyka* I (January, 1954), pp. 40–2 (trans. *CDSP* v, 52, pp. 3–4) for another article written in a similar vein.

34 Bubennov is described by Max Hayward as having been notorious under Stalin for his abject conformity, in 'Conflict and Change in Soviet Literature', in Max Hayward and Leopold Labedz, eds., *Literature and Revolution in Soviet Russia 1917–1962* (London: Oxford University Press, 1963), p. 223. He was later criticized in the *Literaturnaya Entsiklopediya* for having been one of the adherents of the no-conflict theory. Bubennov's part in the Grossman affair demonstrates the fact that he was clearly one of the watchdogs of the board in matters of political reliability.

35 This assessment contrasts with Solzhenitsyn's portrayal of Dement'ev as a rather sinister figure when he had to deal with him in the sixties. See Aleksandr Solzhenitsyn, *Bodalsia telenok s dubom* (Paris: YMCA Press, 1975).

36 A. Metchenko, A. Dement'ev, G. Lomidze, 'Za glubokuiu razrabotku istorii sovetskoi literatury', *Kommunist*, XII (August, 1956), pp. 83–100.

37 Walter N. Vickery, *The Cult of Optimism: Political and Ideological Problems of Recent Soviet Literature* (Bloomington: Indiana University Press, 1963), p. 105.

38 During the previous summer criticism had been expressed with regard to writers who sat on editorial boards of literary journals like 'wedding generals', adding nothing but their names to the publication. See, for example, 'Kto podpisyvaet i kto redaktiruet? – O nepravil'nom stile raboty redkollegii literaturnykh zhurnalov', *Lit. Gaz.*, June 6, 1953, p. 1, and T. Trifonova, 'O zhurnalnoi proze', *Lit. Gaz.*, August 18, 1953, p. 3.

Fedin, Kataev and Sholokhov received no salaries, nor did they have offices there or regularly attend meetings of the editorial board. Indeed, Sholokhov never appeared at the *Novy Mir* offices at all during the time that Tvardovsky was editor (Zaks interview).

39 Vera Panova, *Vremena goda*, in *NM* 11 and 12, 1953.

40 *Izvestiia*, August 30, 1952, pp. 2–3.

41 Z. Boguslavskaia, *Vera Panova: Ocherk tvorchestva* (Moscow: Gosudarstvennoe izdatel'stvo khudozhestvennoi literatury, 1963), p. 90.

42 See, for example, Leonov's treatment of Gratsiansky and the sources of his evil character. This is described later in this chapter in the discussion of Mark Shcheglov's review of Leonov's novel *The Russian Forest*.

43 B. Protopopov and I. Shatunovskii, 'Blight', *Komsomol'skaia Pravda*, November 19, 1953 (trans. in *CDSP* v, 45, pp. 6–8).

44 Boguslavskaia, *Vera Panova*, p. 78.

45 *Ibid.*

46 Lev Abramovich Plotkin, *Tvorchestvo Very Panovoi* (Moscow: Sovetskii pisatel', 1962), pp. 96–7.

47 Sarra Iakovlevna Fradkina, *V mire geroev Very Panovoi: Tvorcheskii portret pisatel'nitsy* (Perm: Permskoe knizhnoe izdatel'stvo, 1961), p. 105.

48 V. Pomerantsev, 'Ob iskrennosti v literature', *NM* 12, 1953, pp. 218–45.

49 Born in Irkutsk in 1907, Pomerantsev completed his studies at the law faculty in his home town and worked variously as a teacher, in a courtroom and as a journalist. After his army duty during the Second World War, he published his first novel, *The Bookseller's Daughter* (*Doch' bukinista* (Moscow: Sovetskii pisatel', 1951)). Other works of fiction followed throughout the fifties. In an interview Grigory Svirsky noted that Pomerantsev had retained many friends in the procuracy from the days of his own legal career. Through these procurators he was able to help a great number of people, including members of the literary community who were in need of legal aid and connections in high places.

Pomerantsev cannot be considered to have been a regular *Novy Mir* contributor. He had reviewed a book in the journal in October, 1950 and did not appear in *Novy Mir* again after his famous article in December, 1953. Except for the half-year following the article on sincerity, Pomerantsev was never again the center of a *cause célèbre*, and it is for this article alone that he will probably go down in literary histories written in the West.

50 The six weeks of waiting constituted the period when the censor can hold up or refuse publication.

51 I. Sats, in a private letter dated February 22, 1974. This excerpt, while giving an interesting insight into the Pomerantsev issue, serves as a reminder of the limitations of relying on personal recollections. All but one of the articles mentioned by Sats were published after Pomerantsev's.

52 Edward Brown noted this stylistic innovation and remarked that Pomerantsev 'abandoned the rigidly paragraphed and patterned system of the

didactic critic to present his ideas impressionistically, moving gently from one idea to another without apparent ulterior purpose, and giving the effect of immediate contact with thought in process' (Edward Brown, *Russian Literature since the Revolution* (New York: Collier Books, 1963), p. 241).

53 Erenburg, *Znamia* 10, 1953, pp. 160–83.

54 Brown, *Russian Literature*, p. 203. The Pereval theorist, A. Lezhnev, in 1927 had stated his preference for an ideologically inferior work over an insincere one (Maguire, *Red Virgin Soil*, p. 234). See also *ibid.* p. 401 for the 1927 platform of the Perevaltsy).

55 Khrushchev used virtually the same story in his statement on literature published in August, 1957. See N. Khrushchev, 'Za tesnuiu sviaz' literatury i iskusstva s zhizn'iu naroda', *Pravda*, August 28, 1957, p. 3. The inequitable taxation system on the kolkhozy referred to by Pomerantsev had already been attacked – and remedies suggested – by Khrushchev in his speech on agriculture at the September plenum.

56 In *Cancer Ward* (New York, 1969) Solzhenitsyn specifically referred twice (chs. 4 and 21) to Pomerantsev's article on sincerity. Without mentioning *Novy Mir* by name, he described 'the magazine with the faded blue cover'. Later in the novel, Demka, one of the young patients, enters into a conversation with Rusanov's daughter on the subject of sincerity in literature.

57 Mikhail Lifshits, 'Dnevnik Marietty Shaginian', *NM* 2, 1954, pp. 206–31. Marietta Shaginyan was already 63 years old and had been an established writer since the 1920s. She was primarily an essayist and had published – and travelled – widely.

58 Sergie L'vov, 'Glavnaia tema pisatelia', *Lit. Gaz.*, December 17, 1953, p. 2.

59 See ch. 1. To the outside reader the Shaginyan review seems less virulent than those of Bubennov and Fadeev, but perhaps more than had been expected of her – hence anger with her was inflamed by disappointment.

60 F. Abramov, 'Liudi kolkhoznoi derevni v poslevoennoi proze', *NM* 4, 1954, pp. 210–31.

61   We reproach our writers, not because they showed the rehabilitation of the kolkhozy after the war and the achievements of the kolkhozy, but because they ignored the hardships of development during that time and the shortcomings of kolkhoz production and life and that they did not trouble themselves with a convincing portrayal of the *transition* of the kolkhozy to the prosperity described by them.

(*NM* 4, 1954, p. 214)

62 Harold Swayze seems to think that Abramov had simply misunderstood the implications of the Party's new agricultural policy, thereby incurring the later censure of the Writers Union, but there is no reason to believe that Abramov had misunderstood anything. Indeed, his criticism shows a very solid understanding of the situation in agriculture. For Swayze's interpretation, see his *Political Control of Literature*, p. 95.

63 The vigorous drive to build hydroelectric stations in the countryside was reported in the contemporary press. According to *Pravda*, in 1948 alone 3,250 rural plants were put into operation ('Leninskii zavet pretvoriaetsia v zhizn'', *Pravda*, January 17, 1949, p. 2). In another article, *Izvestiya* reported that in Kuibyshev Province the local Soviet had demanded improved rural electrification. The result – in three months – was the completion of eight hydroelectric stations, eight sub-stations, and two heating and power plants (A. Stepanov, 'Meropriiatiia ispolkoma po zaprosam deputatov', *Izvestiia*, January 14, 1949, p. 2). Another article in the same month describes a dam and water-power plant on the Kiavar River in Armenia which collective farmers had built ('Industrial'naia baza preobrazovaniia derevni', *Pravda*, January 17, 1949, p. 2).

64 *NM* 4, 1954, p. 215.

65 Edward Crankshaw, *Khrushchev: A Biography* (London: Collins, 1966), p. 180.

66 Mark Shcheglov, 'Bez muzykal'nogo soprovozhdeniia', *NM* 10, 1953, pp. 242–51.

67 Mark Shcheglov, '"Russkii les" Leonida Leonova', *NM* 5, 1954, pp. 220–41.

68 *NM* 10, 1953, p. 242.

69 For example, Shcheglov criticizes much of the dialogue, which, he says, sounds too much like Leonov himself. Furthermore, the evil protagonist, Gratsiansky, is presented so one-sidedly that the reader begins to wonder why the novel's heroes fail to see how grotesque he is.

70 *NM* 5, 1954, p. 240. For further discussion of Shcheglov's review see Max Hayward, 'Potentialities of Freedom: The Restlessness of the Writers' (paper presented at the Conference on Changes in Soviet Society, St Antony's College, Oxford, June 24–9, 1957), p. 12. See also Swayze, *Political Control of Literature*, p. 97; Vickery, *Cult of Optimism*, p. 117.

71 *NM* 5, 1954, p. 226.

72 V. Tendriakov, 'Padenie Ivana Chuprova', *NM* 11, 1953, pp. 104–34.

73 Vasilii Rusakov, 'Sila primera', *NM* 12, 1953, pp. 199–217.

74 B. S. Emel'ianov, 'Nekotorye voprosy sovetskoi komedii', *NM* 12, pp. 251–65.

75 A. Turkov, 'Po shablonu', *NM* 12, 1953, pp. 266–72 (p. 272).

76 See ch. 1.

77 Mark Shcheglov, 'Zhizn' zamechatel'nogo cheloveka', *NM* 1, 1954, pp. 258–63 (see p. 260). The book under review was M. Il'in and E. Segal, *Aleksandr Porfir'evich Borodin*, which had been published by *Molodaya Gvardiya* in 1953.

78 Iu. Karasev, 'Zvezda Vostoka', *NM* 2, 1954, pp. 255–64. Karasev wrote of the lull which had engulfed Uzbek literature for two years.

This 'calm' could not but seize the journal *Zvezda Vostoka*, the organ of the Soviet Writers Union of Uzbekistan. Earlier the journal had published outstanding and frequently interesting works. But in 1952 not one novel written by writers of the republic was published, not

one story, not one play, not one poem. In two issues (no. 8 and no. 11, 1952) there were not even any tales...
Only in the middle of 1953 did the journal finally start to print prose works of any size.
79 Sergei Antonov, 'Novyi sotrudnik', *NM* 3, 1954, pp. 50–9. For a more detailed description of Antonov's story see Dunham, *In Stalin's Time*, pp. 84–6.

3. A temporary setback

1 Pavel Gromov, 'Oshibki Dorofei Kupriianovoi', *Zvezda* 2, 1954, pp. 152–61.
2 *Ibid.* p. 155.
3 'Vremena goda' (a letter by some students at the Gertsen Pedagogical Institute in Leningrad), *Zvezda* 3, 1954, pp. 188–9.
4 Marietta Shaginian, '"Vremena goda" – Zametki o novom romane V. Panovoi', *Izvestiia*, March 28, 1954, p. 3.
5 Z. Berezin, 'Ne vse iasno v romane – pis'mo V. F. Panovoi', *Lit. Gaz.*, May 11, 1954, p. 2. Berezin was a metal-lathe operator from Leningrad.
6 V. Kochetov, 'Kakie eto vremena? Po povodu romana V. Panovoi', *Pravda*, May 27, 1954, p. 2.
7 Boguslavskaia, *Vera Panova*, p. 90.
8 See, for example, Z. Barsuk and I. Dneprov, 'Tenevye storony odnogo talanta', *Lit. Gaz.*, May 29, 1954, p. 3; V. Ozerov, 'Velikie sversheniia i beskryloe opisatel'stvo', *ibid.* June 3, 1954, p. 3; 'V pisatel'skikh organizatsiiakh', *ibid.* June 19, 1954, p. 2.
9 'Za glubuiu ideinost' i masterstvo', *Lit. Gaz.*, June 5, 1954, p. 1.
10 V. Voevodin and I. Metter, 'Delo ob "isporchennoi" rukopisi', *Lit. Gaz.*, June 26, 1954, p. 3.
11 A. Beliashvili, 'Geroi real'nye i geroi pridumannye', *Lit. Gaz.*, July 22, 1954, p. 3.
12 Vitalii Vasilevskii, 'From False Positions', *Lit. Gaz.*, January 30, 1954, p. 3 (trans. in *CDSP* VI, 6, pp. 8–9).
13 L. Skorino, 'Razgovor nachistotu', *Znamia* 2, 1954, pp. 165–74. Skorino had been cited the previous spring as a mature, qualified critic who had reduced her critical work in recent years and now tended toward the odd review of the 'jubilee' type. See 'Rabota kritika', *Lit. Gaz.*, May 21, 1953, p. 3.
14 See ch. 2, p. 21.
15 V. Platonov, 'Novoe v nashei zhizni i literature', *Zvezda* 4, 1954, pp. 148–58.
16 *Ibid.* p. 150.
17 *Ibid.*
18 A. Surkov, 'Pod znamenem sotsialisticheskogo realizma – Navstrechu Vtoromu Vsesoiuznomu s'ezdu pisatelei', *Pravda*, May 25, 1954, pp. 2–3.
19 Leonid Zorin, *Gosti*, *Teatr* 2, 1954, pp. 3–45.
20 Il'ia Erenburg, *Ottepel'*, *Znamia* 5, 1954, pp. 14–87.

21 Boris Pasternak, 'Stikhi iz romana v proze "Doktor Zhivago"', *Znamia* 4, 1954, pp. 92–5.
22 For other articles critical of Pomerantsev see 'Navstrechu Vsesoiuznomu S"ezdu sovetskikh pisatelei' (editorial), *Partiinaia Zhizn'* 4, 1954, pp. 8–14; and V. Ermilov, 'Za sotsialisticheskii realizm', *Pravda*, June 3, 1954, pp. 4–5.
23 Boris Agapov, 'Protiv snobizma v kritike', *Lit. Gaz.*, April 6, 1954, pp. 2–3. Agapov was a member of the editorial board of *Literaturnaya Gazeta* at this time. Later, when Simonov became editor-in-chief of *Novy Mir*, Agapov became an assistant editor of *Novy Mir*.
24 Indeed, Lifshits was mentioned by name only once, at the end of the article, and *Novy Mir* received only one mention.
25 'Navstrechu Vsesoiuznomu s"ezdu sovetskikh pisatelei', *Partiinaia Zhizn'* 4, 1954, pp. 8–14 (see p. 12).
26 T. Trifonova, 'O shtopanykh rukavichkakh i literaturnykh skhemakh', *Lit. Gaz.*, May 25, 1954, p. 3.
27 For other articles criticizing Abramov see 'O kriticheskom otdele zhurnala "Novyi mir"', *Lit. Gaz.*, July 1, 1954, p. 3; and M. Salamatin, 'Khoroshikh i raznykh!', *ibid.* July 6, 1954, p. 2.
28 Z. Kedrina, 'Mnogoobrazie zhizni i literatury', *Lit. Gaz.*, July 29, 1954, pp. 3–4.
29 The discussion of Gratsiansky's character had taken up a mere fraction of Shcheglov's review, in fact.
30 See ch. 2, p. 45.
31 For other articles criticizing Shcheglov see 'Za glubuiu ideinost' i masterstvo!' *Lit. Gaz.*, June 5, 1954, p. 1; and 'O kriticheskom otdele zhurnala "Novyi mir"', *ibid.* July 1, 1954, p. 3.
32 P. Mstislavskii, 'Narodnoe blagosostoianie', *NM* 11, 1953, pp. 174–92.
33 *Ibid.* p. 178.
34 *Ibid.* p. 185.
35 See, for example, the résumé of Bukharin's position in 1928 in Stephen F. Cohen, *Bukharin and the Bolshevik Revolution: A Political Biography 1888–1938* (New York: Alfred A. Knopf, 1973). Cohen writes (p. 295): 'Bukharin reiterated the Right's belief in proportional, "more or less crisis-free development" and a plan that specified and observed "the conditions of *dynamic economic* equilibrium" between industry and agriculture, and within the industrial sector itself.'
36 'Nauka i zhizn'', *Kommunist*, v (March, 1954), pp. 3–13. The March issue of *Kommunist* was published only in April.
37 *Ibid.* pp. 9–10.
38 Ia. Fomenko, 'Led ne tronulsia!', *Lit. Gaz.*, May 18, 1954, pp. 2–3.
39 'Za glubuiu ideinost' i masterstvo', *Lit. Gaz.*, June 5, 1954, p. 1.
40 'Uluchshit' ideino-vospitatel'nuiu rabotu sredi pisatelei', *Lit. Gaz.*, June 15, 1954, pp. 1–2.
41 'O kriticheskom otdele zhurnala "Novyi mir"', *Lit. Gaz.*, July 1, 1954, p. 3.

42 References to the Zhdanov decrees – with their implied 'conservatism' – continued throughout the 1950s.

43 For other articles attacking *Novy Mir* see B. Brainina, 'O rabote kritikov', *Lit. Gaz.*, May 4, 1954, p. 3; and N. Lesiuchevskii, 'Za chistotu marksistko-leninskikh printsipov v literature', *ibid.* June 24, 1954, pp. 2–3.

44 V. Tendriakov, 'Ne ko dvoru', *NM* 6, 1954, pp. 42–94. The review was by Iu. Surovtsev, 'Trudnye puti', *Lit. Gaz.*, July 27, 1954, p. 2.

45 R. Nedosekin, 'Glazami storonnego nabliudatelia', *Moskovskii Komsomolets*, July 17, 1954.

46 'Aktivnost', initsiativa, organizovannost'', *Lit. Gaz.*, July 29, 1954, p. 1.

47 Further, in the same issue of *Literaturnaya Gazeta*, even Kedrina, in her article on 'Variety in Life and Literature', where she criticized Shcheglov severely, in naming influential Soviet writers mentioned Pasternak along with Sholokhov and Leonov.

48 K. Pozdniaev, 'Pervaia povest'', *NM* 7, 1954, pp. 246–51. Pozdniaev reviewed Natal'ia Davydova's 'Budni i prazdniki'.

49 'O sovetskom fol'klore', *NM* 8, 1954, pp. 203–40.

50 N. Leont'ev, 'Volkhvovanie i shamanstvo', *NM* 8, 1953, pp. 227–44. As noted above, I. Sats considered this to be one of the most significant articles to appear in *Novy Mir* in the immediate post-Stalin period.

51 'Blizhe k zhizni' (editorial), *Pravda*, April 12, 1954, p. 1.

52 An article by N. Abalkin, 'Closer Contact with Life', *Pravda*, June 13, 1954, p. 2 (trans. in *CDSP* VI, 24, p. 6), discussed the Third Congress of Latvian Writers. Abalkin attacked the Congress report, which refrained from criticizing the magazine *Karogs* for having reprinted Pomerantsev's 'harmful article and thereby [giving] support to propaganda for views alien to Soviet literature'.

53 M. Sergeenko, M. Podobedov, F. Volokhov, 'Ob odnoi pisatel'skoi konferentsii' (letter to the editor), *Izvestiia*, July 17, 1954, p. 2.

54 'Literatura velikogo naroda', *Izvestiia*, August 8, 1954, p. 1.

55 See ch. 2. p. 29. Conquest writes (*Power and Policy*, p. 247): 'To interpret these trends it seems rational to treat the apparent association of Malenkov and the thaw as real. (Not that there is any need to believe that Malenkov would have defended Pomerantsev and the "extreme" liberalisers, and he may well have agreed to some counteraction.)' Earlier (p. 30), Conquest presents a different example of a dichotomy between government and Party showing openly in a difference of approach in *Izvestiya* and *Pravda*, this time in the autumn of 1954.

56 One indication of this, for instance, is the publication in *Pravda* of Khrushchev's Prague speech with some of the more bellicose points omitted. He further points out that at the Central Committee plenum in June the rapporteurs on agriculture were those Ministers who were concerned, not Khrushchev. Also, the trial of Ryumin (July 2–7, 1954) is a sign, he says, that Malenkov was then in a position to use the Doctors' Plot against his opponents. In pursuing this line of thought

Conquest cites Boris Nicolaevsky's suggestion that Malenkov had
wanted to present Ryumin's crimes as having been the preparation of
a purge against the industrial bureaucrats. Thus, continues Conquest (pp.
245–6), Malenkov was using the Doctors' Plot 'as an object lesson, to
convince a section of the Party that they must rely on him for protection
against opponents who were still dangerous; and that he retained
sufficient control to do this'.

57 Crankshaw, *Khrushchev*, pp. 199–200.

58 For instance, one of Conquest's examples indicating Malenkov's
strengthened position is the appearance of the Deputy Premiers at
Lenin's Tomb on May Day, 1954. The following November – the
anniversary of the Revolution – things were back to normal. Conquest
sees the upgrading of the government in May as a possible Malenkov
move. This timing clearly does not coincide with the fact that the month
of May was a time of concentrated attack in the literary field and would
seem to predate a Khrushchev weakening.

59 'Za vysokuiu ideinost' nashei literatury!' *Lit. Gaz.*, August 17, 1954,
p. 3.

60 Sats was in charge of literary criticism in 1953 and 1954. In a letter he
explained how he was given this post.

> In the summer of 1953, Tvardovsky, travelling to the Far East, left
> his assistant Sergei Sergeevich Smirnov in charge and they asked me
> to take over the criticism department – temporarily until someone else
> could be found, because he understood that this work would prevent
> me from doing my own writing. But he liked the way I ran the
> department and I remained until 1954.

Sats went on to say that while he was head of the department two young
critics began to be published there – Mark Aleksandrovich Shcheglov
and Vladimir Yakovlevich Lakshin.

In his interview, Grigory Svirsky emphasized that Sats was not only
active on the staff – and later on the board – of *Novy Mir*, but that he
was also a great personal friend of Tvardovsky's, and a fellow-drinker.
Sats had been Lunacharsky's personal secretary (and his brother-in-law)
and was, in his own right, highly intelligent and well informed. According
to Svirsky, in the Central Committee it was felt that

> Sats had a bad influence on Tvardovsky. Sats was connected with the
> old Bolsheviks and intelligentsia and therefore at the first opportunity
> they separated Sats from Tvardovsky, although there was a mistake
> in this, of course, because Tvardovsky, as it became clear to everyone,
> was an individual, was himself an unappeasable person, but Sats was
> simply a partner, not at all the leader of new ideas.

61 'Ob oshibkakh zhurnala Novyi mir', Resolution of the Presidium of the
Board of the Union of Soviet Writers, *Lit. Gaz.*, August 17, 1954, p. 3.

62 See p. 60 above.

63 Leopold Labedz, ed., *Solzhenitsyn: A Documentary Record* (London:
Allen Lane, The Penguin Press, 1970), p. 113.

64 See, for example, George Gibian, *Interval of Freedom* (Minneapolis: University of Minnesota Press, 1960), p. 17.

65 In her PhD dissertation, Dina Spechler reviewed Simonov's publishing policy in 1955. See, for example, her résumé of Nikolai Pogodin's play, *We Three Went to the Virgin Lands* (N. Pogodin, 'My vtroem poekhali na tselinu', *NM* 12, 1955, pp. 44–88), which aroused criticism in the press. (Dina Spechler, 'Permitted Dissent in the USSR: *Novy Mir* as an Organ of Social and Political Criticism 1953–1966' (PhD dissertation, Harvard University, 1973), pp. 208–11.)

66 'O romane V. Grossmana "Za pravoe delo"', *Lit. Gaz.*, March 3, 1953, p. 3.

67 Though it should be remembered that Grossman did not 'confess' his 'errors' at the time.

4. *The 'political thaw'*

1 This was only to culminate years later in the appearance (in *Novy Mir*) in November, 1962, of Solzhenitsyn's 'One Day in the Life of Ivan Denisovich' and in other legally published works, as well as in *samizdat* publications.

2 Over a period of time Simonov had removed all the members of Tvardovsky's editorial board, until the only original member left was Konstantin Fedin.

3 Beginning in January, 1958, Agapov was no longer listed as assistant editor, although he remained on the editorial board. Krivitsky alone was assistant editor after this.

4 Agapov was on the *Literaturnaya Gazeta* editorial board until mid March, 1956.

5 Svirsky interview. Svirsky also accused Krivitsky, who was then one of the editors of *Znamya*, of having been instrumental in the KGB confiscation of Vasily Grossman's *For the Just Cause*, Part II.

6 A. Tvardovskii, 'Po sluchaiu iubeleia', *NM* 1, 1965, pp. 3–18.

7 Lavrenev died early in 1959 and Golubov in 1962.

8 A charming autobiographical sketch by Lavrenev was published in *Novy Mir* in April, 1959, following his death; see pp. 61–7 of that issue. An interview with Lavrenev about his latest story appeared in 1958: 'Geroi nevydumannoi povesti', *Lit. Gaz.*, April 8, 1958, p. 3.

 Svirsky characterized Lavrenev as a 'moderately progressive writer with whom, I would think, Simonov was connected by personal friendship...who was never distinguished by any particularly progressive views, but was never particularly distinguished by any base actions'.

9 An illustration of this point can be seen in Michael Glenny's anthology of *Novy Mir* material, from 1925 to 1967 (although one does not have to agree entirely with his choice). Mr Glenny, whose criterion of selection was primarily literary, published only one item – Pasternak's brief poem 'Bread' – from the year 1956. The previous item had been published in 1938 and the following article was in the August, 1961 issue of *Novy*

Mir. See Michael Glenny, ed., '*Novyi Mir*': *A Selection, 1925–1967* (London: Jonathan Cape, 1972).

10 Bruno Iasenskii, 'Zagovor ravnodushnykh', *NM* 5, 1956, pp. 71–96; *ibid.* 6, 1956, pp. 46–120; *ibid.* 7, 1956, pp. 96–143. Bruno Yasensky was a Polish communist writer who had moved to the USSR and had published extensively in *Novy Mir* in the early thirties.

11 Yasensky was a victim of that same wave of arrests which had swept away so many foreign communists living inside Russia – including the entire Central Committee of the Polish Communist Party.

12 'Stikhi dlia detei', *NM* 8, 1956, pp. 119–23.

13 *NM* 9, 1955, pp. 139–40.

14 *NM* 10, 1956, pp. 101–3.

15 *NM* 6, 1956, pp. 133–5; *ibid.* 10, 1956, pp. 104–5.

16 Efim Etkind discussed Zabolotsky's lyrical poetry and his inability to publish most of it until the second half of the fifties. His main published output before this consisted of translations largely of Georgian poetry. (Etkind, *Notes of a Non Conspirator* (Oxford University Press, 1978), p. 145.)

17 *NM* 7, 1956, pp. 90–4.

18 Boris Pasternak, 'Khleb', *NM* 10, 1956, p. 18. Pasternak's poems had already appeared earlier in the thaw in *Znamya* in 1954.

19 *NM* 10, 1956, pp. 101 and 103.

20 *NM* 6, 1956, p. 277.

21 Vladimir Dudintsev, 'Ne khlebom edinym', *NM* 8, 1956, pp. 31–118; *ibid.* 9, 1956, pp. 37–118; *ibid.* 10, 1956, pp. 21–98.

22 For a good summary of the novel in far greater detail, see *Soviet Studies*, VIII (April, 1957), pp. 437–43.

23 *Trud* commented that 'Drozdov and Drozdovism are typical products of the period of the cult of the individual leader', thus placing the blame squarely on Stalin (N. Zhdanov, 'An Incisive Novel about our Times', *Trud*, October 31, 1956, p. 3 (trans. in *CDSP* VIII, 49, pp. 3–4).

24 D. Granin, 'Roman Uilsona "Brat moi, vrag moi"', *NM* 6, 1956, pp. 254–8.

   Another reference to suppression of discoveries in scientific and production circles is pointed out by Vickery. He suggests that an article which appeared in *Kommunist* 14, October, 1956 (G. Glezerman, 'Moral'no-politicheskoe edinstvo sotsialisticheskogo obshchestva i stiranie granei mezhdu klassami', pp. 28–43) was written, at least in part, as an advance defense of Dudintsev's novel (Vickery, *Cult of Optimism*, pp. 83 and 121).

25 D. Granin, 'Sobstvennoe mnenie', *NM* 8, 1956, pp. 129–36.

26 Tendryakov's story, '*Ukhaby*', appeared in *Nash Sovremennik* 2, 1956. The review, by Yu. Kapusto, was in *NM* 9, 1956, pp. 254–7.

27 For Khrushchev's condemnation of Stalin's concept of accelerating the class war, see his Secret Speech in *The Anti-Stalin Campaign and*

International Communism (New York: Columbia University Press, 1956), pp, 11–12, 17–18.

28 Pauir Sevak, 'Nelegkii razgovor', *NM* 6, 1956, pp. 121–32.

29 'Dva pis'ma', *NM* 10, 1956, pp. 181–96. This *Novy Mir* technique of publishing criticism of one of *Novy Mir*'s own items and then following it with a high-powered response voicing the *Novy Mir* point of view was seen in the case of N. Leont'ev's 'Volkhvovanie i shamanstvo', *NM* 8, 1953, and the symposium on folklore in *NM* 8, 1954, pp. 203–4.

30 Semen Kirsanov, 'Sem' dnei nedeli', *NM* 9, 1956, pp. 16–32.

31 *Ibid.* p. 20.

32 *Ibid.* p. 25.

33 *Ibid.* p. 26. He is here referring to 200 g of vodka.

34 *Ibid.* p. 31.

35 For further comments on Kirsanov's poem, see Swayze, *Political Control of Literature*, pp. 169–171, and Gibian, *Interval of Freedom*, pp. 14, 60–2.

36 For example, Swayze discussed the theme of truth and the distortion of truth by officials as it affects the lives of some school children in Liubov' Kabo's 'V trudnom pokhode', *NM* 11, 12, 1956. See Swayze, *Political Control of Literature*, pp. 182–4.

37 S. Zalygin, 'Svideteli', *NM* 7, 1956, pp. 44–85. In the story Zalygin twice referred to the arrest and disappearance of his heroine's second husband. Though the references were brief Zalygin managed to concentrate the pathos of a woman's life in an arbitrary act of the authorities. Tvardovsky discussed Zalygin in his recollections in *Novy Mir* 1, 1965, p. 13. He described him as a writer closely bound to *Novy Mir* whose work was characteristic of the preceding decade.

38 Zhores Medvedev, *Ten Years after Ivan Denisovich* (New York: Alfred A. Knopf, 1973), p. 13.

39 See Ol'ga Berggol'ts, 'Razgovor o lirike', *Lit. Gaz.*, April 16, 1953. Gibian, *Interval of Freedom*, p. 6, considers this the first harbinger of future changes to appear in the Soviet press.

40 Ol'ga Berggol'ts, 'Ispytanie', *NM* 8, 1956, p. 26.

41 Ol'ga Berggol'ts, 'Tot god', *ibid.* p. 28.

42 Ol'ga Berggol'ts, 'Otvet', *ibid.*, Vickery refers briefly to this poem (*Cult of Optimism*, p. 133).

43 K. Simonov, 'Pamiati A. A. Fadeeva', *NM* 6, 1956, pp. 3–6.

44 A similar view was given in an article by V. Pertsov, published in July. He stated that the second variation of the novel, which is an optimistic tragedy, 'in my opinion suffers serious injury' (Pertsov, 'Ne tol'ko ob''iasniat', no i izmeniat'!', *NM* 7, 1956, p. 249). Pertsov was never attacked for this view.

45 *NM* 6, 1956, p. 4.

46 S. Shtut, 'U karty nashei literatury', *NM* 8, 1956, pp. 239–49.

47 *Ibid.* p. 240.

48 *Ibid.* p. 248.

49 Metchenko had had a somewhat liberal reputation in the past, but was marked by a growing conservatism in the postwar years.

50 A. Metchenko, 'Istorizm i dogma', *NM* 12, 1956, pp. 223–38. The December issue of *Novy Mir* was handed in very late, on November 13, 1956, but was passed by the censor much more quickly than usual. By December 1st, the journal had already gone to press. We may assume that recent political events had caused the editorial board temporarily to hold up handing in the dummy – the previous issue had been handed in on October 2nd – but that when it finally reached the censor it was rushed through. This might account for the fact that both Metchenko's and Simonov's articles were accepted.

51 *Ibid.* p. 223.

52 *Ibid.* p. 228.

53 *Ibid.*

54 It was briefly mentioned in two sentences in E. Dolmatovsky's speech at the 3rd plenum of the board of the Writers Union in May. See 'Polozhitel'nyi opyt – na boevuiu pozitsiiu!' *Lit. Gaz.*, May 21, 1957, p. 4.

55 Konstantin Simonov, 'Literaturnye zametki', *NM* 12, 1956, pp. 239–57.

56 One example which Simonov cites to show that a good, salvageable book can be made simply by excluding the parts on Stalin is Pavlenko's '*Schast'e*' (in *ibid.* p. 242).

57 Compare this with Pomerantsev's and Abramov's demands for a truthful presentation of postwar reality in *Novy Mir* several years before. Simonov even uses the same term in his discussion: 'In the majority of cases this was not evidence of the writers' insincerity, because many of them...sincerely believed that it was not the time to write the honest truth, that they could return to it...at a later date, when it was already in the past' (*ibid.*).

58 See ch. 1, pp. 5–6.

59 'Molodaia Gvardiia, na stsene nashikh teatrov', *Kul'tura i Zhizn'*, November 30, 1947.

60 Simonov suggested that the assertion that some of the images of the Bolshevik underground were not typical had actually meant that they were not wholly positive.

61 *NM* 12, 1956, p. 247.

62 *Ibid.*

63 *Ibid.* p. 248.

64 In fact, Simonov grossly understated the case here, for many of the 'anti-patriotic' critics had been arrested or killed.

65 'Ob odnoi antipatrioticheskoi gruppe teatral'nykh kritikov, *Pravda*, January 28, 1949, p. 3.

66 *NM* 12, 1956, p. 251.

67 *Ibid.* p. 257.

68 For more details on Simonov's participation in the anti-cosmopolitan

campaign in 1949 see Gilboa, *Black Years of Soviet Jewry*, pp. 174–5; Swayze, *Political Control of Literature*, pp. 60–1; W. Vickery, 'Zhdanovism (1946–53)', in Hayward and Labedz, eds., *Literature and Revolution*, pp. 109–10.

69 For example, see the essay of Abram Tertz (Andrei Sinyavsky) on socialist realism, which did get published in the West, but never inside the Soviet Union. It was a product of this era. Abram Tertz, *The Trial Begins & On Socialist Realism* (New York: Vintage Books, Random House, 1960).

70 While our subject is specifically *Novy Mir*, it should be noted that it represented the general trends influencing all strata of the literary world during this period.

71 The reasons for this are obvious. An editor is never 'taking a chance' in being more carefully selective in what he publishes. Also, the 'conservative' critic can more safely plunge back into the mainstream without fear of reprisal. While hints of 'liberalization' may sometimes be vague, signs of a return to conservatism are generally clearly visible.

72 In 1953, of course, the onslaught had lasted a shorter time, but this fact was due to the sudden death of Stalin.

73 See V. Ozerov, 'The Spirit of Struggle', *Komsomolskaia Pravda*, January 25, 1957, pp. 1–3 (trans. in *CDSP* IX, 8, pp. 27–8). Ozerov criticized Zalygin for deliberately portraying his ordinary characters as humble and faceless:

> Appearing as rank-and-file ordinary men against a background of the omnipotent heroes bred by the cult of the individual, they sometimes evoked the reader's sympathy. True, their success is illusory since the general reader equally refused to accept both the imposing figures of supermen and the pale shadows of the timid and dull little men misrepresented as our advanced contemporaries... It is precisely such everyday people that populate S. Zalygin's story.

See also I. Rodnianskaia, 'Svidetel' ili uchastnik?', *Lit. Gaz.*, September 18, 1956, p. 3.

74 B. Solov'ev, 'Smelost' podlinnaia i mnimaia', *Lit. Gaz.*, May 14, 1957, pp. 1–3.

75 Of particular interest to the art historian is A. Kamenskii, 'Razmyshleniia u poloten sovetskikh khudozhnikov', *NM* 7, 1956, pp. 190–203. This article was criticized severely in P. Sokolov-Skalia, 'Khudozhnik i narod', *Pravda*, October 15, 1956, pp. 2–3. The critic wrote (p. 2), 'A. Kamensky speaks of socialist realism only ironically and advances in place of this generally accepted term the concept of some kind of "honest and profound realism"'.

76 Berggol'ts was frequently criticized during this period, but the poems were never mentioned.

77 N. Zhdanov, 'An Incisive Novel about our Times', *Trud*, October 31, 1956, p. 3 (trans. in *CDSP* VIII, 49, pp. 3–4). For an example of an early meeting where the novel was received with enthusiasm, see the report on

a meeting of the prose section of the Moscow branch of the Writers Union held October 22, 1956. There appears to have been a good deal of open discussion ('Obsuzhdaem novye knigi', *Lit. Gaz.*, October 27, 1956, pp. 3–4).

78 'Rasskaz, vyzyvaiushchii nedoumenie', *Partiinaia Zhizn'* 17 (September, 1956), pp. 76–8.

79 For reports on the plenum, see 'Plenum pravleniia Moskovskoi pisatel'skoi organizatsii', *Izvestiia*, March 7, 1957, p. 2, and 'Podvodia itogi', *Lit. Gaz.*, March 19, 1957, pp. 1 and 3.

80 *Ibid.* p. 3.

81 For reports on this plenum see 'O nekotorykh voprosakh razvitiia sovetskoi literatury posle XX s"ezda KPSS', *Lit. Gaz.*, May 16, 1957, pp. 1–2; P. Brokva, 'Vospevat' pravdu zhizni, predanno sluzhit' narodu!', *Pravda*, May 17, 1957, p. 3; 'Plenum pravleniia Soiuza pisatelei SSSR', *Pravda*, May 18, 1957, p. 3; 'III plenum pravleniia Soiuza pisatelei SSSR', *Lit. Gaz.*, May 18, 1957, p. 1; Mirzo Tursun-Zade, 'Pafos sozidaniia', *Izvestiia*, May 19, 1957, p. 2; 'Za partiinuiu printsipial'nost', za edinstvo sil sovetskoi literatury!', *Lit. Gaz.*, May 21, 1957, pp. 1–3; 'Za partiinuiu prinsipial'nost', za edinstvo sil sovetskoi literatury!', *ibid.* May 22, 1957, pp. 1–3.

82 *Ibid.* p. 3. For other attacks on Dudintsev see ch. 5, n. 2.

83 Note, for example, 'Instead of plunging into the ocean of the people's life, he preferred to sink into a slimy pond, in order to collect rot and mold from the bottom for his new poem' (I. Riabov, 'Poet Kirsanov's Week', *Ogonek*, February 3, 1957, p. 16 (trans. in *CDSP* IX, 13, pp. 25–6)). For other attacks on Kirsanov see, for example, V. Kiselev, 'Socialist Realism is our Weapon', *Lit. Gaz.*, December 14, 1956, p. 3 (trans. in *CDSP* VIII, 50, pp. 5–6), and 'Poeziia v 1956 godu', *ibid.* January 31, 1957, p. 1.

84 'Eshche raz o rasskaze D. Granina "Sobstvennoe mnenie"', *Partiinaia Zhizn'* 24 (December, 1956), pp. 60–4. By coupling the Zhdanov decree with the 'Magna Carta of Soviet Literature' the author was not lessening the impact of the threat. On the contrary, he was imparting to the 1925 decree a more ominous quality.

Other articles attacking Granin's story include the following: V. Kiselev, *Lit. Gaz.*, December 15, 1956, p. 3; Vl. Basakov, 'O smelosti podlinnoi i mnimoi', *Oktiabr'* 1, 1957, pp. 196–204; 'Partiia i voprosy razvitiia sovetskoi literatury i iskusstva' (editorial), *Kommunist* 3 (February, 1957), p. 16; N. Shamota, 'Problemy sovremennoi literaturnoi kritiki', *Lit. Gaz.*, April 18, 1957, pp. 1–3; B. Solov'ev, 'Smelost' podlinnaia i mnimaia', *ibid.* May 14, 1957, pp. 1–3; B. Markov, 'For Close Ties with Life of the People', *Sovetskaia Rossiia*, October 10, 1957, p. 1 (trans. in *CDSP* IX, 40, pp. 12–13); 'Verno sluzhit' narodu', *Pravda*, October 18, 1957, p. 3; and A. Surkov, *ibid.* December 1, 1957, pp. 2–3. Reports on the plenum of the board of the Writers Union also contained criticism of Granin.

85 'Ideinaia chistota i neprimirimost' – vsegda i vo vsem!', *Lit. Gaz.*, June 6, 1957, p. 3.

86 *Ibid.* See Sytin's report on the third plenary session to a Party meeting of Moscow writers in June.

87 'Writers and their Plans', *Vecherniaia Moskva*, December 6, 1957, p. 2 (trans. in *CDSP* x, 5, p. 39).

88 See mention of his speech at an October meeting of the Leningrad City Party Committee in Markov's article in *Sovetskaya Rossiya*, October 10, 1957, p. 1.

89 A. Vasil'ev and A. Polovnikov, 'Vyshe tvorcheskuiu aktivnost'', *Lit. Gaz.*, February 26, 1957, p. 3.

90 Some of the articles centering on Simonov's *Moskva* stories include Il'ia Kremlev, 'Zametki o zhurnale "Moskva"', *Lit. Gaz.*, July 11, 1957, pp. 1, 3; 'S pozitsii partiinoi printsipal'nosti', *ibid.* August 8, 1957, p. 3; 'V redaktsiiu "Literaturnoi gazety"', *ibid.* August 31, 1957, p. 3, and Aleksei Surkov, 'Etikh dnei ne smolknet slava', *ibid.* October 15, 1957, pp. 1–2. In the August 31st *Lit. Gaz.* Simonov did try to defend his stories in a letter to the editors, which they then answered. Other articles attacking Simonov as the author of the *Novy Mir* articles and as editor of the journal include Vl. Ponedel'nik, 'Sluzhit' narodu – Pisateli obsuzhdaiut itogi plenuma', *Lit. Gaz.*, June 11, 1957, p. 1; and 'Tesnee sviaz' pisatelei s zhizn'iu', *Pravda*, October 3, 1957, p. 2.

91 'Rasskazyvaiut redaktory zhurnalov', *Lit. Gaz.*, January 19, 1957, p. 1.

92 Indeed, at the time the interview was published, Simonov might well have already been writing his apologetic article on socialist realism (K. Simonov, 'O sotsialisticheskom realizme', *NM* 3, 1957, pp. 222–34).

93 'Zametki o zhurnale "Moskva"', *Lit. Gaz.*, July 11, 1957, p. 3.

94 Simonov, like any writer at the time discussing the matter of arrests in the purges, avoided any mention or description of the treatment meted out to prisoners. The reviewer chose to ignore this factor completely and thus questioned Simonov's portrayal. How, he asked, could a soldier like Baburov break so easily?

95 A. Solzhenitsyn, *The First Circle* (New York: Bantam Books, Harper and Row, 1968), pp. 418–19. Note the similarity to Tvardovsky's unseen editor in '*Za dal'yu dal'*', whose writer also writes precisely what he wishes him to. Note, too, the similarity to Simonov's own thoughts described earlier in this chapter (p. 96).

96 K. Simonov, 'V redaktsiiu "Pravdy"', *Pravda*, January 24, 1974, p. 2. Simonov attacked Solzhenitsyn, whose activity, he said, went beyond 'the boundaries of literature and has constantly acquired an openly anti-communist and anti-Soviet character'. Solzhenitsyn was still living in the Soviet Union at the time.

97 For example, in Kaverin's novel, which appeared in *Literaturnaya Moskva* II, pp. 42–91, a central theme involved a woman scientist whose pursuit of a new discovery was thwarted by the scientific bureaucracy in a way distinctly parallel to that of Dudintsev's hero in *Not by Bread*

Alone. Nikolai Zhdanov's story, 'Journey Home' (*Literaturnaia Moskva* II, pp. 404–14), described very sharply the bureaucrat's loss of touch with the common people. These are only two of the many examples one could cite.

98 S. L'vov, 'Posle togo, kak roman prochitan', *NM* 9, 1956, pp. 250–4. L'vov, a frequent literary critic in *Novy Mir* in 1956, is the same reviewer who had given such hearty praise to Vasily Grossman's *For the Just Cause* in *Ogonek* in 1952.

99 As the house organ of the organization, it is not available on a subscription basis to non-Soviet writers and is thus not to be found in any of the well-known collections in the United States.

100 'Narod zhdet novykh knig', *Lit. Gaz.*, May 25, 1957, p. 1.

101 E. Dolmatovskii, 'Polozhitel'nyi opyt – na boevuiu pozitsiiu!', *Lit. Gaz.*, May 21, 1957, p. 4. Dolmatovsky himself was criticized in the report for lacking self-criticism.

102 V. Sytin, 'We will Justify the Party's High Trust', *Vecherniaia Moskva*, June 6, 1957, p. 3 (trans. in *CDSP* IX, 23, p. 20).

5. The return of Tvardovsky

1 This chapter originally appeared, in somewhat different form, in *The Russian Review*, April, 1976, pp. 155–72.

2 This is a widely held explanation found in most works on the period. See, for example, Vera Alexandrova, *A History of Soviet Literature 1917–1964: From Gorky to Solzhenitsyn* (Garden City, New York: Anchor Books, Doubleday and Co., 1964), p. 407. It is also clearly implied in Swayze, *Political Control of Literature*, p. 198. See, too, Spechler, 'Permitted Dissent', p. 320.

3 See, for example, B. Platonov, 'Real'nye geroi i literaturnye skhemy', *Lit. Gaz.*, November 24, 1956, pp. 2–3; N. Kriuchkova, 'O romane "Ne khlebom edinym"', *Izvestiia*, December 2, 1956, p. 2; V. Kiselev, 'Sotsialisticheskii realizm nashe oruzhie', *Lit. Gaz.*, December 15, 1956, p. 3; N. Shamota, 'Problemy sovremennoi literaturnoi kritiki', *ibid.* April 18, 1957, pp. 1–3; 'Slovo druzei', *ibid.* May 4, 1957, p. 2; 'Ideinaia chistota i neprimirimost' – vsegda i vo vsem!', *ibid.* June 6, 1957, p. 3; K. Fedin, 'Pisatel' i zhizn'', *Pravda*, June 16, 1957, pp. 3–4; N. S. Khrushchev, 'Za tesnuiu sviaz' literatury i iskusstva s zhizn'iu naroda', *ibid.* August 28, 1957, pp. 2–4 (also published in *Kommunist* 12 (August 1957), pp. 11–29).

4 Simonov's first attempt to retrieve his position was in his article on socialist realism, 'O sotsialisticheskom realizme', *NM* 3, 1957, pp. 222–34. He then attacked Dudintsev at the March meeting of the board of the Moscow Writers Union: 'Podvodia itogi', *Lit. Gaz.*, March 19, 1957, pp. 1 and 3. Finally, in May, at the third plenary session of the board of the USSR Writers Union, he 'took the criticism levelled at [him] with a sense of Party responsibility and admitted [his] mistakes'. This statement was

made by V. Sytin in reporting on the third plenary session to a Party meeting of Moscow writers in June. See 'Ideinaia chistota i neprimirimost' – vsegda i vo vsem!', *Lit. Gaz.*, June 6, 1957, p. 3.

5 'Glavnaia liniia', *NM* 10, 1957, pp. 3–9.

6 N. Tikhonov, 'Sorokaletie sovetskoi literatury i podgotovka k III s''ezdu pisatelei', *Lit. Gaz.*, February 13, 1958, pp. 1–3.

7 A. Surkov, 'Bor'ba za idealy kommunizma – nashe vysokoe prizvanie', *Pravda*, December 1, 1957, pp. 2–3. The campaign had, however, substantially petered out long before the Surkov article.

8 'Podvodia itogi', *Lit. Gaz.*, March 19, 1957, pp. 1 and 3.

9 *Kommunist* 10, 1957, pp. 13–22. For Swayze's comments see *Political Control of Literature*, p. 195.

10 Conquest, *Power and Policy*, pp. 325–6.

11 'Partiia i voprosy razvitiia sovetskoi literatury i iskusstva', *Kommunist* 3 (February, 1957), p. 14.

12 *Ibid.* pp. 14–15.

13 *Ibid.* p. 16.

14 Unlike the literary journals, *Kommunist* did not list the date when it first turned in rough copy of the issue to be put in type. All that we know is that *Kommunist* 3, 1957, was sent to the press on February 23rd. The timing here is delicate, for it was in February that Shepilov returned to the Secretariat of the Central Committee.

15 Polikarpov has been described as 'a man of extremely conservative, Stalinist views'. See Z. Medvedev, *Ten Years after*, p. 8. Other sources corroborate this assessment.

16 D. T. Shepilov, 'For Further Flowering of Soviet Art', *Pravda* and *Izvestiia*, March 3, 1957, pp. 3–4 (trans. in *CDSP* IX, 13, pp. 15–21, 40).

17 D. T. Shepilov, 'Create for the Good and Happiness of the People', *Pravda*, April 4, 1957, pp. 4–5 (trans. in *CDSP* IX, 13, pp. 15–21, 40).

18 'Postanovlenie plenuma TsK KPSS – Ob antipartiinoi gruppe Malenkova G. M., Kaganovicha L. M., Molotova V. M.', *Pravda*, July 4, 1957, pp. 1–2.

19 'Za leninskuiu printsipial'nost' v voprosakh literatury i iskusstva', *Kommunist* 10 (July, 1957), pp. 13–22.

20 *Ibid.* p. 16.

21 *Ibid.* p. 21.

22 Swayze, for example, asserts: 'In mid-summer 1957, the drive for orthodoxy in the ideological realm entered its decisive and final phase. With the defeat of opponents in the Party Presidium, Khrushchev perhaps found it possible to devote greater energy to outstanding problems in the cultural realm' (*Political Control of Literature*, p. 195).

23 *Kommunist* 12 (August, 1957), pp. 11–29; *Pravda*, August 28, 1957, pp. 3–4.

24 It is true, however, that the decision to publish Khrushchev's statements on literature was the result of his establishment as sole legitimate leader of the Party. This could have been considered the appropriate time to

come out with a strong statement of literary policy in order to establish
a Party literary position in more or less official terms.

25 However accurately Khrushchev's memoirs may or may not reflect
historical fact, the following passage suggests that he did indeed feel a
genuine respect for Tvardovsky: 'Thus, Tvardovsky gave us some great
art, but he ended up without recognition, without honor. I think it's
impossible not to recognize Tvardovsky. Some may not recognize a man
while he's alive, but the people have already recognized him' (*Khrushchev
Remembers: The Last Testament* (London: Andre Deutsch, 1974), p. 76).

26 In October, 1957, Tvardovsky was reported as participating in a three-
day discussion in Rome (A. Surkov, 'Italianskie vstrechi', *Pravda*,
October 30, 1957, p. 6). In January, 1958, he published a poem in *Pravda*
for the first time in years ('Razgovor s Padunom', *Pravda*, January 19,
1958, p. 6). The poem was praised by Khrushchev at a reception ('In
Honor of the Soviet People's Intelligentsia', *Pravda* and *Izvestiia*,
February 9, 1958, pp. 3–4; trans. in *CDSP* x, 6, pp. 3–7). He then
published more poems in *Pravda*: 'Eshche o Sibiri', February 9, 1958,
p. 4; 'Front i tyl' (a chapter from '*Za dal'yu dal*''), February 23, 1958;
'Starozhil', April 13, 1958, p. 6. In 'Perechityvaia Tvardovskogo' (*NM*
3, 1958, pp. 191–202), K. Vanshenkin cited Tvardovsky as his favorite
poet. Some lines from Tvardovsky's '*Za dal'yu dal*'' were quoted and
referred to positively in a long article by Iu. Laptev, 'V nogu s
vremenem', *Lit. Gaz.*, June 14, 1958, p. 3.

27 *Pravda*, June 8, 1958, p. 3.

28 It is true that *Novy Mir*, as a 'thick journal', had always contained
non-literary sections, but the issues in 1957–58 had a much greater
proportion of these – and they proved to be a very dull addition.

29 In a conversation with me at his New Haven, Connecticut home in the
spring of 1969, Arkady Belinkov used this term in referring to *Novy Mir*.

30 Vladimir Lakshin, who was a member of Tvardovsky's editorial board
later, writes of the 1958 return that Tvardovsky chose his board with
great care, especially inviting those 'whose literary taste he trusted, whose
social–moral beliefs were close to his' (Vladimir Lakshin, 'Solzhenitsyn,
Tvardovskii i "Novyi Mir"'', *XX-i Vek* 2, 1977, p. 180).

In his interview, Boris Zaks recalled the preparations for Tvardovsky's
return to *Novy Mir*. Zaks had just come back to Moscow from a spring
vacation in Yalta when Tvardovsky telephoned and asked if he could
meet him at the little square near the *Novy Mir* offices. (Zaks had
remained on the staff under Simonov.) 'I came out of the editorial offices
onto the square, and under my windows and those of Krivitsky we sat
on a bench and planned the future editorial board!' This was at the end
of May or the very beginning of June, that is, about a month before the
first journal under Tvardovsky's renewed editorship.

31 V. Nekrasov, 'Pervoe znakomstvo', *NM* 7, 1958, pp. 142–81.

32 Nekrasov was to carry this even further a few years later in his delightful
'On Both Sides of the Ocean', which Tvardovsky also published.

33 S. Marshak, 'Zametki o masterstve', *NM* 7, 1958, pp. 195–210.
34 *Ibid.* p. 195.
35 A. Tvardovskii, 'Iz liriki raznykh let', *NM* 7, 1958, pp. 28–37.
36 *Ibid.* p. 36.
37 *Ibid.* p. 37.
38 For a detailed account of the attacks, see Robert Conquest, *The Pasternak Affair: Courage of Genius* (London: Collins and Harvill Press, 1961). Khrushchev, in his memoirs, intimates that officials other than himself brought pressure to bear on Pasternak. In retrospect, he recalled, The decision to use police methods put a whole different coloration on the affair and left a bad aftertaste for a long time to come...I said, 'Let's go ahead and publish the book so that Pasternak will be able to go abroad and pick up his award. We'll give him a passport and some hard currency to make the trip.'...In connection with *Doctor Zhivago*, some might say it's too late for me to express regret that the book wasn't published. Yes, maybe it is too late. But better late than never. (*Khrushchev Remembers*, p. 77) In her book, Olga Ivinskaya described the pressures on Pasternak during this period. See *A Captive of Time* (London: Collins and Harvill Press, 1978).
39 Mark Shcheglov had died in the autumn of 1956.
40 Emmanuil Kazakevich, 'Serdtse druga', *NM* 1, 1953, pp. 3–125.
41 Indeed, Vera Dunham sees the year 1959 as ushering in 'a new wave of liberalism'. See 'Insights from Soviet Literature', *The Journal of Conflict Resolution*, VIII, 4 (December, 1964), p. 397. The premonition of it, seen in Tvardovsky's appointment, would be consistent with this.

6. *The literary process*

1 Any details of the operation of *Novy Mir* refer to the period 1952–8, unless otherwise noted.
2 Robert Conquest, *The Politics of Ideas in the USSR* (London: The Bodley Head, 1967), p. 82.
3 Solzhenitsyn relates, for example, that towards the end of 1969, an instructor from the Central Committee called Tvardovsky to talk over changing the editorial board and removing Lakshin, Khitrov and Kondratovich (Solzhenitsyn, *Bodalsia*, p. 290). Z. Medvedev gives an instance, however, of the Union's secretariat having met without Tvardovsky in February, 1970, to carry out the reorganization of *Novy Mir* (*Ten Years after*, p. 125).
4 Being part of the Union secretariat did not necessarily imply an active role in running the Union. There were many secretaries, only a limited number of whom received official salaries and participated actively on the staff.
5 Z. Medvedev, *Ten Years after*, p. 120. On the same point (appointments, or *nomenklatura*, made by the Party Central Committee Secretariat) see

Abdurakhman Avtorkhanov, *The Communist Party Apparatus* (Chicago: Henry Regnery Co., 1966), pp. 211–12.

6 Z. Medvedev, *Ten Years after*, p. 119.

7 I am grateful to Veronika Shtain, Boris Zaks and the late Igor' Aleksandrovich Sats for providing me with the basic facts on the *Novy Mir* setup.

8 See ch. 2, p. 32 and n. 38.

9 In his letter of February 22, 1974, Sats explained the collective nature of work at *Novy Mir*: 'Under Tvardovsky the work was collective, although in controversial situations it was he who decided...I read not only criticism, but all the sections – that is the way we did it.' See ch. 7 for the debate on how much democracy existed at *Novy Mir*.

10 Sats had originally been a member of the board of *Literaturny Kritik*, a journal which, in some ways, had bridged the gap between the old *Krasnaya Nov'* literary criticism traditions and those of *Novy Mir* later. *Literaturny Kritik*, founded in 1933, had been disbanded by decree of the Central Committee in 1940.

11 Lifshits, too, had been on the editorial board of *Literaturny Kritik* in the thirties. Both he and Sats, incidentally, were early members of the Communist Party.

12 'The majority of the editorial board members [after Tvardovsky's return in 1958] were friends and collaborators of long standing' (Lakshin, 'Solzhenitsyn, Tvardovskii i "Novyi Mir"', p. 180).

13 Z. Medvedev, *Ten Years after*, p. 119.

14 In responding to Solzhenitsyn's comments on her father, V. A. Tvardovskaya commented, *inter alia*, on the journal as an entire world. It was characterized by more than the editor himself. The composite character of the journal included the circle of authors, scholars, publicists drawn to a particular journal and, beyond that, the circle of authors of criticism, articles, reviews and, of course, the broad spectrum of readers from all over the Soviet Union who sent in their comments. (A. Tvardovskaia, 'Otkrytoe pis'mo A. I. Solzhenitsynu po povodu ego knigi "Bodalsia telenok s dubom, ocherki literaturnoi zhizni"', published in Italian in *L'Unità*, June 24, 1975. The source used here is the one circulated in Russian in *samizdat*.)

15 See ch. 2, pp. 23–4.

16 When in doubt editors can consult with numerous higher authorities in the Writers Union or the Party *apparat* in order to insure themselves against error. (See also Virta's comment on the state of drama, ch. 1, p. 5.)

17 Translated in Priscilla Johnson, *Khrushchev and the Arts*, documents selected and edited by Priscilla Johnson and Leopold Labedz (Cambridge, Mass.: The MIT Press, 1965), p. 254.

18 For a discussion of the ideological rationale of the system of socialist realism and literary control, see Conquest, *Politics of Ideas*, ch. 1, and

Swayze, *Political Control of Literature*, ch. 1. For the demands of socialist realism, see Rufus W. Mathewson, *The Positive Hero in Russian Literature* (New York: Columbia University Press, 1958).

19 See, for example, Conquest, *Power and Policy*, pp. 38–41, on the allocation of departments among the various Secretaries and the staffing of these departments.

20 Z. Medvedev, *Ten Years after*, p. 8. Priscilla Johnson reports on the fact that when Polikarpov appeared at a meeting of the Academy of Fine Arts in the autumn of 1962, 'he was hooted off stage to jeers about his record under Stalin' (*Khrushchev and the Arts*, p. 7). Zaks spoke of Polikarpov as 'a completely crazy person, a bundle of nerves, this tragic figure... He was used to doing whatever he was told and he suddenly rose high under Khrushchev, who did things which made Polikarpov's hair stand on end and he had to transmit them!'

21 Zaks interview.

22 These dates are somewhat problematic, as sources such as *Who's Who in the USSR* and the US State Department's *Directory of Soviet Officials* vary on specific dates of appointments. But they do not alter the basic argument.

23 *The Soviet Censorship*, Studies on the Soviet Union, XI (N.S.), 2 (Munich: Institute for the Study of the USSR, 1971), p. 17. See n. 46, ch. 1, for a refutation of this. (Burg and Feifer, on the contrary, without mentioning a source, suggest implausibly that 'because [Ovechkin's sketch] was kept from Stalin for fear of provoking his wrath, Tvardovsky escaped attack' (David Burg and George Feifer, *Solzhenitsyn* (New York: Stein and Day, 1973), p. 159.) In an interview in Jerusalem in June, 1978 (referred to hereafter as the 'Dar interview'), David Dar asserted his belief that Stalin 'read everything'. The second half of *Sputniki*, by Dar's wife, Vera Panova, was not published because Stalin would not permit it. This indicates that he read it in manuscript. Dar went on to say that Brezhnev probably reads nothing. Khrushchev, while he did not read either, did take note of what others told him.

24 The publication of Zoshchenko's story is considered to have provoked – at least to some degree – Zhdanov's attack on him in 1946.

25 Z. Medvedev, *Ten Years after*, p. 8. In fact, the Commission on Ideology as such had probably not been set up at the time, but the man whom Tvardovsky sought to avoid – Polikarpov – was the official on cultural matters at the Central Committee nevertheless.

26 Dar interview. Dar suggested that this was far more important than Glavlit censorship. He said that when he first read Solzhenitsyn's letter saying that the censorship was destroying everything, he understood how inexperienced Solzhenitsyn was. In the last thirty or forty years, he argued, the censorship has played no role. It is not the censorship that forbids books, but the Party organs. Before handing a manuscript in to the type-setter, the editor sends it to the *obkom* of the local Party. Every

obkom (Moscow, Leningrad) has a section for literature and art. It is after the Party perusal that the manuscript is sent to the censor, and then back to the *obkom*.

27 See ch. 2, p. 29.
28 For a thorough discussion of both of these laws, see Conquest, *Politics of Ideas*. The book contains a long – and excellent – review of the contents of the censorship regulations as well as a look at the workings of Glavlit. For an enlightening view of the censorship in the Smolensk district before World War II, see the chapter on this subject in Merle Fainsod, *Smolensk under Soviet Rule* (Harvard University Press, 1958), pp. 364–77. On the censorship, see also M. Friedberg, 'Keeping up with the Censor', *Problems of Communism* XIII (November–December, 1964), pp. 22–31. The 1931 Decree can be found in Leonid Grigorevich Fogelevich, *Osnovnye direktivy i zakonodatel'stvo o pechate*, 6th edn (State Publishing House, Moscow, 1937).
29 Quoted in Conquest, *Politics of Ideas*, p. 43. See this book for the specific functions as defined in the law.
30 *Ibid.* p. 44.
31 Boris Zaks, as 'responsible secretary' of the *Novy Mir* editorial board, maintained the journal's contacts with Glavlit, which was located at the Khudozhestvennaya literatura publishing house (GIKhL). The main office was located elsewhere, occupying an entire large floor of a big building. It was to the main office that Zaks would be invited in the case of a complicated problem. He himself never met with the head of Glavlit, but at his meetings there a few less high-ranking people would sit around the table: 'a huge table at the head of which sat the deputy head of Glavlit, Stepan Petrovich Avetisian...flanked by Galina Konstantinov-na...the section head, Lidia Nikolaevna, the assistant section head and, last, Emilia – our censor at that time' (Zaks interview).
32 The information about printing up galleys for censor's approval is given by Leonid Finkelstein in *The Soviet Censorship*, p. 56. These details, as applied to *Novy Mir*, were substantially corroborated by the Zaks interview.
33 Serial numbers for other journals, *Oktyabr'*, for instance, correspond with those of *Novy Mir* and are interspersed in the progression. Interestingly, *Oktyabr'* gives only the date the journal was printed, and not the 'handed in for compositing' date.
34 See Lakshin, 'Solzhenitsyn', p. 153.
35 *The Soviet Censorship*, p. 130. Zaks stressed that the censor at the lowest level is a mere 'pawn', that he makes only the most minor decisions. If he is in any doubt, he consults his superior who, if not sure, consults his superior, and so on. 'And if it is very serious, then the chief himself will do nothing, but goes to the Central Committee.'

Zaks did describe one particular censor who worked with *Novy Mir* for a few years. She was 'a girl who finished Moscow University and...was simply assigned to work at Glavlit. She worked for two or three years and at the first opportunity she fled and went to work at some journal. She was even at Tvardovsky's funeral. She was very oppressed by the work at Glavlit: you get all kinds of people there.'

36 Z. Medvedev, *Ten Years after*, p. 17. For a comment on Stalin and Soviet censorship, see William O. McCagg, *Stalin Embattled, 1943–1948* (Detroit: Wayne State University Press, 1978), p. 216.

37 Translated in Johnson, *Khrushchev and the Arts*, p. 267.

38 *The Soviet Censorship*, p. 2. Boris Zaks discussed the nature of Glavlit's work in the sixties. In political and current affairs, the censor knew 'what to cross out'. But with creative literature the problem was more complex and they never knew how to handle it.

> They could never catch the devil by the tail. Think about this: Tvardovsky was editor of *Novy Mir* from 1958 until the beginning of 1970, and look: all during this time every issue of *Novy Mir* was read by Glavlit, and not just once nor at just one level, but at several, and what was the result? All the same – every issue of *Novy Mir* was criticized strongly in the press. Literally every one. It would be asked: What has Glavlit been doing? Where are the results of its work? Here was a tragicomic situation: it had the colossal strength to coerce the journal into the necessary ideological channel, but the results were not achieved. (Zaks interview)

39 For a unique example of the kind of censorship, qualitative and quantitative, which a piece of Soviet writing might be forced to undergo, see A. Anatoli (Kuznetsov), *Babi Yar: A Document in the Form of a Novel*, trans. by David Floyd (New York: Farrar, Straus and Giroux, 1970). Censored material appears in the text in bold-face type.

40 For a thorough investigation of the workings of the Soviet Writers Union, see Swayze, *Political Control of Literature*, ch. 6, 'Bureaucratic Controls and Literary Production', pp. 224–58.

41 Abdurakhman Avtorkhanov, *Communist Party Apparatus*, p. 201.

42 *The Soviet Censorship*, p. 16. P. N. Demichev was, at the time, the member of the Central Committee Secretariat whose responsibility was propaganda and ideology. He became a Secretary in October, 1961. In November, 1964, he also became a candidate member of the Presidium. (His later appointment as Minister of Culture in December, 1974, and concomitant removal from the Secretariat, was considered a demotion.)

43 According to Conquest (*Politics of Ideas*, p. 81), this may have resulted from the fact that the Writers Union has proved to be a relatively strong body of its kind.

44 *Ibid.*

45 See ch. 4, p. 106.

46 For a rare example of literary discussion within the Moscow branch of the Writers Union, see Labedz, ed., *Solzhenitsyn*, pp. 45–63.

47 For a more recent example of such debate, see the condensed stenographic report of the December 21, 1977 meeting of the Creative Section of the

Moscow branch of the RSFSR Writers Union, in the *samizdat* journal *Poiski* 3, 1978.

48 For an example of an open Party meeting in the early 1950s see, 'Let Us Overcome the Lag in Dramaturgy', *Sovetskoe Iskusstvo*, April 19, 1952, p. 2 (trans. in *CDSP* IV, 14, pp. 8–9).

49 See ch. 1, pp. 13–14, for a more extensive discussion of this.

50 Z. Medvedev, *Ten Years after*, p. 63. See also Solzhenitsyn, *Bodalsia*, pp. 187–93, for a full description.

51 Solzhenitsyn, *Bodalsia*, pp. 201–2.

52 Svirsky emphasized that orders never came written, but were always given by telephone: 'It is always emphasized that this is the editor's business, freedom of speech, the editor has his rights, etc., etc.'

53 Z. Medvedev, *Ten Years after*, pp. 73–4. Voronkov is an excellent example of the intricate crosswires connecting political and literary spheres. He had been, since the mid 1950s, a secretary of the Writers Union board for creative organizational matters. A writer with a modest output, Voronkov was considered primarily a Party functionary in the administration of the Union. (In late 1970 he was appointed Deputy Minister of Culture.)

54 Solzhenitsyn, *Bodalsia*, p. 218.

55 Z. Medvedev, *Ten Years after*, p. 76. Solzhenitsyn's account, p. 220, ends with the *Central Committee* deciding against publishing the novel.

56 Lakshin, for example, states that Tvardovsky's influence 'up above' should not be overemphasized. He never once met or talked to Stalin, for example. Nor was he on such terms with Khrushchev that he could simply go to him easily on a sensitive issue (Lakshin, 'Solzhenitsyn', p. 153).

57 See, for example, Etkind, *Notes of a Non-Conspirator*, p. 172. Here he lists, 'from the bottom up', the various people who can ban a book or at least hinder its progress:

The editor
The head of the editorial staff
The chief editor
The first reader
The second reader
The director
The censor (or 'employee of Glavlit')
The District or Regional Committee of the Party
The Committee for Publications of the RFSFR
The Committee for Publications of the USSR
The Propaganda Section or the Cultural Section of the Central Committee of the Party
The KGB

7. Conclusions

1 Solzhenitsyn, *Bodalsia*, p. 266. Solzhenitsyn felt that the journal was a poor second to what one could read in *samizdat*. He had very ambivalent feelings about the quality of the journal. See, for example, *Bodalsia*, p. 22, where Solzhenitsyn claims that *Novy Mir* did not differ significantly from the other journals. On the other hand, see *ibid*. p. 290, where Solzhenitsyn tries to convince Tvardovsky not to resign (after Solzhenitsyn's expulsion from the Writers Union). Solzhenitsyn refers here to *Novy Mir* as the only honorable witness of contemporary times, saying that in every issue there are two or three good articles and that even if there were only one the journal would be valuable.

2 *NM* 11, 1962, pp. 8–74.

3 *NM* 1, 1966, pp. 69–76.

4 *NM* 1, 1963, pp. 42–63.

5 *NM* 1, 1963, pp. 9–42.

6 See, for example, the novel of F. Abramov, *Dve zimy i tri leta*, *NM* 1, 2, 3, 1968.

7 For an excellent summary of developments in the sixties, see Dina Spechler's article in Paul Cocks, Robert V. Daniels, and Nancy Heer, eds., *The Dynamics of Soviet Politics* (Harvard University Press, 1976), pp. 28–50.

8 See, for example, Tvardovsky's own reference to his speaking 'harshly' to Konstantin Fedin in his letter to the latter, published in Labedz, ed., *Solzhenitsyn*, p. 113.

9 See pp. 155, 157.

10 Solzhenitsyn, *Bodalsia*, pp. 171–2, describes the dismissal, Tvardovsky's reaction and his decision to remain editor.

11 *Samizdat* is, of course, also a vehicle for non-liberal, nationalistic, anti-semitic and other forms of expression in the Soviet Union, but in these roles it does not replace any of *Novy Mir*'s functions.

12 Z. Medvedev makes a similar point in *Ten Years after*, p. 5.

13 It should be noted that in recent years there have been a number of books, published in very small quantities – for experts only – on subjects which would not be permitted in ordinary printings for the public.

14 Merle Fainsod, *How Russia is Ruled*, rev. edn (Harvard University Press, 1964), pp. 235–7.

15 Quoted in Fainsod, *How Russia is Ruled*, p. 235.

16 *Ibid*. p. 237.

17 A. Dement'ev and N. Dikushina, 'Proidennyi put'', *NM* 1, 1965, pp. 236–54.

18 'Iz literaturnykh arkhivov', *NM* 5, 1964, pp. 200–17.

19 A. Tvardovskii, 'Po sluchaiu iubeleia', *NM* 1, 1965, pp. 3–18.

20 Nik. Smirnov, 'Pervye gody "Novogo miri"', *NM* 7, 1964, pp. 185–97.

21 Feliks Svetov, in discussing the book, goes so far as to describe it as 'a novel with its clear artistic and philosophical conceptions in time and

history, compositionally built and completed with a plot, with tension...'
He sees Solzhenitsyn and Tvardovsky as the two principal protagonists,
presented with their contrasting personalities, their friendship and
repulsion (F. Svetov, 'Razdelenie...', *Vestnik Russkogo Khristianskogo
Dvizheniia* 121, 1977, pp. 203–4).

22 Excerpts of the poem appeared in *Posev* 10 (October, 1969, pp. 52–5),
to Tvardovsky's annoyance. According to *Posev*, the entire poem had
been prepared for publication in *Novy Mir*, and was then withdrawn on
orders of the censor. Tvardovsky repudiated *Posev*'s publication of a
version of the poem. Roy Medvedev writes, 'One day this work will
certainly be considered one of the most outstanding achievements of
Soviet poetry of the sixties, but in 1969 it was on two occasions removed
from the journal in page proofs and was not included in the five-volume
edition of Tvardovsky's works. (Many other interesting poems and
critical articles were also deleted from the *Collected Works* in spite of
insistent protest by the author.)' (*On Socialist Democracy* (London:
Macmillan, 1975), p. 180.) For an interesting glimpse of Tvardovsky
from the thirties to the fifties, see the collection of letters he exchanged
with the poet M.V. Isakovsky in *Druzhba Narodov* 7, 1976, pp. 246–67;
ibid. 8, 1976, pp. 253–74; and *ibid.* 9, 1976, pp. 247–66. Also, see letters
to various writers written between 1947 and 1969 in 'Trebovatel'naia
dobrota', *Sovetskaia Rossiia*, June 22, 1980, p. 4.

23 Phrased slightly differently in Solzhenitsyn, *Bodalsia*, p. 344.

24 A. Tvardovskaia, 'Otkrytoe pis'mo A. I. Solzhenitsynu'.

25 Solzhenitsyn, *Bodalsia*, pp. 215–16.

26 Lakshin, 'Solzhenitsyn', p. 173.

27 Roi Medvedev, 'Tvardovskii i Solzhenitsyn', dated May 1–19, 1975;
September 1–5, 1975, *samizdat* typescript.

28 Medvedev wrote this in response to what he felt was an erroneous image
of Tvardovsky projected by Solzhenitsyn.

29 Sinyavsky interview.

30 Sinyavsky reviewed a volume of Pasternak's poetry in *NM* 3, 1962,
pp. 261–3.

31 Boris Pasternak, *Stikhotvoreniia i poemy* (Moscow: Sovetskii pisatel',
1965). The fifty-page introduction to this volume was written by
Sinyavsky.

32 In *Bodalsya*, Solzhenitsyn expressed his annoyance that Tvardovsky had
failed to discuss his, Solzhenitsyn's, predicament in an interview with the
Neue Züricher Zeitung (p. 143). Also, see ch. 5, footnote on p. 117.

33 Tvardovskaia, 'Otkrytoe pis'mo A. I. Solzhenitsynu'.

34 Lakshin, 'Solzhenitsyn', pp. 200–1.

35 Solzhenitsyn, *Bodalsia*, p. 218. Solzhenitsyn writes that after a meeting
with Voronkov, Tvardovsky announced that he would publish *Cancer
Ward*, though no promise of publication had been given to him.
Tvardovsky, according to Solzhenitsyn, was 'sitting on a streetcar
without buying a ticket!' (p. 220).

36 Lakshin, 'Solzhenitsyn', p. 210.
37 *Ibid.* p. 165.
38 Tvardovskaia, 'Otkrytoe pis'mo A. I. Solzhenitsynu'.
39 Translated in Labedz, ed., *Solzhenitsyn*, pp. 38, 40.
40 This is an obvious reference to Solzhenitsyn's article, 'Repentance and Self-limitation in the Life of Nations', in A. Solzhenitsyn, ed., *From under the Rubble* (London: William Collins & Sons, 1975).
41 See, for example, Solzhenitsyn, *Bodalsia*, p. 227, where Tvardovsky asks Solzhenitsyn to respond properly to the publication of *Cancer Ward* abroad. If he does the wrong thing, they might close *Novy Mir*.
42 Lakshin, 'Solzhenitsyn', p. 216.
43 Note, for example, his continued use of Shcheglov's articles; his announcements of the future appearance of more works by Grossman and Kazakevich; his staunch defense of Solzhenitsyn in the mid sixties.
44 Solzhenitsyn, *Bodalsia*, p. 288.
45 *Ibid.* pp. 288–9. Solzhenitsyn writes that Tvardovsky was even more struck by Solzhenitsyn's expulsion than he was. He saw it, further, as a tragedy for *Novy Mir*'s position and even spoke of resigning (p. 290).
46 Sinyavsky interview. Sinyavsky pointed out that in the case of Solzhenitsyn, while the journal did not publish *Cancer Ward*, they did pay the author a substantial sum.
47 Solzhenitsyn, *Bodalsia*, p. 303. Dar, in his interview, stated that Simonov had fostered a much more democratic atmosphere in the *Novy Mir* offices: they drank tea together, shared money; he would sit in the bathtub dictating through the door. His feeling was that at Tvardovsky's *Novy Mir*, in the sixties, decisions were made by the triumvirate of Tvardovsky, Dement'ev (who handled Party and rural topics) and Lakshin (who represented the liberal intelligentsia).

Zaks, too, contrasts Simonov and Tvardovsky, but with opposite results. Simonov's editorial management gave an air of democracy, according to Zaks (who had remained at *Novy Mir* and hence worked on Simonov's staff as well), because his meetings included both board and staff and they were encouraged to speak up on every issue. 'But this meeting never made any serious decisions...Because when the [broad] forum was over, he and Krivitsky would lock themselves up and those two decided everything.'
48 Lakshin, 'Solzhenitsyn', p. 175.
49 *Ibid.* p. 174. This view of spontaneity at *Novy Mir* is corroborated by Boris Zaks. He describes the frequent sporadic meetings of editors, held whenever the necessity arose (as distinct from occasional formal sittings).
50 *Ibid.*
51 See Lakshin, 'Solzhenitsyn', pp. 183–4, on Anna Berzer's view that these men could have kept the manuscript of 'One Day in the Life of Ivan Denisovich' from Tvardovsky. Lakshin is convinced that they would never have deliberately concealed it from him. He does agree with

Solzhenitsyn, however, that, in spite of her editorial skill, Tvardovsky did not care for Berzer.

52 *Ibid.* p. 176.

53 Lakshin recalls arguments, for example, over Tvardovsky's articles on Bunin and Isakovsky, (Lakshin, 'Solzhenitsyn', p. 177).

54 Roi Medvedev, 'Tvardovskii i Solzhenitsyn', p. 2.

55 Solzhenitsyn, *Bodalsia*, pp. 304–5. Solzhenitsyn gives other examples (e.g. p. 294) where Tvardovsky is shown to be in such a state that, on the one hand, he renounces Solzhenitsyn during a conversation with Demichev at the Writers Union and, on the other, he is almost ready to leave *Novy Mir*. The tension, clearly, was tremendous.

56 *Ibid.* p. 122.

57 See, for example, *ibid.* p. 66, where he discussed the post-22nd Congress issues of *Novy Mir* and expresses, in a strongly worded passage, the view that *Novy Mir* was far from doing the most possible.

58 Svetov, 'Razdelenie...', pp. 199–200.

59 Roi Medvedev, 'Tvardovskii i Solzhenitsyn', p. 4.

60 *Ibid.* p. 5. Medvedev offers other examples of Tvardovsky's courage in literary maneuvering: for instance that one day Tvardovsky snubbed a Secretary of the CPSU Central Committee, Demichev, when the latter was trying to read in public a letter addressed to Tvardovsky which for some reason was in the safe of the Central Committee Secretariat. As a sign of protest, Tvardovsky pointedly got up and walked out. According to Medvedev (p. 9), Tvardovsky had frequently had confrontations with Demichev and with his predecessor Il'ichev, and it was often this very bravery and sharpness that rescued *Novy Mir* and its authors. Tvardovsky's defense of Solzhenitsyn may be viewed in the light of Zaks' statement in his interview: 'Tvardovsky loved talent. He fell in love with talent. With Solzhenitsyn's...He was absolutely in love! – only with the talent because in general Solzhenitsyn is such a reserved person...But for his talent he was willing to forgive everything.'

61 Lakshin, 'Solzhenitsyn', p. 168. In his interview, Sinyavsky referred to Tvardovsky's 'well known courage' in deciding to publish Sinyavsky's attack on Sofronov. Tvardovsky felt, according to Sinyavsky, that in some ways, in the old, Stalinist days, he had even helped to get people like Sofronov published. He said jokingly that he himself was guilty, so to speak, of helping them stand on their own feet: 'I never thought they'd turn out like this' (Sinyavsky interview).

62 Lakshin, 'Solzhenitsyn', p. 210.

63 *Ibid.* p. 212.

64 Dar, in his interview, said that, like every *muzhik*, Tvardovsky dearly loved a few members of the intelligentsia – for example, Lakshin. Dar, however, asserted that Tvardovsky could be sharp and unpleasant and didn't have many friends. This is in contrast to Lakshin's insistence ('Solzhenitsyn', p. 180) that Solzhenitsyn was wrong in saying that the editor had no, or few, friends. He recalled, *inter alia*, Tvardovsky's

friendship with Marshak, Sokolov-Mikitov, Kazakevich, and recalls great feelings of comradeship at the *Novy Mir* offices among Tvardovsky's circle. Nekrasov was apparently also a good friend of Tvardovsky's. In his unpublished article, Sats, too, reaffirmed that Tvardovsky had close friendships, naming Lakshin in particular.

65 Comments on Tvardovsky's friendship with Kazakevich were made to me by a well-known Soviet writer.

66 Lakshin writes that while many different types worked at *Novy Mir*, he cannot think of one who did not respect Tvardovsky ('Solzhenitsyn', p. 175). Later in the same article he writes that in the literary world in general Tvardovsky was respected and rather feared, but that one cannot say that everyone loved him. This is why Lakshin fears that anything negative that Solzhenitsyn says about Tvardovsky falls on fertile soil (pp. 215–16).

67 Solzhenitsyn, *Bodalsia*, p. 214.

68 Lakshin, 'Solzhenitsyn', pp. 171–2.

69 Sinyavsky interview.

70 Lakshin, 'Solzhenitsyn', pp. 171–2. Dar, in his interview, also spoke of Tvardovsky's drinking bouts, his visits to the Dar home, drinking and becoming very gloomy and candid, yet always on his guard if someone else were present. He would, said Dar, drink himself into moody depression. Dar recalled one particular night when Tvardovsky, already drunk, rang their bell at 2 a.m. He complained that one could not do anything, that the whole generation had sold out in vain. This was in 1953. Later the same night, according to Dar, Tvardovsky went on to the home of Mikhail Slonimsky and said that there was nothing to do in literature, that every courageous person should commit suicide.

71 Etkind, *Sovetskii pisatel' i smert'*, pp. 141, 142.

72 Solzhenitsyn, *Bodalsia*, p. 309.

73 *Ibid.* p. 303n.

Select bibliography

Reference books

Bol'shaia sovetskaia entsiklopediia, 2nd edn.
Brainina, B. Ia., and Dmitrieva, A. N., eds. *Sovetskie pisateli: Avtobiografii.* Moscow: Khudozhestvennaia literatura, 1966 and 1972.
Fogelevich, Leonid Grigorevich. *Osnovnye direktivy i zakonodatel'stvo o pechate*, 6th edn. Moscow: State Publishing House, 1937.
Gorokhoff, Boris I. *Publishing in the USSR*. [Bloomington:] Indiana University Publications, 1959.
Harkins, William E. *Dictionary of Russian Literature*. Patterson, New Jersey: Littlefield, Adams and Company, 1959.
Kratkaia literaturnaia entsiklopediia, 7 vols. Moscow: Sovetskaia entsiklopediia, 1962–1972.
Levytskii, Borys. *The Political Elite*. Distributed by the Hoover Institution on War, Revolution and Peace, Stanford University, 1970.
Literaturnaia entsiklopediia. Moscow, 1934.
Soviet Political Leaders: Personnel in the Communist Party, Government, and Mass Organizations of the USSR and the 15 Soviet Republics. [Washington, D.C.?] July, 1957.
Sovetskie pisateli: Avtobiografii b dvukh tomakh. Moscow: Gosudarstvennoe izdatel'stvo khudozhestvennoi literatury, 1959.
US Department of State: Bureau of Intelligence and Research. *Directory of Soviet Officials*. Washington, D.C., 1960, 1963, 1966.
Who's Who in the USSR 1960/61. New York: The Scarecrow Press, Inc., 1962.

Books and articles

Alexandrova, Vera. *A History of Soviet Literature 1917–1964: From Gorky to Solzhenitsyn*. Garden City, New York: Anchor Books, Doubleday and Co., 1964.
'Soviet Literature since Stalin', *Problems of Communism*, III (July–August, 1954), pp. 11–14.
'Soviet Youth in Life and Literature', *Problems of Communism*, VIII (July–August, 1959), pp. 30–5.
Avtorkhanov, Abdurakhman. *The Communist Party Apparatus*. Chicago, Henry Regnery Co., 1966.

Blake, Patricia, and Hayward, Max, eds. *Dissonant Voices in Soviet Literature*. New York: Harper and Row, 1964.

Boborykin, V. 'Biografiia romana: V tvorcheskoi laboratorii A. Fadeeva', *Voprosy literatury* 5, 1971, pp. 129–43.

Bocharov, A. *Vasilii Grossman: Kritiko-biograficheskii ocherk*. Moscow: Sovetskii pisatel', 1970.

Boffa, Giuseppe. *Inside the Khrushchev Era*. Translated by Carl Marzani. London: George Allen and Unwin, 1960.

Boguslavskaia, Zoia Borisovna. *Vera Panova: Ocherk tvorchestva*. Moscow: Gosudarstvennoe izdatel'stvo khudozhestvennoi literatury, 1963.

Breslauer, George. 'Khrushchev Reconsidered', *Problems of Communism*, XXV (September–October, 1976), pp. 18–33.

Brown, Archie, and Kaser, Michael, eds. *The Soviet Union since the Fall of Khrushchev*. New York: The Free Press, 1975.

Brown, Deming. 'Muffled Voice of Russian Liberalism', *New York Times Magazine*, December 19, 1965, pp. 10–11.

Soviet Russian Literature since Stalin. Cambridge, 1978.

Brown, Edward J. 'Not by Bread Alone by Vladimir Dudintsev', *The American Slavic and East European Review*, XVII (September, 1958), pp. 378–80.

The Proletarian Episode in Russian Literature. New York: Columbia University Press, 1953.

Russian Literature since the Revolution. New York: Collier Books, 1963.

Burg, David, and Feifer, George. *Solzhenitsyn*. New York: Stein and Day, 1973.

Carlisle, Olga. *Voices in the Snow*. New York: Random House, 1962.

Cocks, Paul, Daniels, Robert V., and Heer, Nancy, eds. *The Dynamics of Soviet Politics*. Harvard University Press, 1976.

Cohen, Stephen F. *Bukharin and the Bolshevik Revolution: A Political Biography 1888–1938*. New York: Alfred A. Knopf, 1973.

Conquest, Robert. 'After Khrushchev: A Conservative Restoration?', *Problems of Communism*, XII (September–October, 1963), pp. 41–6.

The Pasternak Affair: Courage of Genius. London: Collins and Harvill Press, 1961.

The Politics of Ideas in the USSR. London: The Bodley Head, 1967.

Power and Policy in the USSR. London: Macmillan, 1962.

Crankshaw, Edward. *Khrushchev: A Biography*. London: Collins, 1966.

Dementyev, A. 'New Novel by Vera Panova', *Soviet Literature* 3, 1954, pp. 136–8.

Dressler, Alfred. 'Party and Writers: 1956–58', *Soviet Studies*, X (April, 1959), pp. 417–32.

Dunham, Vera Sandomirsky. 'Insights from Soviet Literature', *The Journal of Conflict Resolution*, VIII (December, 1964), pp. 386–410.

In Stalin's Time: Middleclass Values in Soviet Fiction. New York: Cambridge University Press, 1976.

Ehrenburg, Ilya. *People, Years, Life*, vol. v: *The War 1941–45*. Translated by Tatiana Shebunina in collaboration with Yvonne Kapp. London: MacGibbon and Kee, 1964.

Erlich, Victor. 'Soviet Literary Criticism: Past and Present', *Problems of Communism*, vii (January–February, 1958), pp. 35–43.

Etkind, Efim. *Notes of a Non-Conspirator*. Oxford University Press, 1978.

'Sovetskii pisatel' i smert'', *Vremia i my* 26, 1978, pp. 132–44.

Fainsod, Merle. *How Russia is Ruled*, revised edn. Harvard University Press, 1964.

Smolensk under Soviet Rule. Harvard University Press, 1958.

Fitzpatrick, Sheila. 'Culture and Politics under Stalin: A Reappraisal', *Slavic Review*, xxxv, 2 (June, 1976), pp. 211–31.

Fleron, Frederic J., Jr, ed. *Communist Studies and the Social Sciences: Essays on Methodology and Empirical Theory*. Chicago: Rand McNally and Co., 1969.

Fradkina, Sarra Iakovlevna. *V mire geroev Very Panovoi: Tvorcheskii portret pisatel'nitsy*. Perm: Permskoe knizhnoe izdatel'stvo, 1961.

Friedberg, Maurice. *A Decade of Euphoria: Western Literature in Post-Stalin Russia, 1954–64*. Bloomington: Indiana University Press, 1977.

'Keeping Up with the Censor', *Problems of Communism*, xiii (November–December, 1964), pp. 22–31.

'What Price Censorship?', *Problems of Communism*, xvii (September–October, 1968), pp. 18–23.

Gerstenmaier, Cornelia. *The Voices of the Silent*. Translated by Susan Hecker. New York: Hart Publishing Co., 1972.

Gibian, George. 'Ferment and Reaction: 1956–57', *Problems of Communism*, vii (January–February. 1958), pp. 21–7.

Interval of Freedom: Soviet Literature during the Thaw 1954–1957. Minneapolis: University of Minnesota Press, 1960.

Gilboa, Yehoshua A. *The Black Years of Soviet Jewry 1939–1953*. Translated by Yosef Shachter and Dov Ben-Abba. Boston: Little, Brown, 1971.

Glenny, Michael, ed. *Novyi Mir: A Selection, 1925–1967*. London: Jonathan Cape, 1972.

Grossman, Joan Delaney. 'Khrushchev's Anti-Religious Policy and the Campaign of 1954', *Soviet Studies*, xxiv (January, 1973), pp. 374–86.

Grossman, Vasilii. *Forever Flowing*. Translated by Thomas P. Whitney. New York: Harper and Row, 1972.

Za pravoe delo. Moscow: Voennoe izdatel'stvo, 1955; *Za pravoe delo*. Moscow: Sovetskii pisatel', 1964.

Harris, Jonathan. 'The Origins of the Conflict between Malenkov and Zhdanov: 1939–1941', *Slavic Review*, xxxv, 2 (June, 1976), pp. 211–31.

Hayward, Max. 'Pasternak's "Dr Zhivago"', *Encounter*, x (May, 1958), pp. 38–48.

'Potentialities for Freedom: The Restlessness of the Writers'. Paper presented at the Conference on Changes in Soviet Society at St Antony's College, Oxford, June 24–9, 1957.

'Soviet Literature in the Doldrums', *Problems of Communism*, VIII (July–August, 1959), pp. 11–16.

Hayward, Max, and Crowley, Edward L., eds. *Soviet Literature in the Sixties*. New York: Frederick A. Praeger, 1964.

Hayward, Max, and Labedz, Leopold, eds. *Literature and Revolution in Soviet Russia 1917–1962*. London: Oxford University Press, 1963.

Hough, Jerry F. 'The Soviet System: Petrification or Pluralism?', *Problems of Communism*, XXI (March–April, 1972), pp. 25–45.

Hough, Jerry, and Fainsod, Merle. *How the Soviet Union is Governed*. Harvard University Press, 1979.

Iashin, Aleksandr. 'Bobrishnyi ugor', *Oktiabr'* 1, 1980, pp. 148–79; *Oktiabr'* 2, 1980, pp. 159–83.

Institut russkoi literatury. *Istoriia russkogo sovetsogo romana*. Moscow: Izdatel'stvo nauka, 1965.

Institute for the Study of the USSR. *The Soviet Censorship*. Studies on the Soviet Union, vol. XI (N.S.), no. 2. Munich, 1971.

Ivinskaya, Olga. *A Captive of Time*. London: Collins and Harvill Press, 1978.

Johnson, Priscilla. *Khrushchev and the Arts: The Politics of Soviet Culture, 1962–1964*. Cambridge, Mass.: The MIT Press, 1965.

Katkov, George. *The Trial of Bukharin*. New York: Stein and Day, 1970.

Khrushchev, Nikita. *Khrushchev Remembers: The Last Testament*. London: Andre Deutsch, 1974.

Kondratovich, Aleksei. 'Poezdka v Pakhru', *Moskva* 9, 1976, pp. 201–13. 'Uroki Tvardovskogo', *Molodaia gvardiia* 2, 1979, pp. 307–21.

Kruglak, Theodore E. *The Two Faces of TASS*. Minneapolis: University of Minnesota Press, 1962.

(Kuznetsov), A. Anatoli. *Babi Yar: A Document in the Form of a Novel*. Translated by David Floyd. New York: Farrar, Straus and Giroux, 1970.

Labedz, Leopold, ed. *Solzhenitsyn: A Documentary Record*. London: Allen Lane, The Penguin Press, 1970.

Lakshin, Vladimir. 'Solzhenitsyn, Tvardovskii i "Novyi mir": Pisatel', redaktor i zhurnal', *XX-i Vek* 2, 1977, pp. 151–218.

Laqueur, Walter Z., and Lichtheim, George. *The Soviet Cultural Scene 1956–1957*. New York: Atlantic, 1958.

Leonhard, Wolfgang. *The Kremlin since Stalin*. Translated by Elizabeth Wiskemann and Marian Jackson. New York: Frederick A. Praeger, 1962.

Linden, Carl, 'Khrushchev and the Party Battle', *Problems of Communism*, XII (September–October, 1963), pp. 27–35. *Khrushchev and the Soviet Leadership, 1957–1964*. Baltimore: Johns Hopkins Press, 1966.

Literaturnaia Moskva. 2 vols. Moscow: Gosudarstvennoe izdatel'stvo khudozhestvennoi literatury, 1956.

L'vov, Sergei. 'Rozhdenie epopei', *Ogonek*, 47, 1952, p. 24.

M., J. 'A Difficult Spring Follows the Thaw', *Soviet Studies*, VIII (January, 1957), pp. 279–98.

McCagg, William O. *Stalin Embattled, 1943–1948*. Detroit: Wayne State University Press, 1978.

McLean, Hugh, 'How Writers Rise from the Dead', *Problems of Communism*, XIX (March–April, 1970), pp. 14–25.

McLean, Hugh, and Vickery, W., eds. *The Year of Protest 1956*. New York: Vintage Books, 1961.

Maguire, Robert A. 'Literary Conflicts in the 1920s', *Survey*, Winter, 1972, pp. 98–127.

Red Virgin Soil: Soviet Literature in the 1920s. Princeton University Press, 1968.

Mandelstam, Nadezhda. *Hope Abandoned*. Translated by Max Hayward. New York: Atheneum, 1974.

Mathewson, Rufus W. *The Positive Hero in Russian Literature*. New York: Columbia University Press, 1958.

Medvedev, Roy A. *On Socialist Democracy*. London: Macmillan, 1975.
'Tvardovskii i Solzhenitsyn: Predvaritel'nye zamechaniia.' Unpublished article.

Medvedev, Roy, and Medvedev, Zhores. *Khrushchev: The Years in Power*. London: Oxford University Press, 1977.

Medvedev, Zhores A. *Desiat' let posle 'Odnogo dnia Ivana Denisovicha'*, London: Macmillan, 1973. (English translation: *Ten Years after Ivan Denisovich*. New York: Alfred A. Knopf, 1973.)

Mihajlov, Mihajlo. *Russian Themes*. Translated by Marija Mihajlov. New York: Farrar, Straus and Giroux, 1968.

Nekrasov, Viktor. 'Isaichu…', *Kontinent*, no. 18 (1978), pp. 3–5.

Pasternak, Boris. *Stikhotvoreniia i poemy*. Moscow: Sovetskii pisatel', 1965.

Pethybridge, Roger. *A Key to Soviet Politics: The Crisis of the Anti-Party Group*. New York: Frederick A. Praeger, 1962.

Ploss, Sidney. *Conflict and Decision-Making in Soviet Russia: A Case Study of Agricultural Policy 1953–1963*. Princeton University Press, 1965.

Plotkin, Lev Abramovich, *Tvorchestvo Very Panovoi*. Moscow: Sovetskii pisatel', 1962.

Rubin, Burton, 'Plekhanov and Soviet Literary Criticism', *The American Slavic and East European Review*, XV (December, 1956), pp. 527–42.

Ruehle, Juergen. 'The Soviet Theater: Part II', *Problems of Communism*, IX (January–February, 1960), pp. 40–9.

Ruge, Gerd, 'Conversations in Moscow', *Encounter*, XI (October, 1958), pp. 20–31.

Rush, Myron. *The Rise of Khrushchev*. Washington, D.C.: Public Affairs Press, 1958.

Russian Institute. *The Anti-Stalin Campaign and International Communism*. New York: Columbia University Press, 1956.

S., R., '*Kommunist* Answers the Writers', *Soviet Studies*, IX (July, 1957), pp. 111–16.

'A Note on the Congresses of Artists', *Soviet Studies*, IX (July, 1957), pp. 108–11.

'Two Literary Treatments of Pressing Social Problems', *Soviet Studies*, VIII (April, 1957), pp. 437–48.

Sats, I. A. 'O stat'e F. Svetova "Razdelenie..."'. Unpublished article.

Scriven, Tom. 'The "Literary Opposition"', *Problems of Communism*, VII (January–February, 1958), pp. 28–34.

'Literature and the Peasant', *Problems of Communism*, VIII (November–December, 1959), pp. 19–21.

Shub, Boris, 'Humanity Deleted: Alexander Fadeyev Rewrites a Novel', *Problems of Communism* I, 1952, pp. 13–17.

Shulman, Marshall D. *Stalin's Foreign Policy Reappraised*. Harvard University Press, 1963.

Simmons, Ernest J., ed. *Continuity and Change in Russian and Soviet Thought*. Harvard University Press, 1955.

Simmons, George W., ed. *Soviet Leaders*. New York: Thomas Y. Crowell, 1967.

Sinyavsky, Andrei. 'The Literary Process in Russia', *Kontinent*, 1976, pp. 77–118.

Skilling, H. Gordon, and Griffiths, Franklyn, eds. *Interest Groups in Soviet Politics*. Princeton University Press, 1971.

Skorino, L. 'Razgovor nachistotu (Po povodu stat'i V. Pomerantseva "Ob iskrennosti v literature")', *Znamia* 2, 1954, pp. 165–74.

Solzhenitsyn, Aleksandr. *Bodalsia telenok s dubom*. Paris: YMCA Press, 1975.

Cancer Ward. New York: Bantam Books, 1969.

The First Circle. New York: Bantam Books, Harper and Row, 1968.

Solzhenitsyn, Aleksandr, ed. *From under the Rubble*. London: William Collins and Sons, 1975.

Spechler, Dina. 'Permitted Dissent in the USSR: *Novy Mir* as an Organ of Social and Political Criticism 1953–1966', unpublished PhD dissertation, Harvard University, 1973.

Stillman, Edmund, ed. *Bitter Harvest*. New York: Praeger, 1959.

Struve, Gleb. *Russian Literature under Lenin and Stalin 1917–1953*. Norman, Oklahoma: University of Oklahoma Press, 1971.

'The Second Congress of Soviet Writers', *Problems of Communism*, IV (March–April, 1955), pp. 3–11.

Svetov, F. 'Razdelenie...(Posle "Ocherkov literaturnoi zhizni" A. Solzhenitsyna "Bodalsia telenok s dubom")', *Vestnik russkogo khristianskogo dvizheniia*, 121, 1977, pp. 195–236.

Svirsky, Grigory. *Hostages: The Personal Testimony of a Soviet Jew*. London: The Bodley Head, 1976.

Swayze, Harold. *Political Control of Literature in the USSR 1946–1959*. Harvard University Press, 1962.

Tatu, Michel. *Le Pouvoir en URSS: Du déclin de Khrouchtchev à la direction collective*. Paris: Editions Bernard Grasset, 1967.

Tertz, Abram [Andrei Sinyavsky]. *The Trial Begins & On Socialist Realism.* New York: Vintage Books, Random House, 1960.

Tvardovskaia, V. A. 'Otkrytoe pis'mo A. I. Solzhenitsynu po povodu ego knigi "Bodalsia telenok s dubom, ocherki literaturnoi zhizni"'. Unpublished in Russian. (Published in Italian in *L'Unità*, June 24, 1975.)

Tvardovskii, A. T. *O samon glavnom.* Moscow: Sovetskaia Rossiia, 1974.

'Po pravu pamiati'. Unpublished poem.

'Po pravu pamiati'. Different version of poem, published in part in *Posev* 10, 1969, p. 52–5.

Sobranie sochinenii. Moscow: Khudozhestvennaia literatura, 1976.

Tyorkin and the Stovemakers. Translated by Anthony Rudolf. Cheadle, England: Carcanet Press, 1974.

Tvardovskii, A. T., and Isakovskii, M. V. 'Iz perepiski dvukh poetov', *Druzhba narodov* 7, 1976, pp. 246–67; *Druzhba narodov* 8, 1976, pp. 253–74; *Druzhba narodov* 9, 1976, pp. 247–66.

Tvardovskii, Ivan. 'Na khutore Zagor'e', *Sovetskaia Rossiia*, June 1, 1980, p. 4.

Vickery, Walter N. *The Cult of Optimism: Political and Ideological Problems of Recent Soviet Literature.* Bloomington: Indiana University Press, 1963.

Willen, Paul. 'The Crisis in Soviet Drama', *Problems of Communism*, II (January, 1953), pp. 18–26.

Interviews and correspondence

Arkady Belinkov. Interview. Spring, 1969. New Haven, Connecticut.

David Dar. Interview. June, 1978. Jerusalem, Israel.

Igor Sats. Letter. February 22, 1974.

Veronika and Yury Shtain. Interview. January, 1974. New York City.

Andrei Sinyavsky. Interview. October 24, 1977. Jerusalem, Israel.

Grigory Svirsky. Interview. Spring 1974. Jerusalem, Israel.

Boris Zaks. Interview. August 10, 1980. Kauneonga, New York.

Index